New Works
in Accounting
History

Richard P. Brief, *Series Editor*

Leonard N. Stern School of Business
New York University

A Garland Series

THE DECISION-USEFULNESS THEORY OF ACCOUNTING

A Limited History

George J. Staubus

Garland Publishing, Inc.
A member of the Taylor & Francis Group
New York & London 1999

Published in 2000 by
Garland Publishing Inc.
A Member of the Taylor & Francis Group
19 Union Square West
New York, NY 10003

10   9   8   7   6   5   4   3   2   1

Library of Congress Cataloging-in-Publication Data

Staubus, George J.
      The decision-usefulness theory of accounting : a limited history / George
J. Staubus.
            p. cm. — (New works in accounting history)
      Includes bibliographical references.
      ISBN 0-8153-3444-3 (alk. paper)
      1. Accounting—History—United States. 2. Accounting. I. Title.
II. Series.
HF5616.U5 S72 1999
657'.0973—dc21   99-052286

Printed on acid-free, 250-year-life paper
Manufactured in the United States of America

Acknowledgments

"The Residual Equity Point of View in Accounting," originally published January 1959, and "Alternative Asset Flow Concepts," originally published July 1966 are reprinted with the permission of the American Accounting Association and *The Accounting Review.*

"The Multiple-Criteria Approach to Making Accounting Decisions," originally published autumn, 1976, and "Cash Flow Accounting and Liquidity: Cash Flow Potential and Wealth," originally published spring, 1989, are reprinted with the permission of *Accounting and Business Research.*

FASB Research Report, *Economic Consequences of Financial Accounting Standards* is copyrighted by the Financial Accounting Standards Board, 401 Merritt 7, P. O. Box 5116, Norwalk, Connecticut 06856-5116. U.S.A. Portions are reprinted with permission. Complete copies of this document are available from the FASB.

"The Relevance of Evidence of Cash Flows," from R. R. Sterling, ed., *Asset Valuation and Income Determination* and portions of *Making Accounting Decisions* are reprinted with the permission of Scholars Book Company.

Preface

This is an historical work, designed to show how the decision-usefulness theory of accounting was developed, mostly during the third quarter of the twentieth century in America. It is limited—not a rounded treatment of history—because a proper treatment is a bigger project than I am prepared to undertake at this time. I shall suggest to the reader some neglected sources of which he/she should be aware. This book is limited to reprints of my own works along with current commentaries on related developments. It is also limited to decision-usefulness theory in financial accounting, although, in my opinion, very few substantive changes would be required to make it fit managerial accounting. It is not a restatement of the theory, except for the summary in Part III. I intend for the book to show how the theory started in a crude, poorly articulated, and incomplete form, then gradually was developed into a more complete and somewhat better exposed form.

One notable aspect of the development of decision-usefulness theory is the use of the term itself. I do not know who first applied that name to it. Certainly, the body of theory was fairly well developed and publicized before anyone, to my knowledge, called it decision-usefulness theory. For many years, I called it a theory of accounting to investors. In this work, the term refers to a coherent set of general statements summarizing the essence of a specified body of knowledge or beliefs (a theory), in particular, one starting with the objective of providing financial information regarding an enterprise for use in making economic decisions. Even today, the term is not widely used, mainly because accounting theory is not widely discussed, even among accountants, even among teachers of accounting.

With or without the appellation, the decision-usefulness theory of accounting is now generally accepted among those few people interested in accounting theory. There is no recognizable alternative. It has been the most important development in accounting thought in the second half of the twentieth century. At midcentury, a researcher could have found no evidence of its existence. In 1999 it is generally accepted by the accounting standards-setting bodies in the major English-speaking countries and by those who interact with those standards setters. In view of that rapid rise to a dominant position in accounting thought, a history of its evolution seems worthwhile. Finding none in the literature, I decided to assemble a few materials to tell the story as I know it. In my view, the body of accounting literature should include such a work.

The lack of a history of decision-usefulness theory may be surprising to those who accept the above characterization of its acceptance. One explanation for that absence is the degree of stealth with which it conquered accounting thought. Associated with that stealth was the absence of a name; an idea without a name can spread without being recognized. Also, resistance to the implications of the decision-usefulness objective, especially current measurements, by preparers of financial statements—a prominent feature of the American standards-setting environment in the nineteen-seventies—was easier to justify in the absence of a saleable name for the opposition. "Decision usefulness" is so socially acceptable; better not to use the term if you do not like its implications. Aside from the absence of a name and its stealthy spread, the lack of a written history is hard to explain.

Lack of decision-usefulness history may be partially explained by a peculiarity of the major "authoritative body" pronouncements that contributed so much to its acceptance. Prominent among those pronouncements were:

1. *A Statement of Basic Accounting Theory*, prepared by a special purpose committee of The American Accounting Association and published by the Association in 1966.

2. "Basic Concepts and Accounting Principles Underlying Financial Statements of Business Enterprises," *Statement of the Accounting Principles Board No. 4*, American Institute of Certified Public Accountants, October 1970.

3. *Objectives of Financial Statements*, Report of the Study Group on the Objectives of Financial Statements, American Institute of Certified Public Accountants, October 1973.

4. *Statements of Financial Accounting Concepts Nos. 1, 2, 5, and 6*, Financial Accounting Standards Board, 1978-1985.

The peculiarity is that these documents did not include a report of a literature search such as is customary in academic treatises. No recognition of the preceding literature on decision-usefulness theory appeared in those publications, with one minor exception. The preface to the third publication listed above mentioned the first two committee reports as well as a co-authored document published by the Accountancy Research Foundation (Australia) in 1972 (without identifying the authors—W. J. Kenley and G. J. Staubus). But none of the contents were discussed. Those groups assigned responsibility for the compilation of fundamental accounting concepts have been poor historians.

Decision-usefulness theory has played a major role in the evolution of accounting thought. At mid-century, no broad theory of accounting had been developed. By far the most widely recognized theory was Paton and Littleton's *An Introduction to Corporate Accounting Standards* (1940), a work that contributed a great deal to coherent thinking about accounting. A few other thoughtful works were published in the first half of the century, but they did not gain the favorable recognition of a significant portion of the accounting community. A big gap was the absence of a pervasive objective—a gap that even *An Introduction to Corporate Accounting Standards* failed to fill. What that work did well was teach accounting for nonmonetary assets by matching their costs with associated revenues. That was a valuable contribution in the context of its time. From today's perspective, it is not a broad theory of accounting.

The key to the decision-usefulness theory is the decision-usefulness objective. It is the base on which a coherent, broad structure of ideas has been built. No other such structure of accounting ideas has been developed, to my knowledge. Like most social science theories, it is made up of a mixture of normative and descriptive propositions. Because the decision usefulness objective is not generally accepted by those doing accounting, the theory can easily be viewed as normative. At the same time, it is substantially accurate as a general description of current accounting practice, and practice has slowly moved closer to agreement with the theory in the second half of the twentieth century. In the absence of a theory of generally accepted accounting principles, no alternative to the decision-usefulness theory exists. Its evolution is an appropriate object for study by those interested in accounting thought.

Now, three apologies are appropriate. These pages have been assembled and connected with the objective of telling the story of the development of the decision-usefulness theory a I know it. To achieve that objective, early dates, with one exception, have taken precedence over clarity of exposition in the selection of work to be reprinted. This book is not intended to offer a state-of-the-art version of the theory. Unfortunately, the only relatively fully-developed statements of the theory in the American literature with which I am acquainted are Staubus, *Making Accounting Decisions* (MAD) (1977) and Financial Accounting Standards Board, *Statements of Financial Accounting Concepts, Nos. 1, 2, 5,* and *6* (1978-85). There is room for improvement. I apologize for not doing that job.

Secondly, I have not prepared an index—on cost-benefit grounds. A partial substitute is the subsections on Locations of Theory Features in the introductory commentaries in both Parts I and II.

Finally, I apologize for my inadequate acknowledgments of the contributions of five great accountants to the development and acceptance of the decision-usefulness theory. Raymond J. Chambers and Robert R. Sterling have stimulated the thinking of so many serious students of accounting theory (including myself) that nothing I could say would add or detract from their places in accounting history. In another setting, Oscar S. Gellein and Robert T. Sprouse, Board members, and Reed K. Storey of the staff at the Financial Accounting Standards Board in the nineteen-seventies led the Board and the world of accounting standards setters to the adoption of the decision-usefulness theory in the Board's conceptual framework. Their leadership overcame strong resistance by preparers and a few of their allies.

The materials reprinted in this volume consist of two sets: the work done in the nineteen-fifties, and the work done in the nineteen-seventies. The "first edition" was the fruit of my Ph. D. dissertation research, including the portion approved by my committee for the dissertation itself and the omitted chapters that were polished up for inclusion in *A Theory of Accounting to Investors* (ATOATI). That work was finished in 1959, published in 1961. After some eight years of work on decision-usefulness theory as applied primarily to financial accounting, I concentrated on related areas for the next ten years. In the 1969-70 academic year, I returned to decision-usefulness theory in financial accounting. A series of papers published in the years 1970 through 1976 and the full second version—*Making Accounting Decisions* (1977)—resulted from that second period of concentration on the theory. To minimize duplication, the materials reprinted here in Part II are limited to those that represent significant increments to those included in Part I. A complete list of my publications is included at the end of the book to supplement the list of references.

I am grateful for the assistance of those who worked with me on the preparation of this book. I would be pleased to hear from and to respond to anyone who cares to comment on the material presented here or on other matters relevant to the development of the decision-usefulness theory of accounting.

George J. Staubus
Walter A. Haas School of Business
University of California, Berkeley,
CA 94720-1900
staubus@haas.berkeley.edu

Contents

iii   Preface

1   I. In the Beginning: the Nineteen-Fifties Edition

3   A. Commentary on Nineteen-Fifties Developments

9   B. Diagrammatic Outline: Features of the Theory

11   C. Excerpts from *An Accounting Concept of Revenue* (University of Chicago, Dissertation, 1954)

41   D. The Residual Equity Point of View in Accounting *The Accounting Review* (January 1959)

53   E. *A Theory of Accounting to Investors* Chapters I, III, IV, VI (University of California Press, 1961)

155   II. Maturity of the Theory: The Nineteen-Seventies Edition

157   A. Commentary

161   B. Criteria for Making Accounting Choices
163   1. Introduction
168   2. The Multiple-Criteria Approach to Making Accounting Decisions, *Accounting and Business Research* (Autumn 1976)
181   3. Effects via Other Parties, section of Chapter III *Making Accounting Decisions* (Scholars Book Co., 1977)
191   4. Introduction, *Economic Consequences* (Financial Accounting Standards Board, 1978)

197   C. The Evidential Approach to Measurement of
           Cash Flow Potential
199   1. Introduction
203   2. The Relevance of Evidence of Cash Flows,
              from R.R. Sterling, ed., *Asset Valuation and Income
              Determination* (Scholars Book Company, 1971)
233   3. Summary of Relevance Appraisals
              Section of Chapter VII, *Making Accounting Decisions*
240   4. The Magnate/Financio Case
              from Chapter VIII, *Making Accounting Decisions*

243   D. Historical Cash Flows
245   1. Introduction
247   2. Alternative Asset Flow Concepts,
              The Accounting Review, (July 1966)
263   3. Cash Flow Accounting and Liquidity:
              Cash Flow Potential and Wealth, *Accounting and Business
              Research* (Spring 1989)

273   E. Inflation Accounting in Decision-Usefulness Theory
275   1. Introduction
279   2. Common Unit Accounting, Chapter IX,
              Making Accounting Decision

331   III. Summary of the Decision-Usefulness Theory of Accounting
          to Investors

335   IV. Impact

341   V. Publications of George J. Staubus

347   Reference

In the Beginning:
The Nineteen-Fifties Edition

Commentary on Nineteen-Fifties Developments

Accounting literature available in 1951 omitted the objective of providing information useful in making decisions. In fact, no statement of any objective of accounting could be found in the documents prepared by the professional associations' committees charged with responsibility for setting out important concepts and principles of accounting, such as the American Institute of Accountants' Committee on Accounting Procedure and the Executive Committee of the American Accounting Association. Nor had any individual writer identified decision usefulness as the objective of accounting. It followed that no one had sought to build a theory, or conceptual framework, on that basis. Several writers had given attention to users or uses of financial statements, but none tied his comments to the decision-usefulness objective or to a theory structure. With hindsight, that "objective gap" is widely recognized as a critical flaw in the principles of accounting, circa 1950. How could a profession serve the public if its members did not know what they were trying to do?

That was the setting in which I, a Ph. D. student in the School of Business at the University of Chicago, confronted the dissertation topic I had chosen: an examination of the revenue concept. My objective was to define revenue. Then I encountered a logical roadblock. My inclination was distinctly normative, but to say how something should be done required an answer to the question: for what purpose? That is how I got involved in a search for an objective, or objectives, of accounting. Finding none in the literature, I was on my own.

The work started with an analysis of the users of accounting outputs and the uses they made of those outputs. This led to the conclusion that all users sought information for decisions, in the broad sense that included management control. Not wishing to deal with managerial accounting, I chose to concentrate on external reporting which led to the concentration on investors (owners and creditors). The rest of it followed logically: the cash flow orientation, the residual equity focal point, the future-oriented concepts of assets and "specific equities" (liabilities) as positive and negative components of the residual equity calculation, the future-oriented analysis of measurement methods applicable to stocks concepts, including the measurement of real holding gains and losses on both monetary and nonmonetary net asset items (constant dollar accounting)—all of these followed from the decision-usefulness objective and investor focus. The main features of the decision-usefulness theory of accounting to investors fell into place.

The dissertation committee was not satisfied with the first draft. For a project that specified revenue as the topic, my manuscript proposing a theory of accounting to investors seemed to range too far afield, although my chairman did encourage me to pursue my broader ambition after finishing the dissertation. So the more balance sheet-oriented sections — especially the definitions and measurement of assets and liabilities — were omitted. The decision-usefulness objective, users and uses, investors' interest in the future cash flows of the enterprise, the residual equity focal point, and "constant dollar accounting," — all of these basic features of decision-usefulness theory remained in the dissertation in some form, some place. Unfortunately, the revenue focus, my committee's restrictions, and perhaps my own impatience resulted in a poor presentation of the decision-usefulness theory. It was accepted by the committee (Marshall Ketchum, Kullervo Louhi, and William J. Vatter, Chm.) in December, 1953 and the Ph. D. degree was awarded in the March, 1954 commencement ceremony.

With the dissertation out of the way, the revenue constraint was removed. I returned to the broader theory of accounting to investors and completed a draft during a fall semester, 1955 partial sabbatical leave. Subsequent months saw some polishing of the manuscript and circulation among a limited number of acquaintances (very limited in those pre-xerography days), including one former president of the American Accounting Association, who commented: "This is an excellent piece of work and should by all means be published" but "the new terminology and the precise reasoning involved makes it rather tough going." Another year was spent on correspondence with, and reviewing of the manuscript by officers of the American Accounting Association.

The Executive Committee finally declined to publish it. Most of 1958 and 1959 was spent on similar exchanges with The University of Chicago Press, the Bureau (later Institute) of Business and Economic Research on the Berkeley Campus, and the University of California Press. My disappointment and resentment following each return of the manuscript with criticisms were typically followed by reluctant acknowledgment that the result was improvement. Chapter VII was added at the request of one of the reviewing bodies.

Another development during the years of struggle for publication of the whole theory was the preparation and publication of a journal article, "The Residual Equity Point of View in Accounting." As an assistant professor in need of a publications record, I felt that I could present the key ideas of my theory in the guise of a contribution to the ongoing argument over the proper point of view for accountants to take in their work. I felt that my interpretation of the role of the residual equity was more consistent with the interests of users of financial statements than either of the theories recognized in the literature at the time — the proprietary theory and the entity theory — and that a journal editor might find it acceptable if placed in that context rather than presented as a new theory. In fact, the piece was a brief presentation of the bulk of the decision-usefulness theory features appearing in the diagrammatic summary (see below) prior to the criteria for accounting choices and the evidential approach to asset and liability measurement. It was accepted as the lead article in the January 1959 number of *The Accounting Review.*

I finally received notice, March 10, 1960, that *A Theory of Accounting to Investors* (ATOATI) would be published by the University of California Press. It appeared in April, 1961 with a dust jacket announcing the forthcoming publication of *The Theory and Measurement of Business Income* by Edgar Edwards and Philip Bell. Bell, a professor in the Berkeley economics department, was chairman of the committee that had been considering my manuscript and finally approved its publication. I suspect that his interest in accounting was helpful to my cause, although I was not acquainted with him at the

4

time. The book subsequently was republished in Scholars Book Company's accounting classics series and a Japanese translation was published by Hakuto Shobo. Perseverance paid off.

A diagrammatic outline of the decision-usefulness theory of accounting to investors, as visualized in 1999, is presented in EXHIBIT I, p. x. The state of the work as it stood when accepted by the University of California Press in early 1960 differed somewhat in terminology and emphasis. The criteria for making accounting choices was the least developed part at that stage; the section headed "Criteria for the Selection of Measurement Techniques" ran to only a bit over three pages. Relevance was emphasized, but cost and risk of bias were mentioned only briefly (ATOATI, p. 50) and other criteria were not addressed at all. The multiple criteria approach to making accounting decisions was not well developed in my work until 1969-70 while on leave at the University of Kansas. The diagrammatic outline is presented in current form as a reference base for comments on the main features of the theory at various points in this book. A narrative summary appears in Part III below.

Evolution and Acceptance of Major Features of the Theory — The major features of he theory from the decision-usefulness objective through the stocks and flows concepts may be viewed as especially associated with the "nineteen-fifties edition," so a few brief comments on their evolution and subsequent acceptance in the profession are made here. First, the preferred version of the *decision-usefulness objective* has varied over time and context. For example, the broadest version does not limit the decision makers to investors. Managers, regulators and anyone else interested in the financial affairs of the enterprise is included if no group of users is specified. That has not been a very serious issue, however, because attention to the uses made by users other than investors tends to reveal their interest in the same residual equity and future cash flow focal points that interest investors. Limiting the presentation of the theory to accounting to investors permits much greater efficiency of exposition while at the same time covering the interests of those other parties with a similar focus. This means that the interests of owner-managers and managers working to serve owners are covered while the interests of independent managers who view owners as one more group of resource providers to be kept happy are neglected.

Then there are questions regarding adjectives to be used in the objective statement. What kind of information is to be provided? Economic? Financial? What kinds of decisions are to be informed? My answers have varied over the years; the current ones are: **The objective of accounting is to provide financial information regarding an enterprise for use in making decisions. The objective of accounting to investors is to provide financial information regarding an enterprise for use in making investment decisions.** Investors have always included owners and creditors.

The first case of acceptance of the decision-usefulness objective in a carefully-developed statement of broad accounting ideas by a professional accounting body was in the American Accounting Association's *A Statement of Basic Accounting Theory* (ASOBAT) in 1966, where it was advocated enthusiastically and with great influence. It next appeared in *Accounting Principles Board Statement 4*, "Basic Concepts and Accounting Principles Underlying Financial Statements of Business Enterprises," in October 1970 (APB Statement No.4). That document introduced the idea to many practitioners who had not seen the American Accounting Association's report, thereby setting the stage for the next key step. The "Trueblood Committee's" report, *Objectives of Financial Statements* (OFS) (AICPA, October 1973) adopted it wholeheartedly, and that was the basis for the Financial Accounting Standards Board's conceptual framework, which I view as one version of decision-usefulness theory.

Users and uses of accounting information were identified in the 1954 dissertation and no major improvement to the essence of that analysis has been made, to my knowledge. One of the beauties of the decision-usefulness objective is that it raises questions regarding the users and uses (to the extent that they are not addressed in the process of settling on the objective). They are elaborations of the decision-usefulness objective. ASOBAT, APB 4, OFS and the conceptual framework have included them.

The focus on *cash flow-oriented decisions* that was developed in the residual equity article was not picked up in ASOBAT or APB 4. OFS recognized the investor's interest in enterprise cash flows but did not tie that directly to cash flows to the investor. It focused heavily on information for assessing enterprise earning power.

The term *"cash flow potential"* did not appear in my early publications. Instead, there were awkward discussions of cash balance plus rights to future cash receipts plus rights to noncash services, which led to assets, and "future disbursements of cash and distributions of other serviceable things," which became liabilities. The 1967 article expressing disagreement with one aspect of Professor Chambers' views included the term "maximum time-adjusted cash potential." My first use of "cash flow potential" may have been in Kenley and Staubus (1972, p. 59). "The property of an asset that financial statement users would most like to know is its cash flow potential." I continued to focus on it in subsequent publications and now consider it to be an economical term to indicate the property of an asset or liability that makes it important to investors. It has not featured prominently in any of the major documents by the authoritative bodies, although it has been mentioned, e.g. in the FASB's *Statement of Financial Accounting Concepts No. 1, Objectives of Financial Reporting by Business Enterprises* (1978, parag. 41). The role of cash flow potential in the ranking of measurement methods on the relevance criterion is discussed in the commentary on nineteen-seventies works below.

Historical cash flows is an important part of the theory, just as historical income flows are. The funds statement illustrated in ATOATI (p. 136) reflected the net short-term monetary assets concept of funds, the gross (direct) approach to reporting income flows, and the division of line items among recurring events, investment transactions, and financing transactions. In practice, funds statements, circa 1960, focused on working capital, took the indirect (add-back) approach, and showed only the sources and uses classes. The net short-term monetary assets concept of funds was narrowed to a version of "broad cash" in *Making Accounting Decisions*. That funds pool and the three sections of the statement — a feature introduced in ATOATI — are required by today's GAAP, and both the gross (direct) approach and the net (indirect) approach are acceptable.

The *residual equity* concept that has been a major feature of the theory from the beginning was given substantial attention in APB 4 but was ignored in ASOBAT and OFS. It is recognized as "equity" in the FASB's conceptual framework. The Board, after bitter debate in the nineteen-seventies, explicitly chose the asset, liability and equity (balance sheet) approach to the conceptual framework rather than the revenue, expense, and income (matching, or income statement) approach that had been popular since 1940. The division of changes in the residual equity into *revenues, gains, expenses, losses, and transactions with residual equity holders,* based on the scheme for classifying economic events that was developed in the dissertation and ATOATI, was adopted, with some terminological variations, in APB 4 and in FASB Concepts Statement No. 6 (Elements of Financial Statements).

The *future-oriented concepts of assets and liabilities* that were included in the theory in its first stage of development appeared in APB 4 in the guise of economic resources and economic obligations but the definitions of assets and liabilities in that document were of the old-fashioned variety. The FASB adopted — after much controversy — the "future economic benefits" and "future sacrifices of economic benefits" definitions in Concepts Statement No. 3 (replaced by No. 6).

One burden that I took on in the nineteen-fifties, apparently unnecessarily, was an effort to introduce improved terminology. The idea was that the introduction of a drastically different approach to thinking about accounting issues provided an opportunity to introduce more precise terminology. At a time when net worth, surplus, reserve, deferred charges, deferred credits, and profit and loss statement were widely used, when costs could be either expired or unexpired, when it was not clear to what broader categories revenues and expenses belonged, I felt that I could, and should, make an effort to improve the terminology of accounting. With hindsight, I'm not sure it was worthwhile. I had no detectable effect on popular usage, and I believe that that effort, by making the material harder to read, hindered the acceptance of the decision usefulness theory — a more important objective. Even the title — *A Theory of Accounting to Investors* — a determined attempt to emphasize the previously neglected focus on users of financial reports, was awkward. Other terms that probably discouraged potential readers were specific equities to cover liabilities and non-participating preferred stock, intra-actions for the intra-enterprise events that contrast with transactions between enterprises, receipts to include revenue and other inflows of net asset items, and real or real goods items where nonmonetary would have been more clear, although it, too, would have been new. On the other hand, I still believe it was necessary to introduce "accounting to investors" as well as residual equity and, later, cash flow potential, complete-cycle net realizable value, and as-is net realizable value.

Locations of Theory Features in the Nineteen-Fifties Works — I view all of my work on the decision-usefulness theory in the nineteen-fifties as one project. It commenced in 1952 as a dissertation, went through many trials and tribulations, and was finally wound up with the April 1961 publication of ATOATI. The materials reprinted in this volume include about 25 pages from the dissertation that show the earliest (and roughest) versions of many of the features, the January 1959 *Accounting Review* article on the residual equity point of view, and major portions of ATOATI to complete the presentation of the nineteen-fifties developments with a minimum of duplication. The key features of the theory, as they appear in these publications, although not necessarily in portions reprinted here, can be found as follows:

The *decision-usefulness objective* appears in the dissertation on pp. 103-4 and 113;

7

in the residual equity article on p. 4, enumerated paragraphs 2 and 5; and in ATOATI on pp. viii and 11.

Reviews of the *users and uses* of financial statements can be found in the dissertation, pp. 6-18; in the residual equity article, pp.4-6 (covering only investors); and in ATOATI, pp. 11-14 (investors only).

Investors' cash flow-orientation is developed in the dissertation, pp. 9-18 and 88-90, in the residual equity article, pp. 6-8; and in ATOATI, pp. 11-14. The concept of *cash flow potential* had its crude beginnings in the dissertation, p. 89, in the residual equity article, pp. 7-8 and in ATOATI, pp. 15-20, but the term was not used until 1972 in Kenley and Staubus (p. 59).

Historical cash flows, or alternative versions of funds flows, did not fit the scope of the first two works included herein, but were attended to on pp. 134-8 in ATOATI.

The nature of the *residual equity* and all investors' interest in it was addressed in the dissertation, pp. 91-94, throughout the residual equity article, and in ATOATI, Chapter II, which is omitted here because it overlaps the earlier residual equity article.

Assets and liabilities (specific equities) were the subject of Chapter III of ATOATI. The complete scheme for classifying economic events and identifying *revenues, expenses, gains and losses,* as classes of *receipts and costs,* received a great deal of attention in the dissertation (Chapter IV) and in ATOATI (Chapter IV).

The *criteria for accounting choices* were not well developed in the nineteen-fifties work. Only pp. 48-51 of ATOATI were devoted to them. Relevance to the problem of predicting future returns to investors; reliability, and cost, as well as the general idea of employing several criteria in choosing from among alternative possible measurement methods were clearly recognized, but the multiple criteria approach to making accounting decisions was not developed fully until 1970.

The alternative *measurement methods* and their rankings on the relevance criterion were omitted from the dissertation, as mentioned above, but were fairly carefully developed in ATOATI, Chapter III. The *measuring unit* problem was treated properly by today's standards in the dissertation, pp. 92-3, but no careful explanation was retained in the approved version. The reporting of the three effects of inflation on the residual equity was illustrated, but only because it appeared in the same financial statement that reported revenues. ATOATI covered the subject much more satisfactorily, pp. 38-9 and 116-27.

With hindsight, it is clear that selection of the decision-usefulness objective, the selection of investors as the key users, and recognition of their concern with future cash flows were the key steps towards a theory of accounting to investors that could, with time, gain the general acceptance of the theory-oriented accounting community. Those steps were first taken in the dissertation (1952-54) but were not tied together in a systematic manner because my committee objected to such major digressions from the stated topic of the dissertation. Those key features were polished and supplemented in the 1959 residual equity paper and in ATOATI to produce a fairly well-developed decision-usefulness theory of accounting to investors when it was finally submitted to the University of California Press in 1959. General acceptance came slowly, however, and might never have occurred without the participation of a number of excellent communicators, as was pointed out in the preface.

THE DECISION-USEFULNESS THEORY
OF ACCOUNTING TO INVESTORS

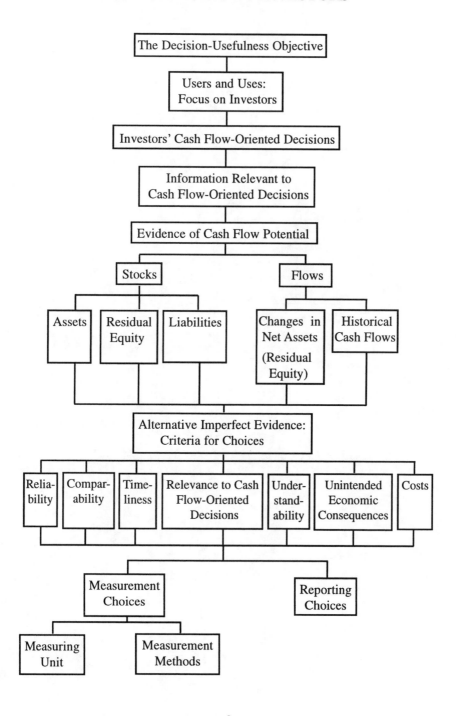

AN ACCOUNTING CONCEPT
OF REVENUE

George J. Staubus

ARNO PRESS

A New York Times Company
New York • 1980

THE UNIVERSITY OF CHICAGO

AN ACCOUNTING CONCEPT OF REVENUE

A DISSERTATION SUBMITTED TO
THE FACULTY OF THE SCHOOL OF BUSINESS
IN CANDIDACY FOR THE DEGREE OF
DOCTOR OF PHILOSOPHY

BY

GEORGE J. STAUBUS

CHICAGO, ILLINOIS

MARCH, 1954

12

TABLE OF CONTENTS

Page

LIST OF TABLES iii

Chapter

I. INTRODUCTION   1

    Uses of "General Purpose" Accounting Reports
    Conclusion

II. EXTANT CONCEPTS OF REVENUE   19

III. THE FIRST CRITERION OF REVENUE--AN INFLOW 30

    Revenue--Inflow or Outgo
    The Meaning of Inflow
    The Recording of Revenue

IV. OTHER CRITERIA OF REVENUE   42

    False Criteria of Revenue
    The Broad Approach--Receipts and Costs
    Revenue as a Type of Receipt
    Conclusion

V. SPECIFIC PROBLEMS IN REVENUE DETERMINATION   66

    Sales of Merchandise
    Disposition of Plant Assets
    Sales of Securities
    The Furnishing of Services
    Receipts of Taxes
    Sundry Economic Events
    Summary

VI. REVENUE IN REPORTS TO INVESTORS   87

    The Need for Dynamic Reports
    The Statement of Changes in the Residual Equity
    The Revenue-and-Expense Statement

VII. SUMMARY 102

    Basic Premises
    Revenue
    Some Implications of the Above Reasoning

BIBLIOGRAPHY 114

ii

13

Uses of "General Purpose" Accounting Reports

Who are the people other than managers who use, or could use, accounting statements? More specifically, in what way are people who can use a firm's accounting statements related to the firm rendering the statements? In addition to the general public,[2] there are taxing authorities and regulatory commissions, customers and suppliers of materials, et cetera; employees and their representatives, and stockholders and creditors; and prospective members of these groups must be included. Let us inquire into the nature of the financial information that these groups would like to have about the firm with which they are connected in these various ways.

The legitimate interests of the general public in business

---

[2]The general public includes everyone who has no particular relationship with the firm other than being a part of the same community.

firms include such things as the effect of the firm on the morals
and health of employees and customers, and the allocation of resources in the society. The health-and-morals aspect surely can
not be reported by the accountant. Perhaps he can aid in the proper
allocation of the society's resources by reporting, to those who do
not know it, the income from their resources, so that they can compare that income with known alternatives, and thereby sell their
resources to the firm that can pay the highest price.

A number of governmental agencies require financial statements from business firms. Most of them prescribe, to some extent,
the accounting methods to be used in preparing the required statements. While their accounting requirements may differ in certain
respects--witness the recent ruling by the Interstate Commerce Commission that railroads may not, in financial statements submitted
to the ICC, use the accelerated amortization rates allowed by the
Bureau of Internal Revenue on assets acquired under certificates
of necessity[1]--the needs of these agencies for accounting information appear to have one thing in common: they all show an interest
in the results of operations as they affect the owners of the business. Since this type of information is also desired by the owners,
and others, a detailed description will be postponed. In so far as
these agencies need financial information different from that supplied to owners, they are likely to want information similar to that
desired by management. Other needs, peculiar to the requiring agen-
cy, are not pertinent to the present discussion, which is concerned

---

[1]United States Interstate Commerce Commission, _Amortization
Accounting for Emergency Carrier Facilities_, Docket No. 30920,
December 21, 1951, p. 8.

only with general-purpose accounting reports.

Customers of a firm engage in a larger dollar volume of transactions with the firm than any other group of parties at interest. Because of this strong relationship, customers could benefit greatly from knowledge of the operations and position of the firm. They presumably are interested in forecasting changes in price, quantity, or quality of the goods supplied by the reporting firm. It is admitted that the future quantity and quality of products can not be reported or even approximated in the accounting statements; changes in these factors result from changes in the quality, quantity, and proportions of the many factors of production that are, or may be, used in producing the specific product, and these latter changes in regard to each product that might be produced by the firm could hardly be summarized in a set of condensed accounting statements. However, firms producing only one distinct product possibly could produce a statement containing some information that would be of aid to customers in predicting price, quality, and quantity of output, if it were considered advantageous to report such information.

Another datum about the firm which customers want is the stability of its rate of output. Stability of production may be limited by labor disturbances, equipment failure, instability of supplies of raw materials, poor production scheduling, or financial weakness. Only one of these factors (financial weakness) can be illuminated very much by accounting statements.

Suppliers would like to have information upon which to base forecasts of prices the firm may be willing to pay for various quan-

tities of the suppliers' products. Accountants and managers do not
now attempt to present this information, but data useful for such
forecasts could be presented in financial reports more effectively
than they now are, if such presentations were desirable. Suppliers
of the firm are usually short-term creditors and as such are interested in the same data in which other short-term creditors are
interested; these needs will be discussed below.

Employees are suppliers of the company and would like to
know the same things that suppliers of materials, etc., would like
to know--a schedule of the prices and quantities (of labor services)
which the firm would be willing to buy in the future. The problem
of telling them this is just as great as it is with suppliers of
materials. Unions, however, often want other information in order
to strengthen their bargaining positions with firms. This information includes labor costs and profits on particular products,
plants, operations, etc., as well as the total return to stockholders and the income-tax collectors.

Creditors and stockholders have very similar needs. They
are all equityholders; and, though the terms of investment may vary
considerably, they are all investors of capital. Suppliers of materials, labor, power, etc., are included in this category. That
is, they share the common position of equityholder--supplier of
goods and services, including command over goods and services in
general (money), with the expectation of future repayment in some
form (usually in money). The time of expected repayment varies,
and each equityholder attempts to predict the firm's ability to repay when such repayment is due or desired. Each equityholder will

have his own point of view; each will be examining the peculiar set
of factors that he thinks bears on the firm's ability to disburse
cash at the time for which his repayment is (implicitly or explicitly) contracted. Since the firm's cash balance at any future date
depends upon its current balance and the cash receipts and cash disbursements between the present date and the future date, equityholders must take into consideration all available indications of
cash transactions during the future period that is in question.
The supplier of materials or labor who expects repayment tomorrow
will have little interest in any element of the firm's financial condition except its cash balance. The bank which lends money on a
ninety-day note will be interested in all of the current assets,
but perhaps a little less in cash than in temporary investments (if
such a borrower would have any), accounts receivable, and inventories of merchandise or finished goods ready for sale, and, in addition, current liabilities and the rates and trends of sales and expenses. The bank that grants an intermediate-term loan (e.g., from
one to four years) will give particular attention to the current
ratio and net working capital, and indications of the firm's earning
power such as recent income, sales rates and trends, expense trends,
and factors that are not usually expressed very well in financial
statements--such as new products, new physical facilities, the
management, and the general business outlook.

Bond buyers are not usually as interested in the current
financial condition of the issuer as are short-term creditors, but
they will want to know about its earnings record (as an indication
of possible earnings under varying conditions), interest and other

fixed charges, the trend of sales and expenses, the ability of the
management, financial policies, the outlook for the industry, prior
liens on assets, the schedule of debt maturities, and the general
record of stability of the firm.

Preferred stock investors will be interested in the stability and level of the firm's past earnings, the trends of sales
and income, and those intangible indications of the future such as
products, management, and the industry outlook. Present and prospective common stock buyers are interested in similar indications
of future earnings with more emphasis on risk factors that may prove
favorable, and somewhat less interest than preferred stock investors
in stability.

All of these comments on the things looked for by prospective and present equityholders indicate that they as a group want
to know as much as they can about the assets, net of "higher ranking" equities, and future "net assets" of the firm in which they
are considering investing, or have already invested, although different members of the group emphasize different individual asset and
equity items, primarily because of the differences in the periods
of time that will elapse before they expect repayment. Since assets
and equities at any future date depend upon present assets and equities and the changes that may arise between now and the future date,
long-term equityholders are especially interested in the processes
identified by such dynamic concepts as expense, revenue, loss, gain,
sales, costs, and production.

The conclusion is that the less current the claim of the
equityholder the further into the future he looks. Nearly all

equityholders need to forecast the firm's cash position, because nearly all of them expect to be paid in cash. They know, however, that there is a turnover of cash, and that they must forecast the cash position of the firm when their respective claims are due to be paid or are desired. Investors who are promised a periodic payment need to forecast from the present until the last of their payments; if they are holders of preferred stock with no indication of when it will be retired, they must look a long way into the future. Holders of common stock have a similar problem. However, if the distributions are cumulative, as in the case of ordinary bonds and cumulative preferred stock, there is less necessity to forecast the stability of the firm's cash position, because if the firm is unable to pay at the scheduled time but is able to "make it up" later little is lost. Of course, it must be remembered that the holders of cumulative securities are, in many cases, very much interested in stability of income, as well as average income, which partially, at least, offsets the advantage of a provision for cumulative distributions. Holders of noncumulative, nonparticipating preferred stock may be more interested in stability of the issuer's cash position than are holders of cumulative shares, but generally the former group does not depend on stability as much as does the latter group. Holders of common stock have the least interest in the stability of the firm's ability to make cash distributions, and the greatest interest in its long-run total ability to pay.

Equityholders are interested in forecasting the pattern of cash inflow into the firm in excess of cash outgo for purposes that rank higher than the payment of their equity in a going concern.

Generally speaking, such a net cash inflow results from economic
events which occur at an earlier date. In a forecast of this net
cash inflow, a summary of those economic events which indicate future net changes in cash is of great value; and the difference between the sum of the net positive effects realized or expected to
result from such events (e.g., the excess of the cash received by
selling merchandise over the cash disbursed in order to obtain and
sell the goods) and the sum of the net negative effects from such
events (e.g., the excess of the cash disbursed in order to obtain
and sell goods over the cash expected to be collected from the buyer)
would be a very useful datum to investors, if only it could be made
available. The rate of its occurrence during the recent past is
important to the equityholders as an indication of its rate of occurrence in the future, which, in turn, is a determinant of future cash
positions. The thing which accountants call "net income" is the
only item in current financial reports which is at all similar to
this net indicated effect of current events upon future cash available to the owners. The well known unreliability and variability
of this datum, however, necessitates analysis of its components and
many other factors by the investor who is to obtain a relatively
clear view of the future of his investment.

These are the needs of the groups in the society. They
arise from the need to make decisions about trading with the firm.
The information that any particular economic unit in the society
needs, in order to make these decisions, may be classified as follows: (1) the benefits it is obtaining from the current relationship, if any, with another economic unit; (2) the benefits that it

possibly could obtain from the best available alternative; and (3) the maximum benefits it possibly could obtain from the present relationship. Looking at this from the point of view of the firm from which this information is desired, we may state these things thus: (1) informing units trading with the firm of what they are getting from it, (2) informing units not at present trading with the firm of what they could extract from it in the future if they traded with it, (3) informing units presently trading with the firm of what they could possibly get from it in the future if they demanded it.

Now, which of these needs should the accountant consider? It is clear that business firms do not want to follow the general policy of attempting to give out all of this information, not only because much of it would be detrimental to the interests of the firm, at least in the eyes of management, but also because much of this information is already available to the interested parties without the special effort of the firm to give it, and often in a more accurate form than the firm could give it. For example, a customer can determine more accurately than the seller the value to him of the goods he buys. The suppliers, employees, and other parties with contractual dollar returns can get a better idea of what they are receiving from the firm than the firm can give them, because the value of money depends upon what is to be purchased with it; the holder of money knows more about his own spending plans than does the previous holder. On the other hand, certain groups do not even know the dollar amount of their shares in the firm's assets unless the firm reports to them. These include the income-taxing authorities and stockholders. For this reason, these parties are more

insistent upon receiving financial reports than are customers, suppliers, and employees.

The firm should give out this information if to do so will
clearly benefit it; if such disclosure would be detrimental to the
firm, secrecy is in order. The following examples should make this
point clear.

1. The firm could not be expected to tell its customers what a
   poor product it is selling to them, but it would not hesitate
   to advertise the (real or imaginary) merits of its products.

2. Prospective purchasers of a new issue of stock could not
   expect a long discourse on the low dividends that the stock
   is likely to pay, but if dividend prospects were good it
   would be eager to explain that situation.

3. Suppliers of materials can not expect notice that the firm
   is willing to pay a higher price, but they should not be
   surprised if they receive complaints that the present price
   is too high and that a lower price would be welcome.

It is evident that the management of a business firm can
not be expected to follow the policy of giving out all information
relative to its trading operations that the parties with whom it
trades desire. However, some of this information is given out to
certain groups. The management finds that it is necessary to provide these groups with certain information consistently, regardless
of its immediate effect on the firm. Who are these groups?

Any group that has the power to enforce its demands for information is likely to get it. The Bureau of Internal Revenue will
get the tax returns it requests; the Interstate Commerce Commission
will get the reports it requires; the Securities and Exchange Commission will get quarterly reports of sales, etc. But since these
bodies all prescribe, to a greater or lesser extent, the form of
the statements desired, it is suggested that their needs should not

be considered in designing "general purpose" statements, except to
the extent that there are economies in using the same data for both
specific and general purposes. Stockholders have, to some extent,
the power to enforce their demands for information. If they do not
have actual control of the management, tradition, to a certain extent, and legal requirements[1] force management to report at least
a limited amount of information to stockholders. Creditors who are
primarily lenders rather than only incidentally lenders (such as
suppliers of materials) are able to require the information they
want with some success. However, no group other than governmental
regulatory bodies and investors of capital has enjoyed any consistent and substantial success in getting the desired information.

Why is it that suppliers of capital who have no vote in the
election of directors are given consideration that customers, employees, and suppliers of materials are not? One reason is that
they simply will not trade with the firm without a certain amount
of information. They are risking their funds (sources of income),
while employees are risking only the current flow of income. They
have very limited means of judging the value of what they receive
in trade (notes or securities), while customers can examine a sample
of the product and usually the whole shipment they are receiving.
Employees, who can quit after sampling the work, know the value, to
themselves, of the money they are receiving. Investors depend upon
the ability of the company to repay after a considerable period of

---

[1]See, for example, Corporations Code--State of California
(1951), Sections 3006-11. On a national scope the Securities and
Exchange Commission has had a tremendous effect upon reporting
methods and procedures.

time has elapsed, while suppliers of materials do not allow a very long time for the firm to change its status. These types of factors are largely responsible for the demands of investors of capital for information and for their uniform refusal to trade without it.

Conclusion

Investors of capital (those parties who become creditors or owners of a firm with the expectation of receiving explicit compensation for the use of their capital) are the people with the greatest need for, and the most forceful arguments for receiving, the information that can be collected in the books of account and presented in financial statements to non-managerial readers. The longer the term of the investment the more uncertain the investor is about his prospects for a return of his capital and a return on his capital, and the further into the future he must forecast the firm's cash position and other aspects of its financial position. Therefore, the more permanent the capital the more emphasis the investor will place upon future events and upon current changes as indications of future events. Every investor wants to forecast the firm's ability to pay (money) when payment is desired, and legitimately expected. However, definite-term investors do not necessarily expect repayment of principal by reduction of total assets; refunding is acceptable and a common practice. Every investor is interested in the firm's ability to pay by converting other assets to cash, or by raising cash from other investors who are willing to commit cash to the undertaking. All investors are interested in the size of the fund of assets available for conversion to cash (through ordinary business activities or by liquidation) for repayment to themselves or lower-ranking equityholders, and the related trends. Therefore, all investors are interested in the correct statement, from their own point of view, of all assets and equities of the firm in which they have invested or are considering investing, and the change in the assets available to them. A certain amount of detail on the change is desirable in order to be able to predict its future course.

The conclusion is that published corporate financial statements should emphasize information for short- and long-term investors, and should not be expected to be general-purpose financial statements at all,[1] just because they are made generally available (through newspapers, statistical services, etc.). Certain information from such statements may be generally useful, but the limitations of one set of statements and the possible harm to the residual equityholders of providing too much information (to others) precludes the use of general-purpose statements that will satisfy everyone.

The chapters which follow will be aimed at developing a concept of revenue which will be of use to accountants in their work of assisting managers of enterprises to report to present and prospective investors in those enterprises. If the enterprise is not a business enterprise, the "investor" may be referred to as a citizen, donor, taxpayer, or patron. That is to say, a concept of revenue must be developed which will be of assistance in reporting to equityholders in nonbusiness enterprises, such as governments and charitable institutions, as well as investors in business firms.

---

[1]As has been pointed out in the text (pp. 7,14), the needs of other parties, especially government agencies, may be identical, in some respects, to the needs of investors. For example, the Securities and Exchange Commission, a regulatory body established to help investors obtain more information about securities, may have requirements which will result in improved reporting to investors, but in this study it is not taken for granted that the SEC requirements are ideal. The practices approved by the SEC, like any other accounting practice, actually must contribute to informative reporting to investors if they are to be considered acceptable practices in accounting to investors, although the force of law may cause their application.

There is one
class of equity that exists in every entity--the residual equity.
The residual equity is that interest in the economic unit which is
affected by changes in total assets which no equityholder has specifically agreed to bear. This equity--the equity of the proprietor
in a sole proprietorship, the partners in a partnership, the common
stockholders in a corporation without contingent or participating
senior securities outstanding--is thus a unique member of the accounting equation.[1]

Three other characteristics of the residual equity contribute
to its distinctiveness. One of these is the non-contractual nature
of most of the changes in it. The amounts of the changes in all
other equities are matters of contract between the equityholder and
the economic unit for which the accounting is done, although the
contract may be broken in a few cases. This is not true of the residual equity; indeed, this is the primary distinguishing characteristic of a residual equity. In the case of the usual type of residual equity in a corporation, for example, only the amount of the
original investment is determined by contract, except for a few uncommon incidents. Most of the changes result from transactions between the corporation and parties other than residual equityholders
in the firm--for example, customers. The stockholders have agreed
to bear the effects of such events, but the amounts of those effects

---

[1]Most business corporations have, as a residual equityholder,
the United States Government (in the fiscal years in which the corporation has a taxable income or a deductible loss). Most business
corporations also have at least one state government as a residual
equityholder.

are not matters of contract.

Another peculiar characteristic of the residual equity is the amount of attention that must be devoted to it in order to make certain that it is stated as accurately as possible. If any asset or any other equity is improperly stated it is very likely that the residual equity is incorrect. The proper determination of the residual equity depends upon the proper determination of all other balances. Now, it is true that if all items on the balance sheet are known to be correct except one, that item is also correct, regardless of what item it may be; but if one asset or one specific (i.e., nonresidual) equity is incorrect, the chances of the compensating error being in any other item are very small except in the case of the residual equity. In other words, if there are two errors in amounts on the balance sheet (and there can never be only one) it is likely that one of them will be in the residual equity. This is an important characteristic of the residual equity.

The other characteristic of the residual equity that is important in this connection is the significance of the changes in this equity, and the components of these changes, to investors. Information about items such as operating income and its components, income taxes, and dividends can be very useful to investors--especially to those who have the most difficulty in appraising their investments, that is, the residual equityholders.

The unique place of the residual equity in the double-entry scheme, the non-contractual nature of the changes in it, the difficulty in accurately determining its amount, and the importance to investors of changes in this equity make the residual equity so

different from all other members of the accounting equation that,
for many purposes, the most useful way of expressing the equation is:
assets minus specific equities equal residual equity.

The Need for Dynamic Reports

The ideal accounting report for investors would be a schedule of all of the future asset distributions to all equityholders. This information would enable the investor to determine the value to him of any equity by applying his discount rate to the known future distributions to the holder of that equity. Since accountants are not omniscient, a schedule of future distributions of assets to equityholders can not be prepared. The inability of accountants to prepare such a schedule, however, does not diminish its desirability. Accountants should attempt to approach the ideal as closely as is possible, subject to limitations set by the cost of preparing such information and the harm that might be done to the junior equities by disclosing certain information to other parties.

To be able to prepare schedules of all future distributions to equityholders would require knowledge of all other future transactions of the firm. If this knowledge were available, the accountant probably would draw up a cash budget for the remainder of the life of the firm; this would allow him to determine exactly when cash distributions to equityholders could be made, and the amounts thereof. If only part of the cash transactions were predictable, the system would break down completely; the amounts of cash available for distribution to equityholders would be indeterminate. This is the situation which the accountant faces.

The information which the accountant actually does have to work with consists of knowledge of a cash balance, a few promised asset distributions, a few definitely expected cash collections, the existence of certain things which are expected to contribute to additional cash collections, and the right of the residual equityholders to participate in additional asset distributions in the amounts and at the times to be determined by their representatives (within limits set by the available fund of assets). The most that the accountant can do with this information is to schedule the collections and distributions which he has some basis for scheduling, apply to each of them a discount rate which is generally accepted as appropriate, and estimate, in a consistent and objective manner, the present values of the effect of other things on future collections and distributions. The sum of the present values of the foreseeable collections and positive effects upon collections, plus cash on hand, minus the present value of the foreseeable distributions and positive effects upon distributions is the present value of the future distributions to the residual equityholders, to the extent that it can be determined; this present value may be consistent with an infinite number of different schedules of distributions to the residual equityholders.

Since this indirect approach (subtracting one total from another) is the approach that must be taken in the real world in order to quantify the residual equity, the result is an estimate of the present value of an indeterminate schedule of future payments. This sounds like an impossible calculation, and it is impossible to calculate this present value accurately by the indirect approach which we must take. But useful estimates of the value of things are commonly made without knowing the time and amounts of the receipts of benefit from them. If carefully made, such estimates surely will be considerably better than none.

The present value of the residual equity in a firm must always be computed by an indirect method; by nature it is the difference between the sum of the positive effects upon it (assets) and the sum of the negative effects (specific equities). This method of calculation is subject to many errors, but there is no other way of doing it. What can be done to eliminate the complete dependence of investors on this calculation?

One thing that can be done is to provide the investor with a schedule (balance sheet) showing the nature and amount of the various items (assets and specific equities) that were taken into consideration in computing the residual equity. This gives the investor some idea of the possibilities for error, gives him an opportunity to make adjustments of valuations upon which he thinks he can improve, and provides some indication of the time distribution of the future collections and distributions involving other parties, and, therefore, himself. This schedule should stress descriptions which will aid the investor in appraising these things. Those factors bearing on the value of the residual equity which can not be quantified in dollars should be described in a narrative report accompanying the balance sheet.

Because of the inability on the part of the accountant to
present either a schedule of future cash distributions to the residual equityholder or a correct present value of these distributions
based on a given interest rate, other data besides that entering
into the formal calculation of the residual equity at a given date,
and the unquantifiable effects upon it, can be of assistance to the
investor who is attempting to determine the amount of any equity.
One type of data which is useful as a supplement to the current
balance sheet in equity analysis work is a past balance sheet, or
a series of balance sheets as of a series of past dates. This will
allow the investor to observe the net changes in the reported
amounts of various net asset items and the net change each period
in the residual equity. While information as to the changes in the
various balance-sheet items during past periods is useful, it would
be much more useful if the reader knew what types of events caused
those changes. The significance of a net change in a balance-sheet
item may depend upon the source or sources of that change. This
means that reports of the increases and decreases in certain balance
sheet items can be very useful to investors.

The Statement of Changes in the Residual Equity

There are several balance-sheet items changes in which can
be reported by causes with the expectation that such a report will
be useful to investors. One of these is the residual equity; a
statement of changes in the residual equity, classified by causes,
often is of great value to the investor. Because the difference
between revenues and expenses is one of the key items on the statement of changes in the residual equity, a suggested form is illus-

trated in Table 1. The form itself is not of any great consequence, but the content of the statement is important.

In addition to the increase-decrease dichotomy, an important basis for classification of items on the statement of changes in the residual equity is time of occurrence. The effects on the residual equity of prior periods' events which were not recognized until the current period, are separated, on the statement, from the effects of current events. The amount of the residual equity as reported on the previous balance sheet, plus and minus the positive and negative corrections of that reported beginning balance, is the corrected beginning balance measured by the measuring unit which was popular at that time. If a different measuring unit, even though called by the same name, is in effect at the reporting date, the balance of the residual equity at the beginning of the period should be stated in terms of that current measuring unit. This adjustment of the beginning balance of the residual equity to state it in current terms has been recognized widely only in recent years as a necessary procedure in the preparation of statements of the greatest usefulness to the sophisticated investor.

The current section of the statement of changes in the residual equity should show all changes which occurred during the accounting period. These may include the difference between total revenues and total expenses, losses, gains,[1] and transactions be-

---

[1]The difference between the costs and receipts involved when a general price-level change occurs is referred to as a "gain" on the statement of changes in the residual equity. A net price-level gain on net money-value equities indicates that a rising price level is assumed. A net price-level loss on net money-value equities would be suffered if the price level declined.

TABLE 1

HYPOTHETICAL CORPORATION STATEMENT OF CHANGES
IN THE RESIDUAL EQUITY, 1954

Decreases			Increases		
			Balance, December 31, 1953, per balance sheet.................		$xxx
Corrections applicable to prior periods:			Corrections applicable to prior periods:		
Correction of federal income tax for 1949...................	$xxx		Correction of allowance for uncollectible receivables, 1953..	$xxx	
Overstatement of inventory, 1953	xxx		Other corrections requiring credits to the residual equity.	xxx	
Other corrections requiring charges to the residual equity	xxx		Total credit corrections.....	$xxx	
			Total debit corrections.....	xxx	
			Net corrections applicable to prior periods............		xxx
Total debit corrections...		$xxx	Corrected balance, December 31,1953		$xxx
			Price level adjustment............		xxx
			Adjusted balance, December 31, 1953		$xxx
Losses:			Excess of revenue over expense (see Table 2),...............		$xxx
Amortization of plant assets not in use...................	$xxx		Net price level gain on net money value equities..............		xxx
Other losses...............	xxx		Net gain due to percentage increase in money value of real value assets greater than percentage increase in general price level....		xxx
Dividends on common stock.........	xxx		Proceeds from issuance of additional shares of common stock........		xxx
Outlay for purchase of common stock held in corporate treasury	xxx		Total current increases.....	$xxx	
			Total current decreases.....	xxx	
			Net current increase........		xxx
Total current decreases...		$xxx	Balance, December 31, 1954.......		$xxx

tween the accounting entity and residual equityholders. The most important consideration in determining the classifications and degree of detail of this section of the statement is that the statement should be useful in predicting future changes in the residual equity. This means that nonrecurring items must be carefully separated from changes which can be expected to occur regularly or often.

Basic Premises

The apparent approval by many accountants of the neglect
being bestowed upon the balance sheet and revenue determination,
while expense measurement is subjected to many misguided attempts
at advancement, suggests the possibility that some basic premises
that underlie accounting to outsiders have been forgotten. Some
may consider it old-fashioned, but, for many of us, it may be worth
our time to go back to the beginning of accounting and try to decide what our field is all about. If we recognize the fact that
accounting is a technique of communication, and that it must involve the communication of some type of information to certain
people for certain uses by those people, it is likely to be recognized that the information is economic in character, that two of

the most important groups of people that should receive that information are managers of the economic unit to which that information pertains and investors in that economic unit, and that the investors want information which will help them make wise investment decisions. Additional exploration at this level is likely to suggest that there are several other groups of people who want economic information about the economic entity, but that conflicts of interest among all of the interested groups, together with the source of the control over the accountant, make it advisable for the latter to view the primary external reports as reports to investors.

Finally, spread through all seven chapters of the study is an insistence that accounting must be oriented to the future if it is to be of maximum usefulness. This is not meant to imply that the accountant should concentrate on forecasting future events to the exclusion of known facts. It does mean, however, that the way in which facts are reported should be colored by a desire to make those facts useful information for making decisions about the future. It has long been agreed that accountants must interpret information as well as record and classify it. This interpretation function should be carried out with a full understanding of the alternatives that are open to the reader of the report. The past is fixed; the future is controllable. The accountant who does not take this into consideration is likely to render reports which are less valuable than those of his fellow-practitioner who emphasizes usefulness more than assurance of not overstating net worth as an attribute of financial statements.

The Accounting Review

VOL. XXXIV   JANUARY, 1959   NO. 1

THE RESIDUAL EQUITY POINT OF VIEW
IN ACCOUNTING

GEORGE J. STAUBUS
Assistant Professor, University of California, Berkeley

THE American Institute of Certified Public Accountants' annual publication *Accounting Trends and Techniques* provides ample evidence that accountants do not agree on the point of view that should be taken in the accumulation of financial information and its presentation in "general purpose" statements. Likewise, a survey of the literature of accounting reveals that writers on accounting theory do not agree on the point of view that should be taken in accounting.

Some accountants believe that they should take the point of view of *proprietors* as a guide in the accumulation and reporting of financial data. Others feel that the point of view of the *entity*[1] is the most use-

ful vantage point for accountants. Another "point of view" that is often used in accounting, although seldom in business accounting, is that embodied in the *fund theory*[2] perhaps best described as a generalized point of view.

Statistics reported in *Accounting Trends and Techniques* indicate that no one of the above points of view has been wholeheartedly accepted by the accounting profession in the United States. That a distinct proprietary point of view is not popular is evidenced by the fact that, in 1956, 523 of 600 companies reviewed by the Institute's staff did not see fit to treat the stockholders' equity differently from creditors' equities on the balance sheet. This point is even more sharply emphasized by the absence of a title for the stockholders' equity section in the balance sheets of 38 of the companies. The lack of

---

[1] Some of the literature espousing the entity theory does not present as clear-cut a point of view as does proprietary literature. A striking example of this is the following paragraphs:

"Looked at through the eyes of the common stockholders the interest on notes, bonds, and other liabilities would seem to be a deduction not unlike that for labor, materials, and other operating charges."

"From the point of view of the enterprise as an economic entity and a center of managerial activity, on the other hand, treatment of interest as a charge analogous to operating costs such as labor and materials is objectionable. To management the cost of operating the undertaking is not affected by the form of capital structure employed, nor by the particular kinds of instruments used in raising the necessary funds. To management the bondholders' dollars and the money furnished by the stockholders become amalgamated in the body of resources subject to administration, and the net income of the enterprise consists of the entire amount available for apportionment among all classes of investors. Interest charges, from this standpoint,

are not operating costs but represent a distribution of income, somewhat akin to dividends." (Paton, W. A. and Littleton, A. C., *An Introduction to Corporate Accounting Standards* [Chicago: American Accounting Association, 1940] pp. 43–4). To the present writer, the points of view of management and the entity are very different, and interest is not a distribution of income from either point of view. The paragraph ends with a statement that expresses the viewpoint of all investors. See Staubus, George J., "Payments for the Use of Capital and the Matching Process," THE ACCOUNTING REVIEW, January, 1952, 104–113.

[2] See Vatter, William J., *The Fund Theory of Accounting and Its Implications for Financial Reports* (Chicago: The University of Chicago Press, 1947).

a trend towards the type of entity theory propounded by Professor Paton and others in recent decades is indicated by the facts that (1) the number of companies using the pure single-step form of income statement—a form that ranks interest[3] abreast of the other major expenses—increased from 13% of those analyzed in 1946 to 40% in 1956; and (2) the number of companies using a form of balance sheet that emphasizes the stockholders' equity section has increased sharply in the last ten years—from 16 to 77.[4]

This article begins with the proposition that the central objective of published financial statements is the presentation of information which will be useful in making investment decisions. An analysis of the informational needs of investors will suggest the importance of predicting the firm's future cash flows. The cash flow analysis will, in turn, lead us to the concept of the residual equity.

BACKGROUND FOR THE RESIDUAL EQUITY POINT OF VIEW

From the standpoint of complete exposition, it would be desirable to discuss some general aspects of accounting to which the author gave some attention before starting the analysis that leads to the residual equity concept. However, in the interest of brevity, that background will be presented in the form of a related series of conclusions.

1. Accounting is an activity. When accountants account they determine the qualitative and quantitative economic effects of events upon a specific entity, they report those effects, and they do several things between determining and reporting economic effects of events, including recording, classifying, and summarizing those effects.

    [3] Leading proponents of the "entity theory" view interest as a distribution of income. See the previous footnote.
    [4] American Institute of Certified Public Accountants, *Accounting Trends and Techniques* (11th ed., New York: American Institute of Certified Public Accountants, 1957).

2. Accounting is performed for a reason or reasons. The basic reason is to provide information that will be useful in making economic decisions—decisions such as those relating to investing, managing, taxing, and regulating.

3. The way accounting is performed should be influenced by the types of information that are needed to make economic decisions; accountants should account in such a way as to be helpful.

4. Accountants employed by the managers of business firms should not be expected consistently to concentrate on being helpful to parties who are bargaining with the firm, such as suppliers, employees, and customers. On the other hand, there are strong reasons why accountants must attempt to be helpful to three broad groups: managers, investors (including all parties who must make decisions regarding committing assets to the enterprise with the expectation of a return of assets later), and governmental agencies.

5. Managers need a great deal of routine and non-routine information, some of which will be the same as that needed by investors, but most of which will be specialized. Governmental agencies typically either prescribe their needs or accept the same information that is provided to investors. To the extent that the accountant is free to choose the methods he uses in the preparation of "general purpose accounting statements," he should make those choices consistent with the *major objective of providing information that will be useful in making investment decisions.*

This series of propositions may be used as the base for a discussion of the informational needs of investors, a topic that leads us through a consideration of cash flows to the residual equity concept.

THE PROBLEMS FACING INVESTORS

The investor group includes owners, whether they be proprietors, partners, common stockholders, or preferred stockholders, and creditors, including those who lend under various contractual arrangements such as debenture bonds, income bonds, mortgage bonds, collateral trust bonds, equipment trust certificates, mortgage notes, and oral or implied credit arrangements. There may be some question about the suitability of the term "investors" to include parties such as suppliers of materials and services and tax collectors who wait for their receipts from the debtor. While the essence of the investment relationship surely is the commitment of assets to the enterprise activities with the expectation, or at least hope, of repayment of a larger amount in the future, it can easily be argued that investors include only those who do so for the primary purpose of earning a return for the use of capital by the other party, and that parties who are willing to wait for payment, if necessary, in order to sell their commodities or services at a satisfactory price are not investors. While the suppliers, employees and tax collectors who wait for payment have other informational needs in their specific capacities, to the extent that they have to make the same economic decisions as investors, it is convenient to include them in the investor group. (Tax collectors, of course, usually do not make any decisions about commitment of assets to the undertaking or how long to wait for payment from the particular taxpayer.) The reader may prefer to think of certain creditors as "involuntary investors," or "incidental investors."

The economic decisions that must be made by prospective investors (and by present investors) revolve around the single major alternative of investing or not investing (or continuing the relationship or terminating it). If the investment relationship involves a transferable security, we commonly speak of the prospective investor's problem as whether he should buy or not buy, while the present investor who holds a transferable security may decide whether to sell or to "hold." In addition to these major problems that an investor may have, he may occasionally face the alternative of converting his investment arrangement into a different form, such as from a credit arrangement to an ownership relationship. This problem, however, does not add anything to the informational needs of investors as a group, because the information required to make this decision was already needed by creditors and by owners for deciding whether they should hold or sell.

A slightly different but related class of problems may face the prospective investor who has some control over the terms of the investment relationship. A bank or insurance company, for example, when planning an intermediate term loan to a business firm, may consider various restrictive covenants such as limitations upon dividend payments in order to maintain working capital at a certain level. Also, the period of the loan, the interest rate, and the schedule of repayments may require specific decisions.

INFORMATION NEEDED BY INVESTORS

What information does the investor need to solve these problems? In the basic situation, the problem is to choose between two alternative courses of action. Whenever a decision must be made to do this or that, the person making the decision must have information about the advantages and disadvantages of each possible course of action. These advantages and disadvantages should be stated in such ways that the relative weights of each factor can be judged. If the decision is entirely an economic one, the weights of the advantages and disadvantages may be stated in monetary terms.

While it cannot be argued that investment decisions are always based entirely upon economic considerations, it can be suggested that it is appropriate for us to limit our discussion to the economic advantages and disadvantages of the alternatives facing the investor. To the (prospective) investor who has not yet commenced the investment relationship, *one possible course of action is to refrain from investing in the particular arrangement* in question. The advantages and disadvantages of not investing are the advantages and disadvantages of whatever alternative use of money he would select. The provision of information about this alternative is outside the realm of the accountant who is accounting for the activities of the particular firm, even though that information regarding the "opportunity cost" of investing in this firm is essential to the investor.

The second possible course of action available to the prospective investor is to invest in the firm. The *disadvantage of investing* (the cost) can be measured by the amount of money to be invested or by the money equivalent of the non-monetary assets the investor transfers to the firm. If the investor is buying the rights of a previous investor, the firm has no opportunity to provide information about the cost of the investment, but if the investor is negotiating directly with the firm, the latter does have the opportunity to provide information about the price the investor must pay, although that information is not likely to be thought of as accounting information since it is not accumulated in the accounting process.

The economic *advantages of investing* may be thought of as the cash receipts by the investor from the firm because of the investment relationship.[5] In some cases investors may enjoy additional advantages such as increased receipts from another investment arrangement because of this one but information about such advantages, should not be expected from the firm in which the investment is being made. *If the*

---

[5] Receipts by an investor of assets other than cash are a possibility, but they are not likely to be planned. It seems reasonable to focus our attention upon cash receipts.

firm can provide any accounting information which will be of assistance in making a choice between investing and not investing, it must be information related to the times and amounts of the investor's future cash receipts from the investment relationship.

Present investors, like prospective investors, typically have two relevant choices; they may continue the existing investment relationship, or they may terminate it. Information relating directly to the advantages and disadvantages of termination of the investment relationship usually is not within the accountant's jurisdiction. The disadvantage of continuation is the receipt that could be enjoyed by termination. The advantages of continuation are the future cash receipts to be enjoyed by maintaining the investment relationship. Thus, information relating to the times and amounts of future cash receipts from the investment relationship is just as valuable to the present investor as it is to the prospective investor.

CASH BALANCE AND CASH FLOWS

Can accountants provide any information which will be of value to investors in judging the future cash receipts from the investment relationship? These future transfers of money from the firm to the investor depend upon (1) the *firm's ability to disburse cash* for this purpose, (2) the *legal status* of the investor's expectations, and (3) the *management's willingness* to pay the investor. Factors (2) and (3) are seldom of great negative significance; if the legal obligation to pay is clear, and if the firm is able to pay, unwillingness is not likely to prevent the disbursement. Likewise, if the management is willing and able to make the disbursement, such as a cash dividend to common stockholders, the lack of a legal obligation to pay is of little significance. Occasionally, however, one of these factors will offset the positive effects of the other two.

In considering the accountant's role in providing information to an investor regarding the latter's future cash receipts, we should first note that information about the second factor, the legal status of the investor's expectations, is outside the scope of the accounting process. Investors usually obtain this information in legal form without reference to an accounting report. Willingness to pay, on the other hand, is more closely related to economic factors that are more nearly subject to measurement and reporting. Dividend payments, for example, often depend upon the views of the board of directors with respect to the need to retain money to provide for obligatory cash disbursements in the immediate future, the application of cash to replacement or expansion of productive facilities, premature debt retirement, dividend equalization, and other possible uses of money. Some light may be shed on some of these possible future uses of money, by accounting reports such as funds statements, income statements, and balance sheets, thus helping the investor predict his own receipts of money from the firm.

The other important determinant of cash receipts by investors is the firm's ability to pay. Ability to disburse cash, as distinguished from willingness to do so, must mean the possession of money—a cash balance of the firm. From the point of view of all investors together, the times when they expect cash receipts from the firm are likely to include a representative scattering of dates from the present to the end of their investment relationships, and since the sale value of investors' interests will depend upon future prospects at the time of sale, they are interested in cash transfers from the firm to their successors. Investors, then, want information pertaining to the cash position of the firm for the period of their investment relationship with the firm and for a period well beyond.

Since all business enterprises have at least one owner-investor, and since owner-investors may be interested in receiving benefits from the business (in the form of cash) for its entire remaining life, or at least a very long time, the accountant must assume that a firm's *investors, as a group, are vitally interested in any evidence of the future course of the firm's cash balance and, hence, any evidence of the firm's future cash receipts and disbursements.*

The interest that investors have in the future cash transactions and balances of the firm cannot be denied. The cash balance of the firm immediately prior to the time the disbursement to the investor is due or expected and the prospective cash transactions shortly after that time are crucial factors in the determination of whether or not the payment will be made. If investors knew these data relating to all possible cash transfers from the firm to them, they would have nearly ideal information on which to base an investment decision. While it is clear that investors' desire for such information about the firm's cash transactions, and its value to them, is great, it is also clear that the concept is an idealistic one. In the real world of limited information about the future, a substitute must be found.

CASH EQUATIONS

Present cash balance plus future cash receipts equal future cash disbursements. We know that this cash equation holds, because cash disbursements cannot exceed what is available, and all cash received will be claimed by someone as long as money is desired and there are owners of the business. The impossibility of obtaining the data to fill out the cash equation results in accountants using a substitute for it: *assets equal liabilities plus proprietorship,* or *assets equal equities.* Assets include the present cash balance plus future cash receipts that are considered reasonably definite, plus other things that can either contribute to cash receipts or reduce cash disbursements. Equities include future cash disbursements plus other future relinquishments of assets. From the structural point of view, the basic equation of accounting (a practical, useful activity) is assets equal equities, but its usefulness will not be fully understood until it is recognized that its importance to investors in a money economy is derived from the fact that it is the most attainable substitute for the idealistic cash equation.

THE RESIDUAL EQUITY

Another way of looking at the cash equation is to distinguish between required cash disbursements and the remaining cash balance that is available for making payments that do not have a definite schedule. Thus, *present cash balance plus future cash receipts equal future definite cash disbursements plus future indefinite cash disbursements.* And, by subtraction, *present cash balance plus future cash receipts minus future definite cash disbursements equal future indefinite cash disbursements.* When this equation is converted to the practical form involving assets and liabilities, it becomes: *assets minus liabilities equal residual* (an equity). In the broader and more practical form, present cash balance plus future cash receipts are replaced by assets, and future definite cash disbursements become liabilities. The residue of assets left over after deducting the definite claims against the total asset pool will be claimed by somebody, because assets are desirable, just as we can be certain that all cash available will be disbursed eventually. In what are thought of as normal business situations, the claimants of the residue of assets (the holders of the residual equity) are owners. In non-business organizations, the residual equityholders may be citizens or members. In "abnormal" business situations, the

owners' equity, as reported in the balance sheet, may be reduced to nothing by losses; at that point, the general creditors become residual equityholders.

It is obvious that the residual equity concept is similar to proprietorship. However, there are three distinctions between the concepts. One is the above-noted fact that creditors can be residual equityholders. Another is that every accounting entity has a residual equity. In any business, non-profit institution, government, or other organization there is always some person or group of persons who have the right to benefit from the residue of assets. Finally, preferred stockholders are normally thought of as owners and as proprietors, whereas typically they do not qualify as residual equityholders. Thus, the holder of cumulative shares with a preference both with respect to dividends and in liquidation (the most common variety of preferred stock) cannot be thought of as a residual equityholder as long as the firm's earnings and net worth positions more than cover the preferred claims. Other types of preferred shares have a less clear-cut position.

The residual equity may be defined as the equitable interest in organization assets which will absorb the effect upon those assets of any economic event that no interested party has specifically agreed to absorb. For example, a cash sale of merchandise at a price in excess of the carrying value of the goods has an effect upon assets which some equityholder or group of equityholders must absorb. Since no equityholder has made a specific agreement to absorb the effect of this particular sale, the equity of the proprietor, partners, or common stockholders will be affected (unless unusual circumstances have eliminated their equities). These equityholders who absorb the favorable effect of the sale are residual equityholders. By contrast, purchases of goods and services on credit (at least those used in production), payments for goods and services, borrowing, and repaying loans all have effects upon the firm's assets which some equityholder has specifically agreed to absorb; those equityholders are not residual equityholders. For example, the purchase of goods on account has a favorable effect upon assets, and a particular equityholder (the supplier) has agreed to, and does, accept that favorable effect; his equity is increased. Uninsured casualty losses and changes in prices of assets held are economic events which no party has specifically agreed to bear; the equityholder who is affected is a residual equityholder.

THE SIGNIFICANCE OF THE RESIDUAL EQUITY TO THE INVESTOR

The last cash equation presented in the previous section showed a distinction between definitely required future cash disbursements and indefinite future cash disbursements. A particular investor whose contract calls for one cash transfer from the firm to him, such as a bank that has made a six months' loan, will be concerned with the firm's cash receipts and disbursements between the date of making the contract and the date the cash return is due. The chronological version of that cash equation is: *present cash balance plus future cash receipts up to the date the investor expects a receipt minus future cash disbursements up to the date the investor expects a receipt equal the cash balance of the firm on the day the investor expects his receipt.*

The chronological form of the equation reflects the going concern assumption. The equation also may be stated so as to emphasize the investor's position in the event of liquidation. *Present cash balance plus future cash receipts minus future cash disbursements to higher ranking equityholders equal cash balance that will be available to satisfy the investor in question (and lower ranking equityholders).*

Still another point of view towards the cash equation is that of a longterm investor who is concerned about the periodic payments he expects to receive over the life of his investment relationship. To him, *the period's cash receipts minus the period's cash disbursements that rank higher than his claim equal the net cash receipts available to pay him (and lower ranking claimants) a periodic return.* (The "times-interest-earned" measure of bond safety is related to this approach.) This point of view is a conservative and practical one in that it assumes that payments to parties other than intentional investors have a priority over interest and dividend payments. Payments for materials, wages, rents, and utilities must be made if the firm is to continue to have the resources it needs to carry on its operations; payments to investors are not quite so vital since the firm already has the investor's contribution, and failure to make prompt payments for the use of capital is not likely to result in the immediate recall of that capital, although it may in some cases. All of these views of the cash equation involve the notion of a *prior claim*, an important concept in investment analysis.

Prior claims are of great interest to investors who are attempting to predict their prospects for receiving cash from the firm. An opposite concept that is of interest is the *margin of safety, or buffer.* When looking at a balance sheet, any investor can look for equities that rank above his and for equities that rank below his. An important aspect of buffer equities is that they are significant primarily because of inaccuracies in the measurement of assets and equities. In a world of certainty, a margin of safety would not be desired. Like prior claims, the margin of safety concept is important both in liquidation and on a going concern basis.

To any investor, both the claims senior to his own and the claims junior to his are important. Looking at any equity, it may be important as a senior claim or as a junior claim; it may be important to some investors as a senior claim and to others as a junior claim. The residual equity, however, can only be a junior claim. It is important to the holders of all other equities as a buffer. The amount of the residual equity at any time is a buffer in liquidation; the amount of periodic change in the residual equity is a buffer on a going concern basis.

These aspects of the residual equity do not appear unique at first glance. All equities are either prior claims or buffers, and, with few exceptions, all types of equities play one or both of these roles both in the going concern view of the enterprise and when termination is considered. But let us consider the difference between the significance of a change in a higher ranking claim and the significance of a change in a buffer equity.

From the point of view of any equityholder, an increase or a decrease in a higher ranking claim also increases or decreases the firm's resources available for paying the claim, with the possible exception of certain tax liabilities. An increase in a higher ranking claim is undesirable, but the accompanying increase in assets is an offsetting, desirable change, because those assets are likely to increase both the earning power and liquidation value of the business. *The net effect of a change in a senior claim is not very great, in most cases.*

Increases or decreases in a buffer equity are entirely different. From the point of view of the general creditor, for example, an increase in the equity of common stockholders upon the issue of additional shares of stock is not disadvantageous, and the accompanying increase in assets is distinctly advantageous. *A change in a buffer equity is of great significance to any equityholder.*

From the point of view of investors as a

group, the special significance of the residual equity is that it is a buffer to all of them (except residual equityholders) and a claim senior to none. It is also of great significance to the residual equityholders as a measure of their claim. The residual equity is the one item on a balance sheet in which all investors have a strong interest; it provides a common meeting ground, a focal point agreeable to all.

Changes in the residual equity occupy the same focal position on the income statement that the static version of the residual equity does on the balance sheet. All investors are interested in the change in the residual equity due to operations during the period. An accrual of interest, or an accumulation of a preferred dividend, is not an especially newsworthy event; each specific equityholder is well aware of changes in his own equity, and is likely to have fully expected the changes in the other definitely stated equities. The changes in the residual equity, however, are not known in advance, and they are important because they represent the periodic buffer (or deficiency). *The focal point of investors' interest in the income statement is the change in the residual equity;* that figure should be treated accordingly.

THE SIGNIFICANCE OF THE RESIDUAL EQUITY TO ACCOUNTANTS

The residual equity in any economic unit has several characteristics which are of special interest to the accountant. If the economic unit is a business, one of those characteristics is that investors are vitally interested in the amount of, and changes in, the residual equity. Because of the importance to the accountant of investors' needs, he must regard the residual equity in a somewhat different light than he does other equities.

Another characteristic of the residual equity as an object of accounting is that there is one in every accounting entity. No other equity is found in all entities. No asset is so common—not even cash. Every accounting entity must have some equity that bears the effects of changes in total assets that cannot be assigned to any "specific" equity.

An aspect of the residual equity that is of practical significance to accountants is that its holder usually has somewhat more power over the (private) accountant than do the holders of other equities. It must be recognized that this power affects the objectives of accounting. In many cases, the accountant will strive a little harder to please the stockholder than he will to satisfy the bondholder's desires for information, although this should not be true of the independent auditor.

A distinctive feature of the residual equity as a legal and economic claim to assets of the firm is that nearly all of the changes in it are non-contractual in nature. Increases and decreases in bondholders' equities, employees' equities, banks' equities and most of the other equities are determined in time and amount largely by agreement between the management of the firm and the equity-holder. The residual equityholder may contribute assets to the firm according to a contract, but aside from increases in transactions with residual equityholders, that equity goes up and down without the specific consent of the holder; and in sole proprietorships even investments by the owner are not contractual changes in a legal sense.

A peculiarity of the residual equity from the accountant's point of view which is a corollary of the above point is that accounting for it is extremely difficult. Its measurement involves all of the difficulties connected with the measurement of all of the other equities and all of the assets. If there is a quantitative error in the balance sheet, the chances of any particular item being involved are not great unless that item is the residual equity. If there is an error in the measurement of an asset because of lack of knowledge, the residual equity is almost certain to be affected. Most of the difficulties of financial accounting involve the residual equity because of its dependence on the other items. To the accountant, this peculiarity of the residual equity is important.

All of the above-mentioned characteristics of the residual equity—its importance to investors, its presence in every accounting entity, the power that its holders usually have over the accountant, the non-contractural nature of the changes in it, and the difficulties encountered in accounting for it— all of these characteristics of the residual equity are related to its basic nature as the *member of the accounting equation which is dependent upon all other members*. The necessity for properly measuring all assets and other equities in order to determine the amount of the residual equity results in a natural tendency on the part of accountants to focus their attention on the residual equity. The accountant knows that if he properly accounts for the residual equity he probably has properly accounted for most, if not all of the assets and other equities. This near assurance of completeness is very important to the accountant. Together with the significance of the residual equity to investors, this confidence leads the accountant to focus his attention upon the residual equity when he is measuring events as well as when reporting them.

THE RESIDUAL EQUITY IN CURRENT PRACTICE

To say that the accountant focuses his attention upon the residual equity is not meant to imply that he shines no light upon other items. The residual equity, however, receives more attention than any other item. When measuring events, the accountant is often more concerned about the effect of the measurement upon the residual equity than its effect upon the asset or specific equity balance. As evidence of this concern with the amount of the residual equity, ask any accountant which mistake has the more serious effects upon the balance sheet: (1) the omission from inventory of goods that have been received and the omission of the liability for those goods from accounts payable, or (2) the omission from inventory of goods that have been received but the inclusion of the liability in accounts payable, thus resulting in the inventory error being balanced by an error in retained earnings. Both mistakes affect the total assets and total equities, but the second is considered more serious because the particular equity affected is the residual equity.

When he is considering the forms to use in reporting the effects of economic events, the accountant gives even greater emphasis to the residual equity than he does when measuring events. The tendency towards the "new style" of balance sheet, the tendency to consider the income statement to be more important than the balance sheet, and the fairly common practice of presenting a third statement (analysis of retained earnings) which also deals entirely with the residual equity indicate that accountants do focus their attention upon the residual equity when preparing "general purpose" reports.

While it is true that accountants give a lot of attention to the residual equity their reporting often is not clearly focused because they are not consciously attempting to use the viewpoint of residual equityholders. Explicit adoption of the residual equity point of view is likely to result in sharpening and quickening the accountant's analysis of unusual or complex events, and may add clarity to his reports. Explicit recognition of the residual equity provides the accountant with a much more clear-cut point of view than either the viewpoint of all investors, which might be thought of as useful in accounting to investors, or the viewpoint of legal proprietors, one that has long been popular in accounting to investors. Both the investors' viewpoint and the proprietary viewpoint (when it includes preferred and common stockholders) have the disadvantage of attempting to unify the points of view of people who are basically antagonistic to each other. The lowest ranking investors always want to minimize the returns to the higher ranking investors, while the latter want to maximize those returns.

CONCLUSION

There is confusion in the ranks of accountants who are responsible for reporting financial information to investors. Not only is there disagreement regarding the basic point of view to employ in such work, but many accountants do not consistently employ any particular point of view. It is in this setting that the author proposes that the residual equity point of view should be seriously considered by all accountants as a clear-cut vantage point from which to analyze and report the events affecting all accounting entities, corporate or otherwise, business or otherwise. Those who have been friendly to the proprietary theory should see some merit in narrowing the focal area to a single point by excluding preferred stock (unless it is participating preferred). Those who have felt that the distinction between owners' equities, in the legal sense, and creditors' equities is not as important in the large corporation financed by several investor groups as it is in sole proprietorships and partnerships should recognize the unique characteristics of the residual equity that justify singling it out for special treatment. Those who have been impressed by the independence of the institutional type of corporation whose management must attempt to please all parties related to it should prefer the residual equity point of view over the proprietary and "entity" points of view because the former is closer to the pure entity point of view. In the residual equity theory, all investors in a corporation except common stockholders are thought of as outsiders; from the pure entity point of view, all investors are outsiders.

One way of emphasizing the residual equity is to convert the primary expression of the accounting equation, assets equal equities, to the form: *assets minus specific equities (liabilities, including preferred stock) equal the residual equity.* In solving conceptual problems it is often helpful to think of liabilities as negative assets (although this must not be taken as a suggestion that offsetting assets and liabilities is generally acceptable). With the recognition of the importance of the residual equity, the liability category, like the distinction between creditors and owners, loses its significance; it is replaced by specific equities—a category that includes non-participating preferred stock. Assets minus specific equities may be shortened to net assets as an abbreviation; *net assets equal the residual equity.*

The supplementary form of stating the equation should not obscure the basis for double entry accounting. The fact that assets are desirable is the basis for the assumption that all assets will be claimed, and this assumption is the basis for the primary form of the accounting equation: assets equal equities. But in specific instances it may be more helpful to recognize that assets minus specific equities equal the residual equity. The most appropriate form of expressing any equation depends upon the purpose of its use. The distance traveled equals the product of velocity and time, but to the traveler who has no speedometer, velocity equals distance traveled divided by time. To the accountant who has no residual equity meter, residual equity equals assets minus specific equities.

The revised form of the accounting equation has the advantage of emphasizing the dependent position of the residual equity. Focusing attention upon the residual equity is not enough; unless its dependent position in the accounting equation is recognized, accountants may believe that they can measure changes in the residual equity (income) directly. Unfortunately, many seem to be attempting to do so currently. The proper approach to the accurate measurement of the residual equity and changes in it is to make accurate measurements of assets and specific equities (liabilities) and changes in them. The residual equity is a completely dependent figure, a difference. Its measurement must be approached through assets and specific equities.

Publications of the
Institute of Business and Economic Research
University of California

A Theory of
Accounting to Investors

GEORGE J. STAUBUS

UNIVERSITY OF CALIFORNIA PRESS
BERKELEY AND LOS ANGELES · 1961

53

Contents

I. *Establishing the Objective*   1

Current status of accounting to investors—General nature
of accounting—The investment decision—Role of accounting in investment decisions

II. *Significance of the Residual Equity*   17

Investors and cash—Significance of the residual equity to
the investor—Significance of the residual equity to accountants—Conclusion

III. *Assets and Specific Equities*   28

Assets and specific equities defined—Approaches to the
measurement of assets and specific equities—Measurement
at face value—Contractual evidence of future cash movements—Measurement at net realizable value—Replacement cost as evidence—Adjusted historical cost—Original
money cost—Measurement of assets yielding a series of
services—Criteria for the selection of measurement techniques

IV. *Changes in Assets and Equities: Economic Events*   52

Primary classification of changes—Classification of economic events—Significance of the eighteen categories of
events—Types of receipts and costs—Summary

V. *Revenues, Expenses, Gains, and Losses*   75

    Sales of stock in trade—Acquisition and disposition of services—Disposition of plant assets—Disposition of securities—Production—Mining of gold and silver—Tax receipts and costs—Gifts—Casualty and disaster costs—Discoveries—Changes in prices and price levels—Elimination of specific equities—Appraisal of the definitions—Final definitions of revenue, expense, gain, and loss

VI. *Financial Statements for Investors*   105

    Statement of assets and equities—Statement of changes in the residual equity—Revenue and expense statement—Purchases statement—Funds statement—Conclusion

VII. *Rudiments of the Use of Accounting Data in Investment Analysis*   140

    Index   147

I

Establishing the Objective

Man's desires are unlimited, but his means for achieving his ends are limited. Hence, any body of knowledge that can augment his bounty is useful. Accounting theory is such a body of knowledge.

All societies face scarcity relative to wants, but it is in highly organized industrial societies that the accountant's special talents make their contribution toward the achievement of a prodigious output. When decisions are to be made concerning the utilization of labor, capital, and natural resources, accounting can be one source of vital information. More specifically, by providing information that will help managers of an economic unit, such as a business firm, select the most efficient methods of accomplishing the unit's objectives, accounting can contribute to the efficiency with which scarce means are converted to desired ends. And again, by providing information which will help holders of capital select the economic units which can use that capital most effectively and avoid those firms which cannot use it effectively, accounting can make a further contribution to the satisfaction of human wants.

Services to society, such as these, lie at the heart of the accounting function. They explain in broadest terms what accountants as a group can accomplish. Although the individual accountant, working with an individual firm, may not explicitly verbalize this

aspect of his work, it is an obvious consequence when the totality
of accounting endeavor is considered.

To limit the scope of the present project to manageable proportions, I have concentrated on the second of these roles of accounting, that is, providing information to holders of capital funds in
order to help them select the units in the economic organization
that can use those funds effectively. From the point of view of
the individual investor, effective use of capital means use in such
a way that the user is able to pay the investor a satisfactory return.
This is his only practical touchstone. It is this need of the investor to be able to gauge the economic unit's future capacity to
pay that will be our guiding concern.

Recognition of the value of information for making investment
decisions raises two related questions. Are investors receiving
the information they need? If not, can accounting be changed
so that it will provide the needed information? The first question
can be approached from two angles: (1) Do the results of investment operations indicate that they are based on satisfactory information? (2) Has the literature of accounting theory shown
a proper concern for the investor? Reviews of investment results
and accounting theory will suggest that there may be room for
accounting to improve its service to investors.

CURRENT STATUS OF ACCOUNTING TO INVESTORS

Results of investment operations

Although results achieved by investors have been distinctly better
than chance would allow,[1] there is much room for improvement.
Extreme fluctuations in the market values of securities, bad debt
write-offs of firms selling on credit, and refusals to lend to companies that would have had no difficulty repaying loans—all are
signs of defects in the information being used to make investment
decisions.

These poorly based investment decisions have resulted not only

---

[1] Better results than chance would allow means that there is a significant positive
correlation between the "true values," measured on almost any basis one might
suggest, and the prices paid for specific investment rights. For example, there
is a positive correlation between market prices of stocks and discounted values of
those stocks, based on dividends for the next ten years and the market value at
the end of ten years.

in realized or opportunity losses to individual investors, but also in suboptimal allocation of society's capital resources. That is to say, not all losses by individual investors are related to the gains of other investors; some of these losses represent the misapplication of real resources. As long as these losses to individuals and society occur, we must conclude that the information on which investors make their decisions is not ideal. This conclusion does not mean that all blame should be laid at the door of the accounting profession; the potential of accounting as an information service is not that great. But the evidence indicates that accounting has never been consciously directed toward serving the needs of investors.

Accounting theory and the investor

A review of literature by committees of leading accounting organizations and by individuals who have given lifetimes of serious thought to accounting reveals that surprisingly little attention has been paid to the objective of providing information for investment decisions. Accounting writers frequently mention owners, stockholders, creditors, or some other subclassification of investors as readers of financial statements, but they seem to have made no special effort to show the relation between accounting and the problems facing investors. Rather, they have assumed that there is a relation without having bothered to analyze the problems of investors with a view to specifying just what information can be provided by accountants and also be useful to investors.

The American Institute of Certified Public Accountants has in recent years sponsored two reports which might have been expected to include careful analyses of the relation between accounting and investment decisions. In *Changing Concepts of Business Income,* the Study Group on Business Income[2] does not give specific attention to any reason for income determination other than as a basis for taxation and as a basis for computation of contractual obligations.[3] Investment decisions are not given explicit attention.

---

[2] The Study Group on Business Income was sponsored jointly by the American Institute of Accountants and The Rockefeller Foundation.

[3] Study Group on Business Income, *Changing Concepts of Business Income* (New York: The Macmillan Company, 1952), sections 2, 7.

Restatement and Revision of Accounting Research Bulletins
refers to society as a whole and specifically to buyers and sellers of
"an interest in an enterprise":

> . . . the problems in the field of accounting have increasingly come
> to be considered from the standpoint of the buyer or seller of an inter-
> est in an enterprise, with consequent increased recognition of the
> significance of the income statement and a tendency to restrict nar-
> rowly charges and credits to surplus. The fairest possible presentation
> of periodic net income, with neither material overstatement nor
> understatement, is important, since the results of operations are sig-
> nificant not only to prospective buyers of an interest in the enterprise
> but also to prospective sellers.[4]

The Committee should be commended for recognizing investors'
interest in accounting. The "increased recognition of the significance of the income statement" and the "tendency to restrict
narrowly the charges and credits to surplus" may be desirable, too.
The point to be made here, however, is that this admirable effort
by the Institute Committee still omits one step in the reasoning:
it does not establish the connection between investors and the
income statement, or between investors and the "clean surplus"
doctrine. The bulletin does not tell us what information investors
need and how they could use it. The result is recommendations
that seem to be detrimental to the interests of investors, for example, provide for all losses[5] (including losses to prospective
sellers),[6] and anticipate no gains.[7]

Other studies have identified parties considered to be the principal users of accounting statements, but these studies, too, have
stopped short of analyzing the requirements of those parties. Two
of the more penetrating analyses of the technical aspects of ac-

---

[4] Committee on Accounting Procedure, *Restatement and Revision of Accounting
Research Bulletins*, Accounting Research Bulletin No. 43 (New York: American
Institute of Accountants, 1953), p. 7.

[5] *Ibid.*, p. 42.

[6] It can easily be argued that the doctrine of providing for all losses and antici-
pating no gains tends to understate net income, net worth, and the book value of
common shares. To the extent that these data are relied upon, this doctrine could
lead buyers and sellers of securities to undervalue them to the detriment of the
seller and to the benefit of the buyer.

[7] *Ibid.*, p. 11.

counting which have been very influential among academic accountants are in this category. Paton, in his pathfinding *Accounting Theory*, emphasized "the preparation of the important financial statements for the use of managers, investors, *et al.*" [8] He clearly recognized that "It is the function of accounting to record values, classify values, and to organize and present value data in such a fashion that the owners and their representatives may utilize wisely the capital at their disposal." [9] He did not proceed, however, to the next step: determining what "value data" would be helpful to those users.

The Paton and Littleton monograph contains a similar reference to the users of accounting statements.[10] The authors back up this identification of management and investors as users of accounting reports with excellent discussions of the accountant's duty to the absentee investor and of the role of accounting, especially through the net income computation, in aiding the flow of capital into enterprises in which it can be used effectively.[11] Unfortunately, the connections between this view of the accountant's duty to investors and society and the several basic concepts on which the remainder of the monograph is based are never established.

Sanders, Hatfield, and Moore recognized that management, investors and creditors, and governments have need for accounting information about businesses.[12] They reminded their readers

. . . that although accounting statements contain information about the past and the present, investors and credit agencies are constantly trying to read the future in them. While the accountant cannot make himself responsible for these prognostications, yet he must know that his statements will be put to such uses, and should not include anything which will definitely mislead a person of ordinarily intelligent familiarity with such matters, nor omit anything necessary to make the statements complete.[13]

[8] W. A. Paton, *Accounting Theory* (New York: The Ronald Press Co., 1922), p. 5.

[9] *Ibid.*, p. 7.

[10] W. A. Paton and A. C. Littleton, *An Introduction to Corporate Accounting Standards* (Chicago: The American Accounting Association, 1940), p. 1.

[11] *Ibid.*, pp. 1-4.

[12] T. H. Sanders, H. R. Hatfield, and U. Moore, *A Statement of Accounting Principles* (New York: American Institute of Accountants, 1938), p. 4.

[13] *Ibid.*, pp. 21-22.

However, this general expression of the accountant's responsibility to investors and creditors does not seem to carry over into the remainder of the statement. For example, in their discussion of inventory valuation no mention is made of parenthetical or footnote presentation of replacement cost or net realizable value; a last-in, first-out, or base stock measurement of cost is considered adequate for the balance sheet presentation of inventories[14] in spite of the authors' admonition to accountants not to "omit anything necessary to make the statements complete" when they are presented to "investors and credit agencies [who] are constantly trying to read the future in them." A hint of recognition of the needs of readers of accounting statements does not suffice if those needs, like Caesar's good deeds, are soon forgotten.

George O. May has given more attention to the uses of accounting than have any of the above-mentioned writers.[15] Not only does he identify the uses of accounts,[16] but he also points out a common characteristic of their use. "The sole relevance of accounts of the past is as throwing light on the prospects for the future." [17] Considering Mr. May's long experience in public accounting and his sage comments on many key issues of accounting theory, he probably could have constructed a valuable theoretical system if he had started with these observations about the uses of accounts and their relevance to the future, and had made a carefully reasoned analysis of the information needed for those uses. However, he has not, to my knowledge, taken any such systematic approach to the subject.

Publications of the American Accounting Association show an interesting development of a concern for the uses of accounting reports. As late as 1948, the careful deliberations of a special committee and the executive committee produced a statement that

---

[14] *Ibid.*, pp. 73-74.
[15] G. O. May, *Financial Accounting* (New York: The Macmillan Company, 1946). G. O. May, *Business Income and Price Levels—An Accounting Study* (Study Group on Business Income, 1949). G. O. May, "Improvement in Financial Accounts," *Dickinson Lectures in Accounting* (Cambridge: Harvard University Press, 1943).
[16] May, *Financial Accounting*, pp. 19-21. May, *Business Income*, pp. 7-8. May, *Dickinson Lectures*, pp. 4, 12.
[17] May, *Financial Accounting*, p. 8. See also, May, *Dickinson Lectures*, p. 12.

showed no greater interest in the specific uses of corporate financial statements than the reminder, "So many decisions are dependent on interpretations of corporate reports that uniform, objective, and well-defined standards have become a requisite for the use of the reports by persons having an interest in an individual enterprise or in the broader problems relating to the national economy." [18]

The Committee on Concepts and Standards did begin to give a little attention to the uses of accounting reports in its supplementary statements following the release of the comprehensive statement in 1948. In Supplementary Statement No. 2, which dealt with the price-level problem, the Committee noted that ". . . corporate reports are typically prepared primarily for stockholders . . ." and proceeded to list six probable uses of "financial statement data expressed in uniform 'current' dollars . . ." [19] However, most of the uses listed were not of specific concern to investors, the most relevant one being "the analysis of earning power in terms of the current economic backdrop." Supplementary Statement No. 7,[20] on consolidated financial statements, referred to the use of financial statements by investors in the parent company and by minority investors in a subsidiary, and suggested that consolidated statements often are more useful to the former group whereas separate statements of the subsidiary are of greatest interest to the latter. In Supplementary Statement No. 8, the Committee on Concepts and Standards continued its explicit recognition of the users of financial statements.

The potential users of corporate reports include governmental agencies, short- and long-term creditors, labor organizations, stockholders, and potential investors. . . . The interest of some one audience should be identified as primary. Traditionally, this has been the stockholder group. . . . The Committee has been concerned primarily

---

[18] Executive Committee of the American Accounting Association, "Accounting Concepts and Standards Underlying Corporate Financial Statements," *The Accounting Review*, XXIII (1948), p. 339.

[19] Committee on Concepts and Standards of the American Accounting Association, "Price Level Changes and Financial Statements," *Ibid.*, XXVI (1951), p. 470.

[20] Committee on Concepts . . . , "Consolidated Financial Statements," *Ibid.*, XXX (1955), pp. 194-197.

with the use of financial statements (1) in the making of investment decisions and (2) in the exercise of investor control over management.[21]

Much of the Supplementary Statement on disclosure was incorporated in "Accounting and Reporting Standards for Corporate Financial Statements—1957 Revision." This document represents a major improvement over the earlier editions.[22] Perhaps at some future date the appropriate committee of the American Accounting Association will take the next step: inquire into the nature of the information needed by investors in solving their problems.

This brief survey of accounting literature reveals that a number of the basic studies of accounting theory identify investors as users of accounting reports, a smaller number of those studies give specific attention to the problems of investors, and none of the contributions to the literature of accounting begins by identifying investors as major users of accounting information and proceeds with an unbroken chain of reasoning through the problems facing investors and the types of information needed to solve those problems to the forms of reports that can communicate that information to the users.

General Nature of Accounting

The information investors use in making their decisions is inadequate. Furthermore, the accounting profession has shown little interest in relating accounting principles to the needs of investors. These are the weaknesses in current accounting theory and practice. But before we can make a successful analysis of the proper role of accounting in providing information for use in making investment decisions, we must have a clear view of the nature of accounting and some understanding of the decision-making process as it is performed by investors.

The primary characteristic of accounting is that it deals with economic affairs. Some accountants will say that accounting is a

---

[21] Committee on Concepts . . . , "Standards of Disclosure for Published Financial Reports," *Ibid.*, p. 401.
[22] For further discussion of the 1957 Statement, see George J. Staubus, "Comments on 'Accounting and Reporting Standards for Corporate Financial Statements—1957 Revision,'" *Ibid.*, XXXIII (1958), pp. 11-24.

branch of economics; probably even more economists will take this point of view. But this is an irrelevant issue. The point is that its relation to economic events is the most fundamental characteristic of accounting. The subject matter of accounting is economic events.[23]

What does the accountant do with economic events? The first thing he does after learning of an economic event is to analyze it to determine its effects. Such an analysis requires that he ascertain the qualitative and quantitative aspects of those effects. The *qualitative* characteristics of an effect of an economic event include an objective description of the particular thing of value (positive or negative) that is changed, and may include a description of the source or cause of the change. Both the things of value and the causes of changes in things of value are grouped into classes for analytical purposes. The *quantitative* aspect of an effect of an economic event is expressed in terms of the specific monetary unit which is accepted as the standard of value.

As an example, consider the entry,

> Dr. Cash $200
> Cr. Interest Earned $200

which records an accountant's analysis of an economic event. He has determined that one class of valuable things affected was cash and that the amount of the change was +$200. Another thing affected was the owners' equity; it was changed by +$200, and the source class was the earning of interest.

Before making this entry, the accountant had to *identify* the things affected (in this case a check made by Mr. Borrower and the equity of the owners) and the source of the change in the owners' equity (earning interest by lending money to Mr. Borrower). Then the accountant had to *classify* the draft made by Mr. Borrower as Cash and the earning of interest on the loan to Mr. Borrower as Interest Earned. Owners' equity, as an item affected,

---

[23] The term "economic events" is meant to be somewhat broader than "transactions." Transactions include explicit relations between two parties. Economic events include transactions and other occurrences that affect the economic position of the firm, for example, changes in prices of commodities held. The possibility of recording, in the formal accounting system, some of the economic events other than transactions will be considered in subsequent chapters.

is too important and unique to be submerged in a broader category at this stage of the accounting process; it must retain its identity as a class by itself.

The above form of notation is a common shorthand style used by accountants for recording, for future reference, the effects of an economic event. "Interest Earned," in this system of notation, tells the trained accountant both the valuable thing affected (owners' equity) and the source of that effect (the earning of interest).

After the accountant ascertains (identifies, classifies, and measures) the effects of economic events, he may perform several activities related to those effects. The most significant of these activities is the reporting of the effects, that is, communicating his knowledge of them to others. Between the time he ascertains the effects of economic events and the time he reports those effects, the accountant may record, sort, and summarize them. These activities, however, are intermediate mechanical steps which are carried out only to facilitate reporting the effects.

One additional characteristic of accounting must be mentioned. The economic events which the accountant analyzes are first selected from among all known economic events because they affect the specific organization (or economic unit) with which the accountant is concerned. To summarize then, *accounting means identifying, classifying, and measuring, and then reporting, the effects of economic events upon a specific economic unit.*

This statement not only may make some small direct contribution to our understanding of accounting, but it also provides a basis for raising some questions that must be answered by anyone who is to construct a theory of accounting. For example: What is an economic event? Should all economic events affecting the economic unit be reported? What techniques of measurement are applicable to which types of events? How should the economic events and their effects be classified for reporting? What forms of reports are helpful, and how often should they be presented? For what purposes should the reports be presented?

This last question is the most fundamental of all. In answering, we must remember that accounting is a practical activity and must meet a need if it is to continue. It is a useful activity, and its objectives must be thoroughly understood by those who are to participate in it. Accounting is an informative activity; it provides information to assist those who have to make economic decisions. These decisions may be of various types. Decisions relating to investing; decisions relating to buying and selling commodities and services; decisions to produce, to pay, to bill, or to insure; and decisions relating to tax collections—all are likely to be easier to make if accounting reports are available. *The purpose of accounting is to provide information which will be of assistance in making economic decisions.*

The kind of economic decision that needs to be made will determine the usefulness of various items of information. For this reason, specific types of decisions must be considered by the accountant who measures and reports the economic events bearing upon the economic unit. One general class of decisions is related to granting credit to, or investing in the economic unit. The persons making such decisions may be called "investors." Another group of decisions relate to the administration of the affairs of the unit. These decisions are made by managers. Other parties involved in types of decisions relating to an economic unit include employees, suppliers, customers, and governmental taxing and regulatory agencies; those not concerned in any special way may be considered "the general public." These persons who have to make decisions about the economic unit are possible beneficiaries of accountants' work. In order for them to enjoy those benefits, the accountant must consider their needs and wishes for information.

The Investment Decision

Investors commit assets to the undertaking with the expectation of being repaid a larger amount of assets in the future. The investor group includes owners, whether they be proprietors, partners, common or preferred stockholders, and creditors, including those who lend under various contractual arrangements such as bonds, mortgage notes, unsecured promissory notes, and oral or implied credit arrangements.

There may be some question about the suitability of including in the term "investors," suppliers of materials and services and tax collectors who wait for their receipts from the debtor. Although the essence of the investment relation is the commitment of assets to the enterprise activities with the expectation, or at least hope, of repayment of a larger amount in the future, it can be argued that investors include only those who do so for the primary purpose of earning a return on capital, and that sellers of commodities and services (other than use of money) who only incidentally wait for payment are not investors. The suppliers, employees, and tax collectors who wait for payment must be considered separately in any over-all approach to the problem of informing parties interested in an economic unit, but to the extent that they have the same economic decisions to make as investors, they should be included in the investor group. (Tax collectors, of course, usually do not make any decisions about commitment of assets to the undertaking or how long to wait for payment from the particular taxpayer.) The reader may prefer to think of suppliers of materials and services who wait for payment as "involuntary investors," or "incidental investors."

Economic decisions that must be made by present or prospective investors revolve around the single major alternative of investing or not investing (maintaining the relation or terminating it). If the investment relation involves a transferable security, we commonly speak of the prospective investor's problem as whether he should buy or not buy, and the present investor who holds a transferable security may decide whether to sell or to hold. In addition to these major problems that an investor may have, he may occasionally face the alternative of converting his investment arrangement into a different form, such as from a credit arrangement to an owner relation. This problem, however, does not add anything to the informational needs of investors as a group, because the information required to make this decision was already needed by creditors and by owners for deciding whether they should hold or sell.

A slightly different but related class of problems may face the prospective investor who has some control over the terms of the investment relation. A bank or insurance company, for example, when planning an intermediate-term loan to a business firm, may consider various restrictive covenants such as limitations upon dividend payments in order to maintain working capital at a certain level. Also, the interest rate and the schedule of repayments may be open for bargaining.

What information does the investor need to solve these problems? In the basic situation, the problem is to choose between alternative courses of action. Whenever a decision must be made to do this or that, the decision maker must know the advantages and disadvantages of the two (or more) possibilities, and these must be stated in such a way as to permit consideration of the relative weights of each. If the decision is entirely an economic one, the weights of the advantages and disadvantages may be stated in monetary terms.

Although it cannot be argued that investment decisions are always based entirely upon economic considerations, it is appropriate for us to limit our discussion to the economic advantages and disadvantages of the alternatives facing the investor. (Accounting statements are not of any assistance to an investor who is trying to weigh his noneconomic motives for investing.) The investor (prospective investor) who has not yet commenced the investment relation has two possible courses of action: he may invest in the firm or refrain from investing. The present investor has his choice (in many cases) of continuing the investment relation or terminating it. These alternatives and their advantages and disadvantages are summarized in table 1.

The tabular presentation of the advantages and disadvantages of investors' alternatives should be accompanied by several explanatory notes. One qualification relates to the future cash receipts from this investment. Noncash economic returns to an investor are a possibility, but they are not likely to be planned. It is permissible for us to focus our attention on cash receipts. A similar qualification should be made with respect to the present cash disbursement that is listed as the disadvantage of investing. The investor may transfer nonmonetary assets to the firm or previous holder of the security when he invests, in which case the disadvantage of investing could be measured (not necessarily accurately) in monetary terms even though the immediate sacrifice is not monetary in nature. Finally, we should note that investors

TABLE 1

ADVANTAGES AND DISADVANTAGES OF INVESTORS' ALTERNATIVES

Possible course of action	Advantages	Disadvantages
FOR A PROSPECTIVE INVESTOR		
Invest	Future cash receipts from this investment	Present cash disbursement (failure to receive benefits of alternative use of money)
Refrain from investing	No present cash disbursement (receive benefits of alternative use of money)	No future cash receipts from this investment
FOR A PRESENT INVESTOR		
Continue investment relation	Future cash receipts from this investment	No present cash receipt from assignment of existing claim (no benefits of alternative use of money)
Terminate investment relation	Present cash receipt from assignment of existing claim (receive benefits of alternative use of money)	No future cash receipts from this investment

may enjoy advantages from an investment arrangement in addition to returns from the firm in which the investment is made. For example, an investor may receive valuable information as a result of his investment relationship—information which enables him to carry on other activities in a more successful manner.

Whether the reader prefers to think of the disadvantage of investing as the present cash disbursement that must be made or the failure to receive the benefits of an alternative use of the money invested, the number of advantages and disadvantages of investors' alternatives is not great. In fact, they can be reduced to two basic factors: the future cash receipts that will be enjoyed if the investment relation is commenced or continued, but must be sacrificed if the relation is avoided or discontinued; and the present sacrifice of money (or the advantages of alternative uses of it) that must be made if the relation is commenced or continued, but may be avoided if the relation is shunned or is terminated now.

ROLE OF ACCOUNTING IN INVESTMENT DECISIONS

Accountants in the firm in question cannot be expected to provide any information about the advantages of the investor's alternative uses of money, or about the amount of money that would be sacrificed if he invested or would be received if he terminated the investment relationship. If the firm can provide any accounting information which will be of assistance in making investment decisions, it must be information related to the times and amounts of investors' future cash receipts as a result of the investment relation.

Can the accounting process provide any information which will be of value to investors in judging their future cash receipts from the investment relation? To answer this question, we need to consider the factors upon which the investor's future cash receipts depend. They are: (1) the firm's monetary capacity to disburse cash, (2) the management's willingness to pay the investor, and (3) the legal priority of the investor's claim. All three factors must favor the investor if the cash transfer is to be made.

The accountant's role in informing investors about their prospects for cash receipts may be analyzed by referring to these three prerequisites to investment returns. Perhaps the most readily noted point is that information about the third factor, the legal priority of the investor's claim, is outside the scope of the accounting process. Investors usually obtain this information in legal form without reference to an accounting report. Willingness to pay, on the other hand, is more closely related to economic factors that are more nearly subject to measurement and reporting. Dividend payments, for example, often depend upon the views of the board of directors regarding the need to retain money to provide for such things as obligatory cash disbursements in the immediate future, the application of cash to replacement or expansion of productive facilities, premature debt retirement, dividend equalization, and other possible uses of money. Some light may be shed on some of these possible future uses of money by accounting reports such as funds statements, income statements, and balance sheets, thus helping the investor predict management's willingness to disburse cash to him. Note, however, that for the investor to obtain any information regarding the firm's willingness to make a disbursement at any given future date, he must predict the firm's needs beyond that date.

The other important determinant of cash receipts by investors is the firm's capacity to pay. Capacity to disburse cash, as distinguished from willingness to do so, must mean the possession of money—a cash balance of the firm. Capacity to pay a particular investor means a cash balance at least equal in amount to that investor's claim at the date the investor expects to be paid. Since owners do not have claims for specific amounts at specific dates, they need information about the firm's cash balance over an indefinite, but long, future period. Furthermore, since the sale value of investors' interests will depend upon future prospects as seen at the time of sale, investors want to know about cash transfers from the firm to their successors. This extends to a great length the period of time over which the firm's cash balance must be predicted in making investment decisions. In fact, the accountant must assume that a firm's investors, as a group, are vitally interested in any evidence of the future course of the firm's cash balance and, hence, in any evidence of the firm's future cash receipts and disbursements.

We know that accounting typically can provide information relating to some of the firm's future cash movements (e.g., accounts receivable, bonds payable), so we must conclude that it can provide information of value to investors who are trying to predict their future cash receipts from specific investment relations.

III

Assets and Specific Equities

Uncertainty in economic affairs creates a need for accounting data and also makes the furnishing of these data a formidable task. The focal point of this uncertainty is the residual equity. But the quantitative dependence of the residual equity upon assets and specific equities shifts the accountant's attention to these pre-requisite data. To report the amount of the residual equity requires finding and measuring all of the entity's assets and specific equities. To report changes in the residual equity requires measuring the changes in all assets and specific equities. The need for definite concepts of asset and specific equity, and the importance of appropriate measurements of the contents of these categories, must not be underemphasized.

Assets and Specific Equities Defined

The first characteristic of an asset is its desirability. "Utility" and "value" are words that are more commonly used in economic analysis; one of them could be applied here. However, reference to "services" in the discussion of the residual equity has set the pattern for the definitions that follow. Assets can be thought of as stores of services.[1]

Another characteristic of an asset is its relation to a particular economic unit. Accounting involves ascertaining the economic effects of economic events on an organizational unit. An asset must be the asset of a particular accounting entity. Assets are personalistic; they are of potential service to a particular person or group. The adoption of the residual equity point of view suggests the identity of the beneficiaries—residual equity holders[2] in the organization to which the asset belongs.

There is another important characteristic of an asset. Frequently the reporting phase of accounting is more effective if the data in some classifications are added and then reported in summary form. If this is to be done, the events must be measured with one measuring unit in order that the items within classes and the different classes may be consolidated or compared. A monetary unit is commonly used as such a measuring unit. If assets are to be added and included in an equation, they must be subject to measurement with a monetary unit.

Furthermore, if investment decisions are to be based upon the amounts of assets reported, the measurements must be made as accurately as possible. But the desirability of accuracy in measurements is generally understood; references to techniques which will contribute to accuracy—such as basing the measurement upon objective evidence, using a constant measuring unit, and discounting—are unnecessary in a definition of asset. Those techniques will not be discussed until the measurement of assets and equities is given detailed attention.

---

[1] The service aspect of assets has been emphasized by other writers. " 'Service' is the significant element behind the accounts, that is, service-potentialities, which, when exchanged, bring still other service-potentialities into the enterprise." Paton and Littleton, *An Introduction to Corporate Accounting Standards* (Chicago: American Accounting Association, 1940), p. 13. Also, ". . . assets are service potentials, not physical things, legal rights, or money claims." W. J. Vatter, *The Fund Theory of Accounting and Its Implications for Financial Reports* (Chicago: University of Chicago Press, 1947), p. 17.

[2] Residual equity holders here are referred to in the broad sense which includes unplanned residual equity holders. If the planned residual equity has been eliminated by losses, the group that has the fluctuating, uncertain equity is an unplanned residual equity holder group.

An asset of any accounting entity, then, is anything measurable in monetary terms which will be of service, directly or indirectly, to the residual equity holders in that entity.

Specific equities are the opposite of assets in their basic characteristic. Assets *provide* service; specific equities *require* service. Otherwise the two concepts are similar. Both categories must be broad enough to encompass future service flows in noncash form; both must be measurable in monetary terms; both affect the residual equity in a particular accounting entity. A specific equity in any accounting entity is a measurable right to receive specified services from the entity—services which would otherwise accrue to the benefit of the residual equity holders.

APPROACHES TO THE MEASUREMENT OF ASSETS AND SPECIFIC EQUITIES

The summation approach

The first step that should be taken in the development of techniques for measuring assets and specific equities is to select a single clear-cut objective of the measurement process—an objective that is related to the needs of investors and that is consistent with the residual equity point of view. It is unnecessary that all "net asset items" [3] be measured in the same way, but it is reasonable to attempt to measure them all for the same purpose.

What are we trying to measure? If future cash receipts and future cash disbursements of the firm are of primary importance to investors, perhaps we should attempt to determine the amount of cash that will flow into the firm because of the existence of the particular asset being measured. If so, specific equities should be measured by the amounts of cash that will be disbursed because of the existence of the obligation in question. Although this "summation approach" eventually must be rejected, let us explore it further to clarify its defects.

If asset and specific equity measurement is approached with the objective of measuring the sums of future cash receipts and dis-

---

[3] Assets minus specific equities equal net assets; net assets equal residual equity. The term "net asset item" will be used to mean any component of net assets, that is, an asset or a specific equity.

bursements, certain problems are encountered. We have defined an asset in terms of service and measurability, so we must observe the distinction between things which will be of service to the residual equity holders and are measurable, and things which will be of service but are not measurable. If measurability must be related to future cash movements, then many things beneficial or detrimental will be excluded from the asset and specific equity categories. Land, buildings, machinery, and intangible things which will serve the residual equity holders, and some obligations to furnish services or goods are rarely subject to measurement in terms of future cash movements. If there is no contractual or direct evidence of amounts of cash that will be received or disbursed because of the thing in question, it cannot be measured by the summation approach.

Some accountants may suggest that a serviceable thing that does not promise definite cash receipts should be measured on the assumption that the cash disbursement made to obtain it is the present value of the series of equal cash receipts to flow from it. An estimate could be made of the number of periods in which such receipts would be enjoyed, an interest rate could be selected, and the rents of the annuity could be computed. These rents would be the assumed future cash receipts; their sum would be the amount of the asset.

But consider how the purchase of such an asset would affect the firm's assets and equities. The incoming asset, as thus computed, would be greater than its cost, because the undiscounted sum of the rents of an annuity is greater than the present value of those rents. The residual equity would be increased. It is doubtful if this technique of measuring assets would result in the reporting of a residual equity figure that could be helpful to investors as a guide for making investment decisions. It would seem that there would be a substantial difference, to an investor, between residual equity amounts created by purchasing long-lived assets and increases in the residual equity from other events. Valuable things that have very tenuous connections with future cash receipts do not seem to be measurable by this summation approach. If such valuable things are not measurable assets, their purchase would reduce the residual equity. Is this solution acceptable?

75

Other problems in the application of the summation approach to the measurement of net asset items arise in connection with borrowing and lending transactions. By this approach, interest payable and interest receivable would be permitted to affect the residual equity at the time the contract was made rather than as they accrued. If the borrower's liability is measured by the sum of the future cash disbursements called for by the agreement with the lender (principal plus interest), does the excess of the increase in the liability over the increase in cash reduce the residual equity or increase some other asset—one related to future cash receipts from the successful use of the funds borrowed? The latter possibility must be rejected on the ground that there is no knowledge of future cash receipts to measure. The residual equity decrease interpretation suggests that perhaps the management should not have borrowed.

An opposite situation occurs when bonds are purchased. Does the excess of the future receipts on the bond contract over the cash outlay to obtain it increase the residual equity? Can this interpretation be supported by a reasonable expectation that the position of specific equity holders has been improved by an increase in the buffer equity?

This analysis of the summation approach to the measurement of assets and specific equities, that is, adding future cash movements, may be recapitulated as follows: Some substantial bundles of services and obligations to render services would be omitted from the asset and equity groups. And some transactions, such as borrowing, would change the reported residual equity in ways that do not seem reasonable. The conclusion is that we must reject this general approach to the measurement of net asset items. An alternative must be sought.

Current value of the residual equity as goal of measurement
Recognizing that the amounts of assets and specific equities are used to compute the amount of the residual equity, and that the residual equity is the focal point of financial accounting, perhaps we can agree to establish the measurement of the current value of the residual equity as the common goal of the measurement of all assets and specific equities. The current value of the residual

equity is equal to the total of all assets measured on the basis of present values minus the total of the specific equities measured at present values. This approach to measurement would permit computation of the change in the residual equity over a period of time in such a way as to provide useful information about its trend, whereas the erratic changes in the residual equity that would be recorded if the alternative measurement approach were adopted, as discussed above, would not provide much information about the trend of the residual equity.

Some may object to the current residual equity approach to measurement on the grounds that it requires the abandonment of the most relevant information that is available—information about future cash receipts and disbursements that are reasonably certain of coming about. That is not quite correct. When those cash movements are converted to present values by the discounting operation, both the times and the amounts of the movements are considered and are allowed to affect the residual equity. Cash to be received in the very near future is measured at a larger amount per monetary unit to be received than cash to be received in the distant future. This is consistent with the interests of both residual equity holders and specific equity holders; the earlier cash receipts of the firm are the more valuable because that money can be applied to productive uses for a longer period of time before a given date when the equity holder expects to receive money from the firm.

The current residual equity approach to the measurement of assets and specific equities requires that they be measured at current values as nearly as allowed by available information. The current value of a net asset item depends upon the future; an asset has no value if it will be of no future service to the residual equity holders.

The type of evidence available to the accountant regarding the future of net asset items varies. In some cases he may have contractual evidence of a future cash movement. In other cases current market quotations are the best evidence of the item's future serviceability to residual equity holders. In still other situations, current market quotations may not be available and past quotations may have to be used. The accountant who is to measure assets and specific equities must be able to evaluate various types of evidence, choose the one type that is most appropriate in the circumstances, and obtain and utilize the specific data needed for measuring the item on the chosen evidential basis.

MEASUREMENT AT FACE VALUE

The measuring unit of accounting is the monetary unit; in the United States it is the dollar. Within this framework, the easiest measurement to make is a measurement of money. Each piece of currency or coin circulating in the United States today clearly shows its amount. This is acceptable evidence of the amount of potential service to residual equity holders that is embodied in that asset.

CONTRACTUAL EVIDENCE OF FUTURE CASH MOVEMENTS

The face or nominal value of money on hand is suitable evidence of its current value. Written, oral, or implied contracts calling for future cash receipts or disbursements by the firm often are accepted as evidence that future cash movements will occur. But the current values of those future cash movements are not equal to the future amounts.[4] The current value approach requires that the "known" future cash movements be discounted to the measurement date.

Discounting future cash movements means adjusting their amounts downward to compensate for a waiting period. The presentation of rights and obligations calling for future money movements at valuations lower than the sum of those money movements is so generally accepted as to require no explanation in this study. Furthermore, analysis of all the difficulties involved in discounting is beyond the scope of this work. It does seem worth while, nevertheless, to indicate some of the issues that are likely to arise.

The accountant who is to discount a future cash movement must know its amount, its timing, and the appropriate discount rate. Examples of circumstances that may make its amount un-

---

[4] See p. 31 above.

certain are failure of the debtor to perform in accordance with the contract and provision in the contract for alternative amounts as in the case of cash discounts. Timing uncertainties may arise in connection with the custom of not adhering strictly to the credit terms allowed on open accounts. There are several possible sources of discount rates, each of which may have its proper sphere of application. The rate inherent in the initial contract (e.g., the yield rate on bonds payable at the date of their issuance), the current market rate on the particular security owned or owed, and a general market rate of interest such as the "prime rate"—all these are likely to have useful applications in the measurement of net asset items by discounting future cash movements.

MEASUREMENT AT NET REALIZABLE VALUE

Many net asset items do not have a face value nor do they consist of contracts calling for future money movements. Nevertheless, some evidence of their current value to the residual equity holders may be available. If the general way of disposing of the asset is known, and the amount of money for which it could be disposed of in that way at the present is known, and only the time of disposition and the amount for which it will be disposed of at that time are unknown, the information that is available should be used.

This situation is likely to arise in connection with securities or commodities for which a well-organized market exists which allows sales to be made at small and predictable costs of selling. The net realizable value of assets meeting this description is likely to be the best evidence of their serviceability to residual equity holders. This technique falls short of a measurement of what will happen, but it uses all known information about what will happen together with the most recent known measure of the part of the future that is unknown. If the market in which the asset will be sold is known, this information, together with the most recent price for the type of asset in question in that market, and the estimated costs of taking advantage of that price, provide a sound basis for a measurement.

Specific equities also may be measured at net realizable value.

The net realizable value of a specific equity is negative, of course, and is equal to the probable cost of eliminating it currently. For a specific equity which consists of definite future disbursements of cash, measurement at net realizable value is almost the same as determining the market rate of discount relevant to that equity and applying it to the future disbursements; only costs of executing the transaction, such as brokerage, might make the two methods unlike. However, neither discounting specific equities at their own market rate nor measuring them at net realizable value is recommended; either method is likely to result in an occasional change in the residual equity in the opposite direction from the change in the financial community's opinion of the firm's prospects.[5]

One type of specific equity which sometimes can be measured at net realizable value is the obligation to furnish goods or services other than money. Liabilities of this type, often called "deferred credits to income," have a negative net realizable value equal to the cost of discharging them. If that cost is easily determinable, it is an appropriate measure of the specific equity.

REPLACEMENT COST AS EVIDENCE

Replacement cost may be distinguished from net realizable value by the fact that the former looks to the origin of the asset whereas the latter looks to its destination. Both techniques of measurement use current prices. The replacement cost of an asset is the sum of the sacrifices that would have to be made to acquire that asset now if the firm did not already have it. "Fringe" acquisition costs are included in replacement cost.

A difference between net realizable value and replacement cost, other than that related to direct costs of buying and selling such as commissions, transportation, and taxes, indicates that the firm buys in a different market from that in which it sells. Furthermore, if such a difference exists the firm presumably per-

---

[5] If financial analysts lower their opinion of the firm's prospects, measurement of the firm's bonds outstanding at net realizable value is likely to result in a reduction in the amount of that specific equity; the offsetting credit would be to the residual equity.

forms some economic function other than risk-taking and financing. Net realizable value of an asset is the preferable basis for measurement in this type of situation because it takes into consideration the destination of the asset rather than its source. If, however, at the date of the report the functions of the firm are largely unperformed with respect to the goods in question, and if the remaining costs before disposition are not substantially predictable, then the application of the net realizable value basis of measurement would require the use of unknown data; a current view of the asset's past may provide better evidence. Replacement cost may be viewed as relevant evidence of future services to residual equity holders on the assumption that it is related to net realizable value by a normal profit margin which will yield a reasonable rate of return on invested capital.

Replacement cost may be applied to specific equities (in which case it would be "replacement receipt") by determining what net cash receipt could be enjoyed now by undertaking an obligation just like the one in question. For example, if the firm has accepted money in advance on an order for goods not available in deliverable condition, the liability may be measured, at any subsequent date, by ascertaining the net amount (selling price less costs of selling) for which similar goods could be sold now.

A version of replacement cost which may be used as a matter of convenience would involve the revision of original money cost by use of an index of construction costs of the type of asset under consideration. For example, the replacement cost of a reinforced concrete building could be found by dividing the current index number for the construction costs of reinforced concrete buildings by the level of that index at the construction date, and multiplying the quotient by the original money cost of the building. The more specifically the index is related to the asset being measured, the closer this technique could be expected to come to a specifically computed replacement cost. It may be used for finished goods inventories of manufacturers as well as for long-term assets that are not held for sale as units.

The same technique could be used to determine the (negative) net realizable value of specific equities which call for payment by delivering goods which are not on hand. In this case, the present level of the index over the level of the index when an asset of the type called for by the contract was last constructed, multiplied by the cost of construction at that time, would show the estimated present cost of discharging a liability in the way that it is to be discharged. The replacement cost of an asset is the same as the negative net realizable value of a liability which is to be discharged by purchasing, or constructing and delivering, an asset of the type in question.

Adjusted Historical Cost

If an asset is neither money, a claim to money, nor a commodity for which some kind of current market price can be ascertained, the best evidence of its significance to residual equity holders may be a past market price. Typically, an asset that falls into this category is so specialized that the only past market price that can be obtained is the one actually paid upon its acquisition. If the monetary measuring unit has changed since the date of acquisition of the asset, the number of units paid at that time is not the best expression of its cost. Furthermore, the computation of the amount of the residual equity requires the addition of all assets. If the assets are not all measured with the same measuring unit, their sum cannot be expressed in any one figure. Since the assets that are measured on the basis of nominal, contractual, or current market evidence are stated in terms of the current monetary measuring unit, the easiest way to obtain statistical consistency is to adjust any asset amounts that are expressed in terms of an old measuring unit. This can be done with the aid of a broad, general-purpose price index. The level of the index at the date of acquisition of the asset is divided into the current level of the index to obtain an adjustment factor to apply to the original money cost of the asset. Use of this method of measurement can be facilitated by classifying assets by year of acquisition and by length of life.

The adjusted historical cost method of measurement may be applied to specific equities which obligate the firm to furnish services or goods other than money. For example, a magazine publisher could measure his liability for copies to be delivered on paid up subscriptions by adjusting to current dollars the part of the original subscription price which is applicable to the future issues.

ORIGINAL MONEY COST

A method of measuring assets that is generally less informative than those discussed above is original cost in terms of the monetary unit at the date the asset was acquired. In spite of its lack of association with future services to residual equity holders, this method has two very significant merits which must be considered. One is its ease of application, a practical advantage that may be decisive when measuring numerous small assets. A theoretical advantage is that original money cost usually is determined with reference to the future to the extent that the decision to purchase the asset is based on some expected pattern of future services from it. For assets which have been acquired very recently and which do not involve definite claims to future cash receipts, original money cost may provide the best available evidence of their service potential. Unfortunately, however, the amount paid for an asset is seldom more than a minimal guess as to what the future holds in store. Furthermore, the usefulness of this evidence can be expected to diminish with the passage of time, because the circumstances which resulted in a judgment that the asset was worth more than its cost are not likely to endure.

The original money receipt enjoyed upon the creation of a specific equity may be acceptable evidence of the amount of the equity if no other measure is available. Like original money cost, original money receipt is a poor method of measurement by logical standards, but on some occasions it may be the only technique readily available for application. (In addition, we should recognize that original money receipt often is equal to the discounted amount of the specific equity at the time of its origin, for example, when money is borrowed.)

MEASUREMENT OF ASSETS YIELDING A SERIES OF SERVICES

The measurement techniques described above constitute the entire list to be proposed here. The discussion of measurement of assets and specific equities is not complete enough to allow us to move on, however, because it has not included the peculiar problem of the measurement of assets that have yielded part of their limited original store of services, or have been reduced as a store of future services simply by the passage of time. This measurement problem is of particular interest because the more relevant types of evidence discussed above (nominal value, contractual evidence, market quotations related to the likely method of disposition) usually are not readily available, and the cost methods cannot be applied without adjustment for the reduction in the store of services.

Assets subject to physical exhaustion, obsolescence, or arbitrary economic life[6] pose a special group of problems that has long taxed the abilities of accountants, engineers, businessmen, and government officials. The major source of the difficulty is the uniqueness, or at least the relatively specialized nature, of each such asset; the more specialized an asset is, the more difficult it is to find evidence of the monetary equivalent of its service potential. Once an asset has been utilized in the conduct of the organization's operations, it typically takes on such a unique character that another asset which can be said to be the equivalent cannot be readily found. And to find a market in which equivalent assets are frequently exchanged is much more rare.

Needless to say, these assets do not embody claims to definite future money receipts, or at least we are not presently concerned with those that do. Measurement at nominal value or by discounting a series of future money receipts is not feasible in this circumstance.

---

[6] The term "arbitrary economic life" is used here to include cases of contractual or legal limitation on the usefulness of an asset. Patents, copyrights, and leaseholds are good examples.

Net realizable value

Assets yielding a series of services are, in some instances, subject to measurement at net realizable value. However, the unique character of these assets, considering the peculiar physical condition, location, and degree of mobility of each, makes the determination of maximum obtainable selling price and costs of disposition very difficult. Furthermore, the net realizable value method of measurement does not fit amortizable assets as well as it does securities or stock-in-trade, because the amortizable asset typically is not sold as a unit in its present form. Thus net realizable value of an asset of this type is a measure of the amount of money for which it could be disposed of in a market in which it is not likely to be sold.

Net realizable value has its advantages, however, especially when compared with its alternatives—replacement cost or a form of original cost. If we can obtain a market quotation or an offer for the asset that we are attempting to measure, such a quotation has the advantage of reflecting an independent opinion of the current store of services that the asset comprises. In many cases, the fact that the asset's net realizable value reflects its value in a use very similar to its present use makes a measurement based on an invalid assumption as to disposition (sale rather than use) more accurate than a measurement that requires an apportionment of the asset's services among calendar periods (depreciation) as well as an indirect measurement of the value of the total services (valuation at cost.) Net realizable value has the possible additional advantage of reducing the likelihood of overstating the asset. The fact that the asset is retained by the firm is evidence, although not proof, that the management considers it to be worth more in its present use than its net realizable value.

Original money cost

Assets yielding a series of services may be measured by reference to original money cost, adjusted historical cost, or replacement cost. If net realizable value cannot be determined conveniently, one of these cost methods must be chosen. The peculiar feature of this type of measurement is that the valuation to be assigned to the remaining services embodied in the asset is computed indirectly by figuring the costs incurred to date to obtain all services that the asset will ever yield and then deducting the estimated cost of the services received to date. This calculation leaves as a residual the costs incurred to obtain services in the future. This approach, assuming the measurement is to be made by the original money cost technique, can be expressed in mathematical language as follows:

$$A_d = \sum_{p=1}^{d} C_p - \hat{c} \sum_{p=1}^{d} U_p$$

A_d is the asset amount at any date; C_p is the cost incurred in any period in order to obtain future services of the asset; 1 to d is the holding period of the asset to date; $\hat{c}$ is the amortization charge per unit of service received; U_p is the number of units of service received in any period.[7] In traditional accounting language, the value of the asset at any date is equal to the sum of the costs incurred in connection with that asset to date less the depreciation taken to date. The account balance is equal to the sum of the debits minus the sum of the credits.

Charges to the asset account for the costs of obtaining its services seem, at first blush, to be for diverse things. If the asset is a machine, the first thing that has to be done in order to obtain the services of the machine is to acquire it. This may be accomplished by leasing, but the more typical practice is to purchase the machine. Acquisition by purchase usually involves some fringe costs such as transportation, installation, adjustment, and testing, in addition to the agreed purchase price. After the machine has been acquired, further costs must be incurred in order to obtain all the services of the machine. These postacquisition costs include insurance, taxes, interest, maintenance, repairs, and perhaps others. In this connection, the question arises as to which costs should be added to the asset account. The general answer is that any cost incurred in order to obtain services from the asset in the *future* (after the date of cost incurrence) should be capitalized. The wages of the operator, the cost of electricity or other source

---

[7] Cf. Canning's "service unit" formulas. J. B. Canning, *The Economics of Accountancy* (New York: Ronald Press Company, 1929), pp. 279-83, 290-305.

of energy, and other costs which are incurred to obtain *present* services should not be charged to the asset account, but the costs of holding and preserving the future services embodied in the asset must be related to those future services.

Interest cost requires special attention because of the apportionment problem involved in ascertaining the amount related to a particular asset. Apportioning interest cost requires that we determine the total interest cost for the organization during the accounting period and the part of this total that is applicable to the asset, or group of assets, in question. This calculation may be made by computing an asset interest rate from the total interest cost for the period, divided by the total assets to which interest cost is applicable. This rate can then be applied to the account balance of the item in question. Although the computation of the asset interest rate is discussed in detail in chapter v,[8] perhaps we should note at this point that the interest involved is a true cost in the traditional accounting usage of the word. The actual payments, or accruals, to specific equity holders for the use of capital funds are costs of holding assets. In this respect, the method of accounting for amortizable assets advocated here differs from the annuity method of depreciation. The latter approach results in adding "hypothetical interest earned on the asset investment value"[9] to actual costs and assigning the total to the operations utilizing the services of the asset. The method described here is a pure cost approach involving only the type of apportionments that accountants are accustomed to making in situations requiring the division of a single cost or group of costs among several objectives. (Witness traditional depreciation accounting and overhead cost allocation.)

The credits to the asset account represent the costs of the units of service that have been separated from the asset. The calculation of the amount of cost connected with each service unit released begins with recognition that frequently a group of costs is incurred for the purpose of obtaining a group of service units. The service units, such as a mile driven, an hour in operation,

---

[8] See pp. 81-84.
[9] Rufus Wixon (ed.), *Accountants' Handbook* (4th ed.; New York: Ronald Press Company, 1956), Section 17, p. 25.

or a month of availability, may be assumed equal in value at the time of their separation from the group. Accordingly, the cost of each is assumed to be the same as the cost of any other unit emanating from the same asset.[10] The mathematical expression of this idea is:

$$\hat{c} = \frac{\sum_{p=1}^{\hat{n}} \hat{C}_p}{\sum_{p=1}^{\hat{n}} \hat{U}_p}$$

$\hat{c}$ is the estimated cost per unit of service; $\hat{C}_p$ is the estimated cost to be incurred in any period in order to obtain future services of the asset; $\hat{U}_p$ is the estimated number of units of service to be received in any period; $\hat{n}$ is the estimated calendar life of the asset. If the service unit is the availability of the asset during the accounting period, $\hat{U}_p = 1$, and

$$\sum_{p=1}^{\hat{n}} \hat{U}_p = \hat{n}.$$

The cost per unit of service may be computed at various times. Before the asset is acquired, the manager may be interested in estimating the cost per unit of service under alternative methods of obtaining that service, such as leasing or purchasing. In making such a calculation, c is largely an estimate, because all costs, with the possible exception of the invoice price of the asset upon acquisition, are estimates; the unit of service to be received in any period is an estimate, except in those cases in which the availability of the asset during an accounting period constitutes the unit of service; and n is an estimate. As the asset ages, more and more of $\Sigma\ C_p$ and $\Sigma\ U_p$ become known so c can be computed

---

[10] Although it may seem reasonable to assume that a certain type of cost, such as interest or repairs, relates more to the services received during one part of the total life of the asset than to those received at another time, such an assumption surely would have to be accompanied by an assumption that some other cost, such as the original acquisition price, related more to other units of service. This dovetailing pattern of assumed costs is one of the valid explanations for the use of diminishing charge methods of amortization of the acquisition costs (less salvage value) of an asset when maintenance and repair costs are accounted for separately. If the latter are expected to be larger in the later periods of the asset's life, depreciation should be smaller in those periods, thus resulting in an approximately equal total charge per year's service received as the asset ages.

more accurately if the accountant wishes to recompute it. A revision of c would permit a change in the charge to operations per unit of service received as well as a revision of the net asset value, A_d, as computed from the equation,

$$A_d = \sum_{p=1}^{d} C_p - \hat{c} \sum_{p=1}^{d} U_p.$$

Upon retirement of the asset, c can be computed as the "actual" cost per unit of service, subject only to the usual inaccuracies in accounting, as both the total costs and the total units of service become known.

Estimated total costs of obtaining the services of the asset must include, in addition to the invoice price and fringe acquisition costs, the postacquisition costs that are incurred in order to obtain service from the asset in the future, as mentioned on page 42. An additional factor to be considered in the estimation of the total costs is the probable salvage value upon retirement of the asset. The sale price of the retiring asset should not be thought of in connection with the service units yielded by the asset $\left(\sum_{p=1}^{\hat{n}} U_p \right)$, because this salvage value is estimated in monetary units and the services released by the asset before retirement are stated in terms of a different measuring unit. The best view of the salvage value is as a negative cost to be included in the computation of $\sum_{p=1}^{\hat{n}} \hat{C}_p$, although it must be ignored in the computation of $\sum_{p=1}^{d} C_p$. This approach results in retaining the salvage value as a component of the asset value until the asset is retired, rather than assigning it to the units of service received.

Estimated number of units of service to be yielded by the asset may be stated in terms of elapsed calendar periods, time periods in actual use, or a physical measure of usage such as miles. The choice of the measuring unit for service rendered depends upon the cause of the diminution in remaining usefulness. If obsolescence is expected to limit the life of the asset, future usefulness decreases as time goes by whether the asset is used during the period or not. The same conclusion holds if weather limits the asset's life. If use decreases the future usefulness of the asset, then a measure of use should be chosen to express the total estimated service units.[11]

Before going on to explore some additional aspects of the measurement of assets yielding a series of services, a restatement of the presuppositions underlying our discussion seems in order. This technique of capitalizing all costs of acquiring and holding the asset and calculating the amortization charge by dividing the estimated total of such costs by the estimated total units of service to be provided by the asset is based on the following assumptions: (1) The cost of every unit of service is the same, that is, we must incur a group of costs to obtain a group of service units, and specific costs cannot be related to specific service units. (2) Every cost incurred to obtain the services of the asset itself is incurred to obtain future service units. Turning this assumption around, we can say that no cost should be capitalized in a particular asset account unless that cost is incurred to obtain service from the asset in the future. (3) In the particular model presented on the immediately preceding pages, it is assumed that the original money cost of the remaining service units is the best measure of the amount of the asset.

When these assumptions are considered acceptable but the technique described is relaxed because of practical considerations of some kind, it may be appropriate to depart from the equal amortization per unit approach. For example, if taxes, insurance, and interest are not capitalized, the heavier charges to expense in the earlier periods may be offset by an increasing charge method of amortization to obtain asset and residual equity amounts that approximate those computed by the purer approach. Or, if repair and maintenance charges are not capitalized, and if they are expected to have a tendency to increase as the asset ages, a decreasing charge method of amortization may be appropriate to

---

[11] Cases in which both use and the lapse of time diminish the future usefulness of the asset may be dealt with by splitting the asset into two or more parts for the purpose of assigning costs to service units, and applying a time rate to one part and a "units-of-production" rate to the other.

counterbalance, in a rough way, the increasing costs expediently charged to operations.

Adjusted historical cost

The above discussion is based on the assumption of original money cost measurement of the gross amount of the asset. Measurement of amortizable assets by the adjusted historical cost approach does not add any major problems. At each measurement date, both the gross amount of the asset at the previous date $\left(\sum_{p=1}^{d-1} C_p \right)$ and the accumulated amortization $\left(\sum_{p=1}^{d-1} U_p \right)$, or simply the net amount of the asset at the last measurement date (A_{d-1}), must be adjusted by the percentage change in the price index that is being used. At the same time, the unit amortization charge $(\hat{c})$, that is, the estimated unit cost of services provided by the asset, must be adjusted by the percentage change in the price index. Then the amortization for the period may be computed and entered. The current postacquisition costs of holding the asset will have been added to the asset as they were incurred during the period, thus being included at relatively current prices.

Replacement cost

The use of the replacement cost method of measuring the gross amount of an amortizable asset and the application of the amortization technique advocated in the paragraphs above result in somewhat more complicated procedures if both are completely accepted. The calculation of the replacement cost of every postacquisition addition to an asset account during a period of years and the recalculation of the total estimated costs during the life of the asset may be enough work to suggest the abandonment of the replacement cost approach to the measurement of amortizable assets. A more moderate conclusion may be that it is feasible to adjust both the gross amount of the asset and the accumulated amortization, but to adjust each only for the change in the original invoice price or construction cost of the asset, leaving fringe acquisition costs and postacquisition costs unadjusted. In terms of the equations presented on the basis of original money cost measurement, $\hat{c}$ would be changed as $\sum_{p=1}^{\hat{n}} C_p$ is revised or, more specifically, as C_1 is revised. This change in the amortization per unit would be reflected in the negative term in A_d, namely, $\hat{c} \sum_{p=1}^{d} U_p$, the accumulated amortization. C_1 in $\sum_{p=1}^{d} C_p$, the sum of the debits to the asset account, would also be changed by the difference between original money cost and replacement cost of the asset.

Alternatively, a simple version of the replacement cost technique of measurement may be applied to amortizable assets in an approach that omits the capitalization of any postacquisition costs. This expedient would be satisfactory if the postacquisition costs were expected to be relatively small, but it is conceptually inferior to the partial adjustment approach described above. Whether the simple version of replacement cost (omitting the capitalization of postacquisition costs) is preferable to original money cost with proper capitalization of postacquisition costs, depends upon two variables: the percentage by which replacement cost differs from original money cost, and the ratio of postacquisition costs to acquisition costs. A large change in replacement cost favors the simple version of replacement cost, whereas a relatively large amount of postacquisition costs favors the complete original money cost technique.

CRITERIA FOR THE SELECTION OF
MEASUREMENT TECHNIQUES

The significance of the residual equity and its quantitative dependence upon the assets and specific equities place a heavy responsibility upon the accountant who must select techniques for measuring assets and specific equities. Assets are homogeneous in that they are expected to be of service to residual equity holders, directly or indirectly. They differ, however, in other respects, and these differences must be taken into consideration by the accountant who selects the measurement techniques to be used in determining the amounts of assets. Few, if any, accountants would attempt to measure receivables by determining their cost, and not many more would consider it appropriate to measure a patent at acquisition date by discounting its future contributions to cash. There are several techniques of measurement which accountants apply to assets and specific equities; the determination of which one is appropriate for the measurement of a particular net asset item is the responsibility of the working accountant. He should choose that measurement technique the application of which will contribute most to the accurate measurement of the present value of the residual equity. In order to make such a choice, he must be familiar with available measurement techniques.

Unfortunately, not all assets and specific equities can be measured accurately at their present values; in fact, it is questionable if any can be so measured. Currency and coin on hand at the date of counting may be deposited in a bank shortly thereafter and distributed to stockholders as a cash dividend a month later. Measuring those money items by counting their nominal value may not be a measurement of the present value of the benefits they provide to residual equity holders because of two probable inaccuracies: a given amount of money transferred to residual equity holders one month in the future has a present value to them of a little less because of the necessity of waiting for it; likewise a given amount of money is likely to have more or less significance (purchasing power) to the recipient a month hence than it has now. Furthermore, the importance of these inaccuracies varies between different residual equity holders in the same entity. But these shortcomings in measurements of money must be accepted, albeit somewhat ruefully. They result from our inability to predict changes in prices and our inability to predict the timing of all future cash receipts and disbursements.

It may be argued that the services an asset will provide to residual equity holders cannot be measured precisely, but that other things, such as the money investment in assets, can be measured accurately. But even money investment in assets often cannot be measured accurately. The cost of inventories of goods for resale and plant assets for use in the business is often extremely difficult to ascertain. The purchasing, receiving, storing, and manufacturing costs of merchandise and materials are not at all obvious. The money invested in buildings and machinery constructed by the using firm is not easily ascertained. Claims against customers (accounts receivable) present a difficult problem of cost accounting. It is very seldom, if ever, that the money investment in assets can be measured with absolute accuracy.

Even if money investment in assets could be measured accurately, the wisdom of giving such measurements a key role in reports to investors who must choose between future courses of action would not be clear because of the doubtful relevance of those measurements to the investor's problem. We must never lose sight of the fact that investment decisions require judgments regarding the future. Investors rely on the amount of the residual equity and changes therein as a partial basis for making such judgments; they are most concerned with those aspects of past events that portend some part of the future.

The selection of a measurement technique is a selection of the most appropriate type of evidence. The application of a measurement technique involves obtaining specific evidence (of the appropriate type) regarding the potential service, or disservice, of the item being measured. There are two criteria for appraising measurement techniques, one on the conceptual level, the other related to the application of the concept: the relevance of the type of evidence utilized, to the problem of predicting future returns to investors; and the accessibility of the evidence. The latter criterion includes such variables as the difficulties in making estimates and computations, fees to independent appraisers, and the risk that bias may reduce the reliability of the measurements. This criterion can be applied only on a case-by-case basis as the accountant's judgment dictates.

Relevance, on the other hand, is subject to a general analysis. In accordance with the notion that the investor must attempt to predict the firm's capacity and willingness to pay, ownership of money must be considered the best evidence of potential service to residual equity holders. Measurement techniques utilizing other types of evidence may be ranked for relevance on the basis of whether the evidence relates to the future course of the asset (its

TABLE 2

RANKINGS OF MEASUREMENT TECHNIQUES IN ORDER OF THEIR
RELEVANCE TO RESIDUAL EQUITY HOLDERS

Measurement technique	Nature of the evidence utilized	Terminus of asset's life to which amount is related	Relative time of money transaction setting amount	Order of relevance
Counting money	Money	—	—	First
Discounted future money movement	Contract for future money movement	Expiration	In the future	Second
Net realizable value[a]	Market quotation	Expiration	The present	Third
Replacement cost	Market quotation	Origin	The present	Fourth
Adjusted historical cost	Market quotation	Origin	In the past	Fifth
Original money cost	Market quotation	Origin	In the past, with a different measuring unit	Sixth

[a] Net realizable value is more relevant than replacement cost if the market to which the quotation pertains is relevant to the firm. The replacement cost of assets not held for direct sale may be more relevant evidence of their service potential than net realizable value, if the only way the assets can be sold is as scrap.

expiration) or to its origin, the future course being more relevant to the residual equity holder who is trying to predict the future; and the relative timing of the money transaction which is taken as the basis for the amount of the assets.[12] Table 2 summarizes this appraisal of the relevance of evidence utilized in the six different measurement techniques discussed here. Although this table is worded to apply to assets, with a few changes such as replacing "cost" with "receipt," it could apply equally to specific equities.

[12] Every measurement in monetary units is based on one or more money transactions. Adjusted historical cost and original money cost are based on past cash disbursements by the entity. Replacement cost and net realizable value are based on current cash transactions involving other parties. Discounting utilizes information regarding an expected future cash movement. The identity of the parties participating in the transaction is not nearly as important as the timing of the transaction, because there are greater differences in service potential from time to time than there are between different holders of an asset.

IV

Changes in Assets and Equities: Economic Events

Uncertainty in economic affairs results in the impossibility of measuring all assets and specific equities accurately, leading to the inaccurate measurement of the residual equity, which in turn impairs investors' ability to make accurate predictions of their future returns. This suggests that the accountant should strive to supplement his report of the amounts of assets and equities with other data that can be of aid to the investor in predicting his future cash returns.

Accounting deals with the "effects of economic events upon an economic unit." These effects may be thought of either as the changes that take place with the occurrence of economic events (the dynamic view), or as the accumulated results that can be discerned after the occurrence of those events (the static view). The dynamic view of "effects of economic events" can add valuable information to that yielded by the static concepts developed in preceding chapters. The amounts of changes, rates of changes, and sources of changes in assets and equities are useful data. But not all aspects of changes in all assets and equities are equally informative.

PRIMARY CLASSIFICATION OF CHANGES

Without considering the cause of the change or the item that is changed, changes in assets and equities can be divided into two classes. One class consists of changes which bring a new item into existence or which increase the amount of an item which is already on the books. The other class consists of changes which decrease the amount of an item. This is a simple classification which does not require any particular point of view other than the recognition of two mathematical possibilities with respect to changes in quantities. Whether it is an asset or an equity, its quantity can increase or it can decrease.

The increase-decrease classification is not very meaningful by itself. It does begin to take on meaning, however, when we add a point of view that is meaningful in accounting, namely, the residual equity point of view. To the residual equity holder, the most important two-fold classification is not increases in assets and equities and decreases in assets and equities. To the residual equity holder, assets minus specific equities equal the residual equity, and it is increases and decreases in the residual equity that are the most interesting. Since the residual equity can be determined only by first measuring assets and specific equities, the residual equity holder is very much interested in changes in net asset items. Increases in assets and decreases in specific equities constitute one class of changes; decreases in assets and increases in specific equities make up the other class. The first class of changes in net asset items is, *ceteris paribus,* favorable to the residual equity holders; the second class is unfavorable.

These two classifications of changes in assets and specific equities are very important in accounting and in business in general. The objective of specific business activities is to maximize favorable changes in net assets while minimizing unfavorable changes. For the sake of convenience, short symbols for these concepts should be adopted. In view of present terminology, "receipt" and "cost" seem to be the best words. A receipt is an increment in an asset or a decrement in a specific equity of the economic unit, that is, an increment in a net asset item. A cost is a decrement in an asset or an increment in a specific equity of the economic unit, that is, a decrement in a net asset item.

CLASSIFICATION OF ECONOMIC EVENTS

Knowledge of changes in assets and equities is important in accounting for two reasons. One is that one way of ascertaining the amount of an asset or equity item at any time is to adjust the amount determined at a previous time as changes occur. Changes in assets and equities are also important because of their tendency to recur, or rather because some types of changes tend to recur, and thus provide a basis for forecasting future changes. The first reason for the importance of asset and equity changes requires the recording of the effects of the changes, but it does not require that associations be indicated. The second reason requires the recording of a change in such a way as to indicate the nature of the associated change, if any, or other circumstances surrounding the change, because the effect alone does not provide enough information to indicate the likelihood of the change recurring. For example, we cannot predict next month's cash receipts as accurately on the basis of knowledge of total cash receipts of previous months, as we can if we know the sources, as well as the amounts, of the cash receipts in the previous months.

Knowledge of individual changes in assets and equities is not as helpful for predicting the firm's ability to pay investors in the future as is knowledge of economic events which change assets and equities. The accountant should attempt to report economic events of interest to investors, not just the isolated changes in assets and equities. As an illustration, the disposition of a net asset item may change the amount of the residual equity in the firm. The change in the residual equity is of interest to the investors, but the cause of the change is also of interest. For example, if the change has been due to the premature retirement of a specific equity at less than its book value, its significance to the investor would be different than if due to the sale of goods manufactured by the firm for sale. Changes in assets and equities can be reported (net) by comparative statements of their amounts at different dates (comparative balance sheets). Economic events are not reported by such statements.

Many different kinds of economic events may involve the accounting entity. Some of them are of great interest to investors; others are of very little or no interest. Knowledge of some is useful for predicting the firm's ability to pay in the near future; others give indications of benefits to investors in the distant future. A system of classification of economic events, pointing up their differences and similarities from the viewpoint of the residual equity holder, would facilitate the job of reporting.

Differences among economic events

Economic events differ with respect to the asset and equity items affected. If we believe that no two assets or equities are alike, it follows that no two economic events are alike. Classification of economic events for the purpose of reporting to investors requires classification of assets and equities; we cannot limit the number of types of economic events unless we limit the number of asset and equity categories.

So many factors are relevant in the classification of net asset items for general purposes that no complete analysis is attempted here. Let it suffice to say that clerical accuracy, convenience of information needed for routine operating decisions, physical similarities, legal relationships, the prevention of theft, and a host of other factors justifiably affect the classifications which are reflected in general ledger account titles. These classifications are so convenient that it may be excusable to refer to "cash," "accounts payable," and other groupings as if they were individual assets or liabilities rather than groups of assets or liabilities.

Useful as may be the customary groupings for general ledger account purposes, they do not yield the distinctions needed for classifying economic events for reporting to investors. One difficulty is that there are too many such groups; another is that they simply are not designed for, and are not appropriate to, the problem of accounting to investors, being primarily bookkeeping classifications, secondarily managerial accounting groupings, and only incidentally related to the subject of this chapter.

What groupings of assets and specific equities can serve as a basis for classifying economic events? We defined assets and specific equities in terms of future services. By extending this reasoning to their classification, we can see that differences in the nature of the service or in its timing would be of interest to residual equity holders. But the nature of the service received by a residual equity holder is almost always a money transfer; if it is not, that fact is likely to be difficult to determine in advance. The nature of the service to be received by a residual equity holder does not seem to be a satisfactory basis for classifying assets, and it is even less relevant to specific equities.

Other possible bases for classifying net asset items are the timing of their anticipated effects upon the firm's cash balance, and the relation between the services controlled by, or to be rendered by, the firm and its cash balance. Let us consider timing first, although it will prove to be of limited value as a basis for classification of net asset items for the present purpose.

There can be little doubt but that a difference between the times when two assets affect the firm's cash balance is an important difference. It follows that there is a significant difference between economic events if they increase assets that differ substantially in their time relation to cash. Thus a purchase of ninety-day Treasury bills differs from a purchase of twenty-year Treasury bonds involving the same amount of money. The problem is to determine how to group assets and equities so that receipts of all items in the group can be considered similar events if the other sides of the events are similar. If differences among items are the time and directions of their effects upon the cash balance, then specific equities can be grouped with assets, and increases in assets and decreases in specific equities are similar events if the items have the same maturity dates. Grouping asset and equity items on the basis of the length of time until they will affect cash requires that the waiting period for each item be determined and that categories be set up for grouping items.

Both steps are susceptible to perils. For many items, the timing of their effect upon cash is extremely difficult to estimate, for example, goods held for resale and inventories of supplies. Some, like plant assets and bond issues, will affect cash at a number of different times so that they must be split into several parts. To draw lines dividing the items into groups would be completely arbitrary. Timing of effect upon cash is important to investors, but timing, by itself, does not provide any substantive basis for distinguishing between items. To say that the receipt of a promissory note due in three hundred and sixty days is one type of event and that the receipt of a promissory note due in three hundred and seventy days is another type of event is not a helpful distinction. In addition, arbitrary distinctions offer an opportunity for manipulation—a type of manipulation by management which could not be criticized very severely by accountants who establish the lines of division, but which could change the picture presented by the accounting reports. To describe assets and equities so as to indicate the timing of their effects upon cash is helpful, but to use timing as a primary basis of classification and to report the occurrence of economic events on the basis of such a classification would place undue emphasis on a difference of degree at the expense of a fundamental distinction.

The monetary–real goods distinction

Turning to the nature of the relation between the services involved in an asset or specific equity and the firm's cash balance, we encounter a substantive difference among net asset items. A distinction that is important both to the accountant and to the investor is the distinction between monetary net asset items and real net asset items, or "real goods items." [1] Monetary net asset items include monetary assets (money claims) and monetary equities (money obligations). Real net asset items include real goods which are assets, claims to real goods or services, and real specific equities (obligations to deliver real goods or services). Monetary assets include money and rights to receive reasonably definite numbers of units of money within reasonably definite time limits or at times chosen by the holder of the right. Mone-

---

[1] The monetary-real goods distinction may remind the reader of Gilman's proposal to distinguish between cash, deferred charges to cash, and deferred charges to future income. Stephen Gilman, *Accounting Concepts of Profit* (New York: The Ronald Press Company, 1939), pp. 297-301. Gilman, however, did not advocate the use of these classifications on the balance sheet, but he did argue that the basic test of "income realization" is the receipt of cash or a claim to cash. (*Ibid.*, pp. 98-124.)

tary equities will require the relinquishment of monetary assets. Real goods can be used to contribute, directly or indirectly, to the satisfaction of human wants without dependence upon a monetary system. Real specific equities will require the relinquishment of real goods.

Monetary net asset items are genuinely different from real net asset items. Monetary items have a direct quantitative relation to the firm's future cash balance; they are the parts of the practical residual equity equation presented in chapter ii (page 19) which can be expressed in terms used in the idealistic cash equation. The present cash balance, the known future cash receipts, and the known future cash disbursements (all monetary net asset items) are much more closely related to the interests of investors than are the other things that will have favorable or unfavorable effects upon the firm's cash balance.

Another difference between monetary and real net asset items is that monetary items depend upon the value of the measuring unit for their significance to the residual equity holder, whereas the significance of real items is dependent upon many other things but not, to any great extent, upon the value of the measuring unit. This distinction between monetary assets and equities and real assets and equities is important in accounting if the value of the (monetary) measuring unit is variable. The fact that some assets can be expected to become less valuable as the price level rises, whereas others may become either more valuable, less valuable, or maintain the same value, is an important distinction for investment purposes in a changing price level economy.

The monetary-real dichotomy is of immediate concern to the practicing accountant for another reason. When he is accounting for monetary assets and equities, the accountant usually "knows" the future cash movements that will be connected with the item. This means that it is much easier to use a highly relevant technique of measurement with monetary items than with real goods items, the future of which is usually less certain. This difference in measurability means that the future significance of monetary items to investors can be determined with greater certainty than it can for real goods items.

The distinction between monetary items and real goods items

is a useful distinction in accounting. That this distinction can be used to classify economic events meaningfully is manifest when a few examples are considered. Thus, we see that a purchase of government bonds (a monetary asset) for cash is substantially different from the cash purchase of goods for resale (a real goods asset). The cash sale of machinery (a real good) by its manufacturer has a different significance from the collection of a trade account receivable (a monetary asset). The receipt of money from a customer for goods to be delivered in the future (a real specific equity) is viewed by the investor as not at all similar to the receipt of money by borrowing from a bank (which creates a monetary specific equity).

Economic events may be classified on the basis of whether the "receipt" affects a monetary net asset item or a real net asset item. They may also be classified according to the real or monetary nature of the net asset item involved in the "cost." These bases of classification are helpful in grouping economic events for reporting to investors. However, other characteristics of economic events provide additional bases for grouping them.

Two-sided and one-sided events

A third basis of classification of economic events is the number of directions in which net asset items move. A two-sided event involves at least one receipt and one cost; a one-sided event involves a receipt or a cost, but not both (although a one-sided event may be the indirect result of, or indirectly result in, an opposite value flow in the past or in the future).[2]

A two-sided event may be recorded without changing the reported residual equity; a one-sided event must change the reported residual equity. This difference has a distinct bearing on accounting to residual equity holders and other investors who are concerned about the amount of the residual equity.

Transactions and intra-actions

A fourth basis on which economic events may be classified is whether or not another economic unit is involved. On this basis,

---

[2] For example, the gratuitous services provided by the American Red Cross may result, indirectly, in future receipts of contributions by that organization.

an event may be a transaction or an intra-action. A transaction may be defined as an economic event in which something of measurable value is passed voluntarily from one party to another —and perhaps both ways—with both parties aware of the existence and participation of the other. Voluntary passage of consideration would include the payment of taxes but would exclude the payment of fines or the relinquishment of assets by robbery. An intra-action is an economic event that has a measurable effect upon the firm but does not involve the voluntary, explicit participation of two parties known to each other. Examples of intra-actions are the physical destruction of an uninsured asset by wind storm, a robbery, accidental discovery of an asset, production operations,[3] and changes in the amounts of assets or equities due to changes in prices or price levels.

Transactions differ from intra-actions in two ways that are important in accounting to investors. One characteristic of one-sided intra-actions that is especially interesting to investors is that they are completely unpredictable. The occurrence of such an event (e.g., a casualty loss or a change in an asset's market value) in one period provides no basis whatsoever for predicting the future. One-sided transactions (e.g., donations and income tax accruals) though not always regular in the time and amount of their occurrence, have a much greater tendency to recur, and knowledge of them is much more useful for predicting the future than is true of one-sided intra-actions.

Another difference between transactions and intra-actions that is of practical significance to accountants is that intra-actions generally are more difficult for accountants to verify than are transactions. Documentary evidence and the opportunity to have the occurrence of the event confirmed by other parties often are not available if the event does not involve a specific relationship with another party. Although this difficulty of verification does not mean that the event should be ignored, it does suggest the desirability of separate classifications for events that differ in verifiability but are similar otherwise.

---

[3] The use of services in production operations, just as the use of materials, is viewed as an event separate from their acquisition. Use of services and materials would be an intra-action because they are already in the accounting entity; they may be viewed as having been acquired in a previous event—a transaction.

Transactions with residual equity holders

Four bases for distinguishing among economic events have been discussed. Classification of economic events on these bases results in groups of events each of which is homogeneous and each of which has a distinct significance to investors. But there is one more characteristic of economic events that should be isolated. Those transactions between the accounting entity and its residual equity holders (as such) should be set aside in two separate categories before the other four bases of classification are applied. Transactions with residual equity holders which increase the residual equity constitute a distinct class of economic events. Transactions with residual equity holders which decrease the residual equity make up another group of events that should be reported separately.

Eighteen categories of economic events

The use of these bases of classification is summarized in the outline below. Two classes are set aside for transactions with residual equity holders. The remaining economic events are classified according to (1) whether it is a transaction or an intra-action, (2) the number of directions that net asset items move in the event, (3) the real or monetary nature of the receipts, and (4) the real or monetary nature of the cost. The classes are described and examples are given in the outline that follows. This outline is presented as an integral part of the conceptual structure for accounting to investors.

    I. Transactions between the economic unit and its residual equity holders.

(1)   A. Increments in a net asset item and the residual equity. Examples: Investment by proprietor or partners; issue of common stock; assessment of stockholders.

(2)   B. Decrements in a net asset item and the residual equity. Examples: Withdrawal by a proprietor; declaration of a dividend on common stock; corporation's acquisition of its own common stock.

    II. Events other than transactions between the economic unit and its residual equity holders.

A. Transactions
  1. Two-sided
    a. Monetary receipt (increment in a monetary net asset item)

(3)   i. Monetary cost (decrement in a monetary net asset item). Examples: Collection of a note receivable; acquisition of bonds for cash; borrowing money; repaying a loan.

(4)   ii. Real cost (decrement in a real net asset item). Examples: Sale of merchandise; furnishing of a service (purchased services considered assets before being furnished to customer); cash receipt on contract to sell merchandise.

    b. Real receipt (increment in a real net asset item)

(5)   i. Monetary cost. Examples: Purchase of merchandise on account; purchase of equipment for cash.

(6)   ii. Real cost. Examples: Exchange of building lots; exchange of merchandise for truck; delivery of merchandise for which cash has been received previously on contract to sell.

  2. One-sided
    a. Receipt

(7)   i. Monetary receipt. Examples: Receipt of a gift of money; levy of taxes on property owners (from point of view of government).

(8)   ii. Real receipt. Examples: Receipt of gift of real estate; receipt of gift of personal services.

    b. Cost

(9)   i. Monetary cost. Examples: Donation of money to a charitable organization; accrual of income tax (from taxpayer's point of view).

(10)   ii. Real cost. Examples: Contribution of merchandise to a charitable organization; furnishing of services by a charitable organization or government without charging the beneficiary.

B. Intra-actions
  1. Two-sided
    a. Monetary receipt

(11)   i. Monetary cost. Example: A change in the value of money while the firm has monetary assets and equities.

(12) ii. Real cost. Example: Final step in the preparation of gold or silver for sale to the United States Government.[4]

    b. Real receipt

(13) i. Monetary cost. Example: The use of gold or silver industrially.

(14) ii. Real cost. Example: The application of purchased materials, equipment, and services to production operations.

  2. One-sided

    a. Receipt

(15) i. Monetary receipt. Example: Accidental discovery of money.

(16) ii. Real receipt. Examples: Accidental discovery of oil on land owned by the firm; increase in market value of inventory of merchandise.

    b. Cost

(17) i. Monetary cost. Example: Loss of money by robbery.

(18) ii. Real cost. Examples: Destruction of an uninsured building by fire; decline in the market value of an inventory of merchandise.

SIGNIFICANCE OF THE EIGHTEEN CATEGORIES OF EVENTS

The eighteen categories of economic events that might affect a given accounting entity must be analyzed to determine their meaning in accounting to investors. If the residual equity point of view is to be maintained, perhaps the first line of investigation should be an attempt to appraise the relative significance of the different categories of events to the residual equity holders.

Events that change the residual equity

One basis for singling out categories of economic events as significant to the residual equity holders is whether or not those events change the residual equity, or how likely they are to change the residual equity. Although it is clear that the transactions with

---

[4] Precious metals which the government stands ready to purchase at a price that is high enough to stand as a stable market price should be viewed as monetary assets of the holder, if the metal is ready for sale. They have the two important characteristics of monetary assets: their value fluctuates with the value of money, and they are accurately measurable by a relevant technique.

residual equity holders and the one-sided events change the residual equity, whether or not the two-sided events in Part II of the outline change the recorded residual equity depends upon the measurement techniques that are employed. If an incoming asset is recorded at cost (that is, if the amount of the receipt is determined by the amount of the cost, as in the typical purchase transaction), the event does not change the residual equity. If, on the other hand, an incoming asset is recorded at nominal value, as in a cash sale of merchandise, or at discounted value, or at net realizable value, the net asset inflow may not equal the outflow, so the event may change the residual equity. In order that we may tally all of those types of events that are likely to change the recorded amount of the residual equity, we shall make a brief survey of the two-sided events listed in Part II of the outline. (The reader should refer to the outline for a description of each type of event as it is analyzed.)

Starting with two-sided transactions, events in category (3) are not likely to be recorded in such a manner as to change the residual equity; typically, the receipt will equal the cost (if all amounts were up-to-date before recording this event). Category (4), on the other hand, can be expected to include a large number of transactions that affect the residual equity, because the monetary asset that is received (or monetary specific equity that is eliminated) is likely to be measured at nominal value or discounted value, rather than at the amount of the cost involved. The transactions in (5) are not likely to affect the recorded residual equity, because it is not likely that evidence will be available to warrant initial valuation of the real item at any amount other than the monetary cost that was incurred. The transactions in (6), involving real goods items on both sides, can change the residual equity, although the likelihood of the residual equity changing in this way is limited. In most organizations transactions of this nature are rare, and when they do occur there may be no opportunity to measure the receipt on a basis other than cost.

In two-sided intra-actions, the only familiar example of such an event that involves both a monetary receipt and a monetary cost is a fluctuation in the significance of the monetary measuring unit which results in the monetary assets becoming more or less valuable while the monetary specific equities become less or more valuable. These changes in value offset each other to the extent that the monetary assets and monetary specific equities offset each other. When the latter are unequal, the changes in value also are unequal; the difference changes the residual equity.

Category (12) under two-sided intra-actions corresponds to the category of transactions that includes the common sale of merchandise. Since the receipt takes the form of a monetary item, it is almost certain to be subject to measurement on some basis other than cost, thus changing the residual equity. Category (13), like category (5), is not likely to change the residual equity because of the probability that the real receipt will be measured at cost. Type (14) intra-actions occur frequently. Probably most of the receipts must be recorded at cost, but some of them will permit independent measurements. These will affect the residual equity.

This review of the eighteen categories of economic events reveals that fifteen of them [all except (3), (5), and (13)] must be thought of as events which may change the residual equity. If events which may change the residual equity are important to the residual equity holders, we may conclude that residual equity holders are interested in almost all categories of events. Such a conclusion should not be surprising. Indeed, further analysis of the interests of residual equity holders may suggest that the three categories of events that are unlikely to be recorded so as to affect the residual equity are, nevertheless, apt to be of interest to residual equity holders. The determination of which events are of interest to residual equity holders does not terminate the analysis. We must now attempt to differentiate events on the basis of what their effects upon the residual equity mean to residual equity holders.

To begin, we can segregate the first two types of transactions as events which have an entirely different meaning to residual equity holders than do other events. Transactions between the firm and residual equity holders must be given special attention because they affect the residual equity holders in two ways, one of which is favorable, the other unfavorable. The net effect can be appraised only by the residual equity holder himself. A cash dividend, for example, increases a residual equity holder's personal cash balance but decreases his equity in the corporation; the net result may be considered favorable by some stockholders, unfavorable by others.

Recurring types of events

To a residual equity holder, a change in the residual equity implies a change in the schedule of benefits he will receive from the firm. Beyond this significance, some residual equity changes mean a great deal more. Those events which change the residual equity and also suggest the likelihood of future changes in the residual equity are of much greater interest to the residual equity holder than are those events which change the key equity without providing any evidence of future changes. A review of the events that change the residual equity will show that some types of events are much more likely than others to recur and are, therefore, more useful for predicting changes in the residual equity.

The first category of events other than transactions between the economic unit and its residual equity holders that was recognized as affecting the residual equity was category (4) under two-sided transactions. If any of the categories can be considered to include events of a recurring type, this category can. Category (6) in this group, however, clearly is on a different level with respect to the likelihood of these events recurring. The exchange of real goods is likely to be an isolated event which gives no hint of similar events in the future. In addition, it was pointed out previously that more likely than not such a transaction would be recorded so as not to affect the residual equity. The third example of an event that falls into category (6) (fulfilling an obligation to deliver goods) is a recurring type of event, but it is not likely to be recorded so as to affect the residual equity if the rationale of asset and specific equity measurement expounded in chapter iii is followed.[5]

One-sided transactions that involve receipts are extremely rare in business firms; as such they would have to be viewed as non-recurring. But receipts in one-sided transactions are very common, extremely important, and recurrent in some types of organizations,

---

[5] This type of transaction will be given special attention in the next chapter. See table 4.

including some religious and governmental units, and those organizations are important to investors. Receipts in one-sided transactions should be included in the list of categories of recurring events which change the residual equity. Both real receipts (8) and monetary receipts (7) are apt to occur again in the future.

Costs in one-sided transactions, (9) and (10), are common. In business firms, both charitable contributions and taxes (not all of which are one-sided events) are recurring types of transactions which affect the residual equity. Contributions may be in the form of real assets. Nonbusiness organizations have many one-sided transactions which involve costs; often these costs are real costs (including services rendered).

Seven of the eight categories of intra-actions were classed as categories of events which may affect the residual equity; only the two-sided intra-action involving a real receipt and a monetary cost was excluded. The four categories of one-sided intra-actions are quickly recognized as nonrecurring. The first category of two-sided intra-actions also must be viewed as nonrecurring as long as the only example that comes to mind is the price level change. Even if it is conceded that change in the value of the monetary measuring unit is the rule, not the exception, unless we can assume that the change will continue in the same direction as in the past and that the difference between the total monetary assets and the total monetary specific equities of the firm retains the same arithmetical sign, we cannot consider the change in the residual equity from this type of event to be an indication of the future.

Category (12) under two-sided intra-actions is another category that includes an extremely limited variety of events. The nature of monetary assets is such that it is not easy to obtain one unless another party participates in the event. Neither is it easy to eliminate a monetary specific equity without the participation of a second party. If the type of event given as an example is the only one included in this category, it must be recognized that these events have a tendency to recur. Category (14) is very different from category (12) in the number and variety of examples that can be given. Essentially all manufacturing activity and many other events that involve the use of purchased services or materials, without either losing the value of those items or furnishing them to another party, are included in this category. The recurring nature of these events cannot be questioned. The regularity of their effects upon the residual equity is not as clearly discernible. Even if the measurement pattern outlined in the preceding chapter is followed, most of these events will not change the residual equity. Independent measurements of the receipts enjoyed in these events is out of the question in most cases. Since the events in the other categories classified as recurring always affect the residual equity, unless the two sides of a transaction are coincidentally equal, it seems wise to omit this category of events from the group of categories of recurring events that change the residual equity. However, additional attention will be given, in the next chapter, to events in this category.

TYPES OF RECEIPTS AND COSTS

Six categories of economic events have been isolated by the search for events which are of special concern to residual equity holders. The two crucial characteristics possessed by these six categories of events which are thought to be of substantial import to residual equity holders are that these events almost always change the residual equity, and they have a strong tendency to recur, thus providing some evidence of future changes in the residual equity. The six categories of events are:

1. Two-sided transaction involving a monetary receipt and a real cost.

2. One-sided transaction with a monetary receipt.

3. One-sided transaction with a real receipt.

4. One-sided transaction with a monetary cost.

5. One-sided transaction with a real cost.

6. Two-sided intra-action involving a monetary receipt and a real cost.

The prominent role played by these six categories of events in accounting to investors requires that this group of economic events, as well as the receipts and the costs associated therewith, be given specific names to serve as convenient symbols for concepts that have been identified in the preceding analysis. It is suggested that receipts in this group of events be known as "revenues," that the costs in these events be called "expenses," and that the six categories of events be referred to as "revenue-expense events." In addition, we may find it convenient to refer to the one-sided transactions involving receipts simply as "revenue events" or transactions and the one-sided unfavorable transactions as "expense events." The use of these words as labels for these phenomena does not mean that revenue and expense are being permanently defined accordingly. Rather, the naming of the concepts is meant to provide us with short symbols for use in subsequent discussions and to establish hypotheses for investigation.

Perhaps the tentative definitions of revenue and expense should be stated more simply. Revenue is a monetary receipt at a real cost or any receipt in a one-sided transaction. Expense is a real cost of a monetary receipt or any cost in a one-sided transaction.

Fifteen of the eighteen categories of economic events were found capable of affecting the residual equity. Six of the fifteen have been given the name "revenue-expense events." The two categories of events that constitute Class I in the outline clearly are of peculiar significance; they may be called "investments by residual equity holders" and "returns to residual equity holders." These same terms may be used for the receipts and costs that occur in transactions with residual equity holders. Since receipts and costs refer to changes in net asset items, it is clear that the typical transaction with a residual equity holder involves a receipt or a cost but not both, although a combination is possible.

Seven categories of events from Part II of the outline, in addition to revenue-expense events, may change the residual equity. These events and the receipts and costs involved in them should be given names for use in the subsequent discussion. Four of the seven categories are one-sided intra-actions. It is suggested that both the costs in one-sided intra-actions and the events involving costs be referred to as "losses." Similarly the receipts in one-sided intra-actions and the receipt events may be called "gains."

Events in category (6) under two-sided transactions may be called "real exchanges." Any difference between the "exchange receipt" and the "exchange cost" that may be recognized may be thought of as a "net loss" or "net gain." Until additional examples of events falling into category (11) are recognized, those events may be known as "price level fluctuations," and the difference between the "price level receipt" and "price level cost" may be called "net loss" or "net gain." Events in category (14) are "production activities," and any difference that may be recognized between "production receipts" and "production costs," as, for example, when finished goods are valued at net realizable value, may be thought of as "net gain" or "net loss." Sometimes it will be convenient to group all gains and net gains together as gains and all losses and net losses as losses. Needless to say, it will also be convenient to distinguish between gains in different categories of events by the use of preliminary adjectives such as "price level" gain, "production" gain, or "exchange" gain, just as it may be helpful to do so for losses, revenues, and expenses. In some cases, even more precise adjectives may be used such as "fire" loss, "interest" revenue, or "rent" expense.

Three categories of events have been omitted from the discussion so far, because they are not likely to change the residual equity. Two of them are very common types of two-sided transactions. Category (3), involving a monetary receipt and a monetary cost, includes events which may be thought of as "financial exchanges" and receipts and costs which may be called "financial receipts" and "financial costs." Events in category (5) of two-sided transactions are "purchases" and the receipts and costs are "purchase receipts" and "purchase costs." The conversion of monetary assets into real assets in an intra-action may be viewed as a "demonetization" which involves "demonetization receipts" and "demonetization costs." In the rare instance in which an event of one of these three types is recorded so as to change the residual equity, the difference between the receipt and the cost could be called a net gain or net loss, providing it does not represent a correction of a previously erroneous measurement.

SUMMARY

Economic events which an accountant may be able to measure and report have been divided into eighteen categories. The events in each of these categories have been analyzed for the effect they may have upon the residual equity. This analysis disclosed two significant respects in which events differ. First, some may change the residual equity; some do not. Again, of those events which may change the residual equity, some have a tendency to recur; others do not. These characteristics, together with the five bases of classification used to determine the eighteen categories, provided a basis for a partial condensation of the list of events so that only thirteen different types of events were recognized to the extent of assigning different names to the events. (See table 3, column 8. If revenue events, expense events, and revenue-expense events are considered as one type, there are only eleven different types of events.) The assignment of names to the receipts and costs in the thirteen types of events showed nine different types of receipts and nine costs. (See columns 9 and 10, table 3).

Four of these eighteen types of changes in assets and specific equities—revenues, expenses, gains, and losses—are of vital significance to accountants and investors, yet are extremely abstruse. The next chapter will be devoted to these receipts and costs in events which change the residual equity (other than transactions with residual equity holders).

The objectives of chapter v are to familiarize the reader with the concepts of revenue, expense, gain, and loss; to test the tentative outlines of these concepts for their applicability in accounting for specific common and/or controversial kinds of economic events; and to consider revisions of the tentative definitions as may seem appropriate for the development of the most useful concepts of changes in the residual equity. The present chapter will conclude with individual summaries of the four concepts to be examined in detail in the following chapter.

The receipts (increments in net asset items) in the following categories of events are revenue:

1. Two-sided transaction, monetary receipt, real cost.
   Examples: Sale of merchandise; sale of services.
2. One-sided transaction, monetary receipt.
   Examples: Receipt of gift of money; accrual of taxes receivable.
3. One-sided transaction, real receipt.
   Example: Receipt of gift of merchandise.

115

TABLE 3

Summary of Analysis of Eighteen Categories of Economic Events from Point of View of Residual Equity Holders

I^a or II^b	Transaction or intra-action	1 or 2 sides	Nature of receipt	Nature of cost	Change residual equity?	Recurring?	Term for event	Term for receipt	Term for cost	Term for difference
I	Transaction	1	Real or monetary	....	Yes	No	Investment by residual equity holder	Investment by residual equity holder	....	....
I	Transaction	1	....	Real or monetary	Yes	?	Return to residual equity holder	....	Return to residual equity holder	....
II	Transaction	2	Monetary	Monetary	No	Yes	Financial exchange	Financial receipt	Financial cost	None assigned
II	Transaction	2	Monetary	Real	Yes	Yes	Revenue-expense	Revenue	Expense	....
II	Transaction	2	Real	Monetary	No	Yes	Purchase	Purchase receipt	Purchase cost	....
II	Transaction	2	Real	Real	Sometimes	No	Real exchange	Exchange receipt	Exchange cost	Net gain or net loss
II	Transaction	1	Monetary	....	Yes	Yes	Revenue	Revenue	....	....
II	Transaction	1	Real	....	Yes	Yes	Revenue	Revenue	....	....
II	Transaction	1	....	Monetary	Yes	Yes	Expense	....	Expense	....
II	Transaction	1	....	Real	Yes	Yes	Expense	....	Expense	....
II	Intra-action	2	Monetary	Real	Yes	No	Price level fluctuation	Price level receipt	Price level cost	Net gain or net loss
II	Intra-action	2	Real	Monetary	Yes	Yes	Revenue-expense	Revenue	Expense	....
II	Intra-action	2	Monetary	Real	Yes	No	Demonetization	Demonetization receipt	Demonetization cost	None assigned
II	Intra-action	2	Real	Real	Sometimes	Yes	Production activity	Production receipt	Production cost	Net gain or net loss
II	Intra-action	1	Monetary	....	Yes	No	Gain	Gain	....	....
II	Intra-action	1	Real	....	Yes	No	Gain	Gain	....	....
II	Intra-action	1	....	Monetary	Yes	No	Loss	....	Loss	Loss
II	Intra-action	1	....	Real	Yes	No	Loss	....	Loss	Loss

a I indicates transactions between the economic unit and its residual equity holders.
b II indicates events other than transactions between the economic unit and its residual equity holders.

4. Two-sided intra-action, monetary receipt, real cost.
   Example: Production of gold salable to government.

Revenue is thus a monetary receipt at a real cost, or any receipt in a one-sided transaction.

The costs (decrements in net asset items) in the following categories of events are expenses:

1. Two-sided transaction, monetary receipt, real cost.
   Examples: sale of merchandise, sale of services.
2. One-sided transaction, monetary cost.
   Examples: Contribution of money, accrual of income tax payable.
3. One-sided transaction, real cost.
   Example: Contribution of merchandise.
4. Two-sided intra-action, monetary receipt, real cost.
   Example: Production of gold salable to government.

Expense, then, is a real cost of a monetary receipt, or any cost in a one-sided transaction.

The excess of receipts over costs in the following categories of events are gains:

1. Two-sided transaction, real receipt, real cost. Example: Exchange of real estate for real estate.
2. Two-sided intra-action, monetary receipt, monetary cost. Example: Price level fluctuation.
3. Two-sided intra-action, real receipt, real cost. Example: Production of refined sugar.
4. One-sided intra-action, monetary receipt. Example: Discovery of money.
5. One-sided intra-action, real receipt. Example: Accidental discovery of oil.

Gain is therefore the excess of a real receipt over a real cost, the excess of a monetary receipt over a monetary cost, or a receipt in a one-sided intra-action.

The excess of costs over receipts in the following categories of events are losses:

117

1. Two-sided transaction, real receipt, real cost. Example: Exchange of real estate for real estate.
2. Two-sided intra-action, monetary receipt, monetary cost. Example: Price level fluctuation.
3. Two-sided intra-action, real receipt, real cost. Example: Production of refined sugar.
4. One-sided intra-action, monetary cost. Example: Loss of money by theft.
5. One-sided intra-action, real cost. Example: Destruction of building by fire.

Loss is the excess of a real cost over a real receipt, the excess of a monetary cost over a monetary receipt, or a cost in a one-sided intra-action.

VI

Financial Statements for Investors

Accounting was described in chapter i as a process of identifying, classifying, and measuring, and then reporting the effects of economic events upon a specific economic unit. Identification of effects of economic events was discussed in chapters iii, iv, and v; classification was stressed in chapter iv; and measurement was emphasized in chapter iii. Concepts useful in reporting to investors have been developed in several chapters. These steps provide the accountant with the tools needed to describe both the qualitative and the quantitative aspects of the effects of economic events. Now, vehicles for reporting information to investors must be designed. The theme of this chapter will be the presentation of evidence of the firm's future capacity to make cash distributions to investors.

Statements will be constructed which deal with concepts other than the three static and four dynamic concepts that already have been given so much attention. However, the straightforwardness of these additional concepts permits their inclusion in reports without first making lengthy analyses of their nature. In particular, funds transactions and purchases are readily understood after the general discussion of categories of economic events in chapter iv. Nevertheless, the reader should be prepared for statements containing technical data aimed at the professional analyst rather than deliberately simplified statements for the enlightenment of the layman.

STATEMENT OF ASSETS AND EQUITIES

A firm's accountants should prepare, and its management should present to investors, a statement of the firm's assets and equities. The reasons for periodically reporting assets and equities are:

1. The report of the residual equity, measured as accurately as it can be measured, tells the residual equity holders the amount of their equity as determined by accounting techniques, and tells the specific equity holders the amount of the one equity that stands as a common buffer protecting all of them.

2. Reporting specific equities as accurately as they can be measured gives indications of cushions protecting higher ranking specific equity holders. The preferred stockholders' equity provides protection to all creditors, and the equities of general creditors protect those whose claims are given priority in the bankruptcy act.

3. Reporting monetary assets and specific equities indicates the cash balance at the reporting date and the amounts and times of some future money movements, especially those that will occur in the near future and perhaps some very large ones that are scheduled for the distant future.

4. Reporting all assets and specific equities provides some indications of the reliability of the measurement of the residual equity by indicating the nature of the net asset items, the measurement techniques that were used, and alternative amounts that may be relevant to an investor's problem.

5. The statement of assets and equities serves as a base for the dynamic statements.

The next step after recognizing these uses of the information about assets and equities is to design a statement that will perform these functions in the best possible manner.

For the use of the residual equity holders, the statement must show the residual equity in such a fashion that each holder may know the amount of his equity. If there are several residual equity holders in the firm, and if the equity of each is different from that of his colleagues, then the statement should show the equity of each. If, on the other hand, there is only one residual equity holder, there is only one amount to report. If there are many, but each holds a different number of identical units of the residual equity as in a stock corporation, that must be reported in such a manner as to reveal the amount per unit.

The specific equity holders who are interested in the residual equity as a buffer protecting their investments are not interested in any subdivisions of the residual equity total unless the breakdown is based upon differences in the reliability of the various subdivisions as buffers. One such difference in reliability is observed when a distinction is made between the legal capital of a corporation and the remainder of the residual equity. Perhaps another difference in reliability is the distinction between contributed capital in excess of legal capital and the remainder of the residual equity in excess of legal capital, at least in states which do not permit dividends to be paid if such payment will reduce the owners' equity below the contributed capital.

Another basis for difference in reliability of parts of the residual equity may be a contractual agreement between the firm and a group of investors. For example, a bond indenture may prohibit dividend payments to residual equity holders which will reduce the residual equity below a certain amount. That agreement would make part of the residual equity a little firmer type of cushion than the remainder, for it could be eliminated only by losses. The practical importance of this distinction may not be very great, but it and the legal distinctions are the only bases for reporting subdivisions of the residual equity in a corporation, either for the information of specific equity holders or for residual equity holders.

The residual equity is not the only buffer equity. Some specific equity holders in corporations rely upon the residual equity as a first line of defense but have a further cushion in the form of a low-ranking specific equity. The statement of assets and equities must indicate any priorities among specific equities that are important to investors. The distinction between creditors' equities and the equity of holders of preferred stock may be indicated by using appropriate titles. The distinction between claims which have priority in bankruptcy and claims of general creditors may not be important enough to justify reporting it for the typical concern that seems far from the point of liquidation, but occasionally it merits recognition.

One of the most valuable uses of the statement of assets and equities is as a source of information about known money movements that are to occur in the future. If a prospective lender can determine the amounts and times of all money movements involving the prospective borrower during the period for which the loan is scheduled, he has a very sound basis for deciding whether or not to make the loan. The statement of assets and equities is incomplete in this respect so is much less valuable than a complete statement of cash movements that will occur during the period in question, but it can, nevertheless, be of considerable assistance to short-term lenders because of the large proportion of the money movements that can be reported for a brief period in the future. The reporting of large amounts of money that are scheduled to be received or paid in the distant future is also helpful.

To be most helpful, the report of monetary assets and monetary specific equities should indicate the times and amounts of the money movements. The description of each item should include a specific date, series of dates, or a period during which the money will be received or paid unless knowledge of traditional business practice can be relied upon to indicate the timing, as with wages payable; and the items should be arranged in chronological order. Since the amounts of these items that are to be added as assets and equities in the statement should be discounted values, the full amount of the expected cash movement could be indicated parenthetically or in a separate column, if the discount is substantial. If any monetary item is not measured by discounting, the method of measurement must be indicated. If an item may be eliminated by an alternate route, its value by that route should be indicated. For example, the market value and/or call price of bonds payable should be shown.

To give the reader some idea of the reliability of the measurement of the residual equity, both the nature of all net asset items and the amounts at which they are included in the computation must be reported. Monetary items must be clearly distinguished from real items. The measurement technique used must also be made known, especially if it is one of the less relevant ones or if the result of its application changes quickly and substantially.

Although the statement of assets and equities is of value to investors if presented by itself, it is more valuable as an indication of the future if it is accompanied by information about recent changes in the assets and equities. Changes in the items that seem to serve as the best weather vanes for the investor should be reported in separate statements, so that the causes may be indicated. Changes in others can be summarized by the presentation of comparative statements of assets and equities. The inclusion of a column for last period's figures would show the amount and direction of changes in all items and would serve to tie the dynamic statements firmly to the statement of assets and equities.

The conversion of last period's amounts to compensate for the change in the measuring unit is based upon three assumptions. We assume that the change in the measuring unit is so great as to make comparisons of original data misleading.[1] We assume that a general price index of useful accuracy is available for measuring changes in the monetary measuring unit.[2] (Index numbers used in the accompanying statements are, of course, hypothetical.) Finally, we assume that the measuring unit in effect at the date of the latest statement is more familiar to readers of the accountant's reports than is the measuring unit of any earlier date. Thus we convert 1959 data to make them comparable with 1960 rather than the opposite.

A statement of assets and equities is illustrated in table 8. (The reader may add to the amounts as many zeros as he wishes.) The amount of net short-term monetary assets is shown on the statement for two reasons. It is an important datum in its own right to the analyst who is concerned with the firm's short-term capacity to pay. Furthermore, changes in this item are described in another statement—the funds statement—and the comparative figures tie the statement of assets and equities to that dynamic state-

---

[1] For an elementary explanation of the logic of adjusting old economic measurements to current terms, see Perry Mason, *Price Level Changes and Financial Statements* (American Accounting Association, 1956).

[2] For a discussion of the selection of an index for measuring changes in the value of the United States dollar, see R. C. Jones, *Effects of Price Level Changes on Business Income, Capital and Taxes* (American Accounting Association, 1956), pp. 177-81.

TABLE 8

Hypothetical Company Statement of Assets and Equities
December 31, 1960, 1959

Assets and equities	December 31	
	1960	1959[a]
Short-term monetary assets		
Money..	$ 230	$ 180
United States government bonds, at net realizable value....	210	160
Notes receivable, $45.30 due within 40 days..............	45	
Accounts receivable, $257 due on terms net 60 days, deduct $5 for possible uncollectibles and $2 for discount.........	250	220
Note receivable from supplier, $118 due June 15, 1961......	115	
Miscellaneous short-term monetary assets.................	30	140
Total short-term monetary assets.....................	$ 880	$ 700
Short-term monetary specific equities		
Wages payable, at nominal value........................	$ 25	$ 20
Accounts payable, mostly due within 30 days, net..........	110	105
Miscellaneous accrued liabilities.......................	40	40
Federal income tax payable March 15 and June 15, 1961, discounted at 5 per cent...............................	60	40
Note payable to bank, $122 due April 26, 1961.............	120	
Miscellaneous short-term monetary specific equities........	30	80
Total short-term monetary specific equities..............	$ 385	$ 285
Net short-term monetary assets.......................	$ 495	$ 415
Note payable to bank, $122 due April 26, 1961............		$ 120
Bonds payable, $420 maturing July 1, 1975, 2% interest coupons maturing January 1, and July 1, discounted at 5 per cent, less those coupons maturing in 1961 included above as short-term (market value, $345).....................	$ 369	$ 386
5 per cent cumulative preferred stock, at issue price less discounted 1961 dividends included above; market value, $540; liquidation preference, $630.....................	601	632
Total long-term monetary specific equities..............	$ 970	$1,138
Net monetary specific equities.........................	$ 475	$ 723
Real assets		
Inventories		
Finished goods, at net realizable value...................	$ 220	$ 200
Finished goods, at replacement cost.....................	360	375
Partly completed goods, at replacement cost.............	30	25
Materials and parts to be used in manufacturing, at replacement cost......................................	80	75
Supplies, at original money cost.......................	20	20
Services paid for but not yet received, at original money cost	50	47
Machinery and equipment, mostly at adjusted historical cost, remainder at replacement cost new, totaling $340, less amortization...	250	240
Buildings, at replacement cost new, $420, less amortization..	320	315
Land, at adjusted historical cost........................	70	70
Total real assets...................................	$1,400	$1,367

TABLE 8 (*Continued*)

Assets and equities	December 31	
	1960	1959[a]
Real specific equities		
Estimated cost of fulfilling obligations on product warranties	$ 40	$ 40
Net real assets....................................	$1,360	$1,327
Net assets.......................................	$ 885	$ 604
Residual equity of common stockholders		
Legal capital....................................	$ 700	$ 480
Remainder......................................	185	124
Total...	$ 885	$ 604
Equal to $8.85 per share for each share of common stock outstanding.		

[a] The reader should not expect the amounts reported for 1959 to correspond with the amounts of these items reported in last year's statement of assets and equities. All figures on that statement have been multiplied by 1.051 to convert them to December 31, 1960 dollars.

ment. The net figure for all monetary items is also shown. This figure is especially important in connection with predictions of changes in the value of the monetary unit.

Real items are not segregated into short-term and long-term categories. Because of this, the statement of assets and equities does not provide the summary information necessary to compute net short-term assets or the "current ratio." (But if the descriptions of the real items indicate their terms, the analyst can make his own computations.) It is likely that some readers will dislike this feature of the illustrated statement. My position is that monetary items are so different from real items, from the point of view of the investor who is attempting to analyze future cash flows, that they should be merged only in order to compute the residual equity. Indeed, in order to present the maximum of useful detail without excessive length, the accountant may consider presenting two statements of assets and equities. One would be a statement of monetary assets and equities; the other would show the real assets and specific equities, the balance of monetary items appearing on the first statement, and the residual equity.[3]

[3] Cf. William J. Vatter, *The Fund Theory of Accounting and Its Implication for Financial Reports* (Chicago: University of Chicago Press, 1947), pp 96 ff.

Inventories and prepayments differ from short-term monetary assets in that the accountant usually is able to indicate both the amounts and times of future cash flows related to the monetary items whereas he can report neither for the real items. Even in the best of circumstances—when an inventory item can be measured at net realizable value—the analyst cannot rely upon the time and amount of the future money receipt as much as he can if the asset is a monetary item. However, it must be admitted that inventories in this category, for example farm products, are of much greater interest to the short-term analyst than are inventories which can only be measured at cost, for example, women's ready-to-wear merchandise. Inventories and prepayments should be presented in enough detail to permit the analyst to consider them as he sees fit. If he wants to add an inventory of wheat owned by a grain dealer to the short-term monetary assets, he may do so, but the general form of the statement of assets and equities must be based upon the generally significant distinction between monetary items and real items. The fact that some short-term real assets are similar to short-term monetary assets in their meaning to investors is not sufficient justification for grouping all inventories with short-term monetary assets; differences among inventories are too great.

It is rather difficult in a comparative statement to show the timing of the future money flows which constitute the monetary items. The description that fits this year's item may not be appropriate for an item on last year's statement which was similar but due at a different date. If this year's description is reasonably accurate for last year's item, it may be permitted to serve the purpose. Those items on last year's statement that do not fit any of this year's specific descriptions can be accommodated on the miscellaneous line or on a special line if the amount or the nature of the item seems to warrant it.

As a final point regarding the reporting of assets and equities, we should note an important practical aspect of the use of financial statements. Perhaps the most useful figure that analysts hope to work toward is the intrinsic value of the residual equity —what the common stock of a corporation is really worth. This elusive figure is valuable for comparison with the price at which the stock can be obtained and as evidence of the soundness of the senior equities. The discussion of measurement of assets and specific equities in chapter iii was aimed at computing the accounting version of the intrinsic value of the residual equity, that is, the book value of that equity. But in a discussion of how to describe and classify assets and equities, we must not forget that financial analysts are very much concerned with the margin of safety, a crucial concept in the selection of fixed income investments. Since the margin of safety is supposed to indicate the cushion protecting the investor against the effects that unsatisfactory operating conditions may have on the firm, it must be measured under poor conditions.[4]

The financial statements should give the analyst information that is useful in predicting how serious the effects of such conditions could be in the future, but this must be done in the descriptive, parenthetical, and note sections of the statements, not in the basic amounts. The latter must be determined in a manner consistent with the objective of providing evidence of intrinsic value, not margin of safety under adverse conditions. The basic amounts on all statements should be the most accurate figures that can be obtained without leaning toward either underestimation or overestimation. The descriptive, parenthetical, and note information, however, may properly be heavily weighted with pessimism without at all prejudicing its validity, for it is more important that the analyst be apprised as to how bad things can get for the fixed income group than it is for him to judge the best that could be in store for the residual equity holders. The typical bondholder is concerned with the safety of his investment and relies upon the specific returns called for in the bond contract. Failure to receive these expected returns is of much greater concern to him than a favorable or unfavorable fluctuation in returns on common stock is to the risk-taking stock investor because the latter typically is prepared for fluctuations.

---

[4] Benjamin Graham and David L. Dodd, *Security Analysis* (3d ed.; New York: McGraw-Hill, 1951), p. 284.

STATEMENT OF CHANGES IN THE RESIDUAL EQUITY

One of the reasons given for the presentation to investors of a statement of assets and equities is that it serves as a base for dynamic statements. The statement of assets and equities is thought of as a static statement because it shows position, not action, although position depends upon action, both past and future. Dynamic statements show certain events that occurred during a particular period of time.

The statement of assets and equities provides sufficient information for the use of investors in making investment decisions if the data are accurate and complete. If the assets listed included all things which would be of service to the residual equity holders, without any qualification as to measurability, and if the specific equities included all things which would be detrimental to the interests of residual equity holders, and if the residual equity were stated at an amount that represented its worth to all present and prospective residual equity holders, regardless of their alternatives, there would be no need for dynamic statements. Since the facts of life in the real world do not permit an accountant to present a static statement with these merits, the investor can obtain additional evidence of the future of his investment from dynamic statements.

The residual equity is of great concern to investors as a group because it is a buffer equity to all investors other than residual equity holders and because it is the amount of the equity of the latter group. In a world of certainty, specific equity holders would not be interested in a buffer, but in the real world a margin of safety is desired, and the investor's appraisal of a specific equity depends partly upon the margin of safety protecting that equity.

Long-term specific equity holders typically receive interim payments between the time they make their investments and the time they receive their final remittances from the firm. Investors are interested in the firm's ability to make the interim payments without impairing its capital, that is, without reducing its ability to make future payments below the level of that ability at the beginning of the period. The net change in the residual equity during the period, before deducting returns on specific equity investments, is of importance to specific equity holders as the amount the firm could pay to them without impairing its capital. The net change in the residual equity after deducting returns on all investors' equities is the change in the specific equity holders' buffer. These are good reasons for the interest of specific equity holders in changes in the residual equity. The interest of residual equity holders in those changes requires no explanation at this point. All investors are concerned about changes in the residual equity, so the accountant should report them.

What should the residual equity statement (to shorten the title) show? The net change in the residual equity from the end of last period to the end of this period should be determinable from the comparative statement of assets and equities. An explanation of the net change in terms of changes in the asset and specific equity items is also shown on the static statement, but that type of analysis is not the most useful for predicting changes in the residual equity. The investor wants an analysis of the changes in the residual equity that will help him predict future changes in that equity. This requires a breakdown of past changes by cause, that is, on the basis of the nature of the economic events that changed the residual equity.

A net change in the amount of the residual equity reported now as compared with the amount previously reported must be traced to no more than four major groups of causes: changes in the previously reported figure to correct errors and to adjust for a change in the measuring unit; transactions between the firm and its residual equity holders; the difference between revenues and expenses; gains and losses. The first cause is only an explanation of a change in the reported residual equity, not a cause of a genuine change in the residual equity. It may include corrections of such items as the liability for income taxes, the allowance for uncollectible accounts receivable, the estimate of cash discounts that will be collected, or any other case of a discrepancy between the amount of a monetary item as determined by the method of measurement being applied at the time of its disposition and the cash movement that resulted from that item. For example, if bonds payable are purchased in the open market at a price different from their up-to-date book value, that book value should be considered erroneous. The standard for the measurement of monetary items should be discounted future money movements.

The second possible cause of changes in the residual equity is transactions between the firm and the residual equity holders. The appearance of these items on the residual equity statement is not likely to be of great help to residual equity investors for two reasons. First, they are apt to have known about such items before they received the report, either by participation or consultation. Also, they are somewhat like transfers from one pocket to another. Specific equity holders are vitally interested in these changes, of course; to them, they are changes in their buffer.

The gains, the losses, and the difference between total revenues and total expenses are the heart of the residual equity statement from the point of view of the analyst. They are of distinct concern to all investors because they are genuine changes in the residual equity during the period, from any point of view. The transfers and the corrections must be reported, of course, but largely for the sake of completing the reconciliation, whereas the revenue-expense differential, the gains, and the losses are more likely to attract and hold the attention of investors who are attempting to foresee the future.

Reporting changes in prices and price levels on the residual equity statement

Changes in prices and in the measuring unit have been considered in connection with the measurement of assets and specific equities, but only as they affect the amount of the net asset item being measured. Thus when the use of the net realizable value and replacement cost methods of measurement was recommended, the debits and credits that would be required in a double-entry framework of accounts were not considered. Likewise, when the adjusted historical cost method of measurement was discussed, the determination of the amount of the asset was considered, but nothing was said about an entry to record the change from the previous measurement. Since the accompanying residual equity

TABLE 9

HYPOTHETICAL COMPANY RESIDUAL EQUITY STATEMENT
1960, 1959

	1960	1959[a]
Residual equity, January 1, per books.......................	$573	
Corrections, favorable and (unfavorable)		
Additional federal income tax for 1957.....................	(3)	
Other corrections (net)...................................	5	
Corrected balance January 1 in dollars of that date............	$575	
Adjusted balance January 1 in December 31, 1960 dollars (adjustment percentage, 105.1)...................................	$604	$582
Increases during year		
Excess of revenues over expenses...........................	$ 60	$ 40
Price level gain on net monetary equities...................	35	–0–
Other gains...	8	3
Total increases.......................................	$103	$ 43
Decreases during year		
Loss from decrease in real value of real net asset items........	$ 4	$ (2)
Loss from maintaining idle facilities.......................	3	–0–
Other losses..	7	4
Total decreases.......................................	$ 14	$ 2
Net increase during year..............................	$ 89	$ 41
Transfers during year		
To common shareholders as dividends.....................	$(28)	$(19)
From common shareholders upon issue of shares..............	220	–0–
Net transfers..	$192	$(19)
Residual equity, December 31.........................	$885	$604

[a] The reader should not expect the amounts reported for 1959 to correspond with the amounts of these items reported in last year's residual equity statement. Some of the figures on that statement have been changed to correct errors discovered following publication, and all items have been multiplied by 1.051 to convert them to December 31, 1960 dollars.

statement includes three amounts relating to changes in prices and/or price levels, this subject must be dealt with at this time.

In the discussion of changes in assets and equities, price changes and price level changes were listed as economic events. A change in the general price level was said to affect monetary assets and monetary specific equities. The decrease in the purchasing power of money and other monetary assets as prices in general rise, and the decrease in the sacrifice required to pay monetary specific equities as the price level rises (and the "value of the dollar" falls) were viewed as opposite effects. To the extent that there is a balance of monetary assets over monetary specific equities, the unfavorable effect of the reduced purchasing power of the monetary assets would be greater than the favorable effect of the reduction in the sacrifice necessary to eliminate the monetary specific equities. There would be an opposite net effect if the total monetary specific equities exceeded the total monetary assets, or if the price level declined.

This can be illustrated by an example in which it is assumed that all prices move in the same direction by the same percentage. Let the firm start the period in the position indicated by the condensed statement of assets and equities presented in table 10.

TABLE 10

MYTHICAL CORPORATION STATEMENT OF ASSETS AND EQUITIES
January 1, 1960

Monetary assets	$100,000	Monetary equities	$150,000
Real assets	200,000	Residual equity	150,000
Total assets	$300,000	Total equities	$300,000

Now, let the price of everything rise by 10 per cent during the year and retain the same totals of the four categories shown on the above statement (before converting to the new unit of measurement). At the end of the year the assets and equities may be presented, in terms of the new monetary unit, as they appear in table 11.

TABLE 11

MYTHICAL CORPORATION STATEMENT OF ASSETS AND EQUITIES
December 31, 1960

Monetary assets	$100,000	Monetary equities	$150,000
Real assets	220,000	Residual equity	170,000
Total assets	$320,000	Total equities	$320,000

By what amount has the position of the residual equity holders been improved, if any?

The monetary unit shrank by one-eleventh as the price level increased 10 per cent. Eleven of the new units are equal to ten of the old, so 165,000 of the new are equal to 150,000 of the old. The residual equity increased from $150,000 to $170,000, which is $5,000 more than was necessary to represent the original value. The residual equity holders' position has been improved by 5,000 of the monetary measuring unit in use December 31, 1960, that is, 5,000 current dollars as of December 31, 1960.

Looking at the four categories of assets and equities, we see that the real assets are stated at a 10 per cent higher figure than they were at the beginning of the year. The monetary items are unchanged, so the entire change in the real assets is offset by a similar change in the residual equity. This makes it seem that the improvement in the residual equity holders' position was due to the increase in the value of the real assets. But this is not so. The real assets have not increased in real value. They cannot be exchanged for any more commodities and services than they could a year ago. It is the monetary items which have changed in value. The monetary assets will only buy ten-elevenths of the commodities and services they would buy a year ago; it would take 110,000 current dollars to buy the same real goods. The Mythical Corporation has lost 10,000 current dollars on its monetary assets. The monetary equities have also decreased in significance, and since they are undesirable, the change represents an improvement in the residual equity holders' position. It would take 165,000 current dollars of specific equities to represent the same burden as 150,000 of the old style dollars, so the improvement is measured at 15,000 current dollars. The $15,000 gain on monetary specific equities is partly offset by the $10,000 loss on the monetary assets; the remaining $5,000 gain on monetary equities is the real source of the improvement in the residual equity holders' position.

To the extent that monetary assets and monetary equities offset each other, a change in the size of the measuring unit has no net effect upon the residual equity, because the loss suffered on one category of monetary items is exactly offset by a gain on those of opposite sign. And to the extent that real assets and real equities offset each other, the conversion of each to its amount as measured by the new monetary unit offsets the conversion of the other.[5] It is only the excess of monetary equities over monetary assets, or vice versa, that allows a change in the value of the monetary unit to affect the real value of the residual equity. The change in the value of the real assets does not affect the residual equity because the real assets do not change in real value in the situation hypothesized.

Referring again to the Mythical Corporation example, we noted that it would take a residual equity of 165,000 December 31, 1960, dollars to equal the 150,000 January 1, 1960, dollars of residual equity. When the ending residual equity is computed by subtracting specific equities from assets, it is found to be $170,000. For the residual equity statement to account for the difference between the residual equity reported on the December 31, 1959, statement of assets and equities and the residual equity reported in the December 31, 1960, statement of assets and equities, it must first show the $150,000 converted to $165,000 and then report the increase from $165,000 to $170,000 as the price level gain on net monetary equities. The *pro forma* residual equity statement of the Hypothetical Company shows the conversion— in the case of the Mythical Corporation from $150,000 to $165,000 —on the two lines "Corrected balance January 1 in dollars of that date" and "Adjusted balance January 1 in December 31, 1960 dollars (adjustment percentage 105.1)." The price level gain on net monetary equities appears in the section of the residual equity statement that includes genuine increases.

This analysis of price level effects, assuming uniformity of price movements, shows that the $20,000 increase in the reported residual equity from one statement of assets and equities to the next is not caused by the increase in the dollar value of the real assets, but by a real gain on net monetary items and a restatement of the residual equity as measured by a different measuring unit. This point of view can be explained in terms of debit and credit entries as follows:

---

[5] A glance at table 10 or table 11 will remind the reader that equality of monetary assets and monetary equities must be accompanied by equality of real assets and real equities (the residual equity only, in the Mythical Corporation). Likewise, an excess of monetary equities over monetary assets must be balanced by an excess of real assets over real equities.

1. The adjustment of the real assets to state them at their new monetary value consistent with the change in the price level requires a debit to real assets for $20,000. The offsetting credit should not be made in the residual equity account because there has been no change in the real value of the real assets. So let us hold the credit entry in a temporary suspense account.

2. The restatement of the residual equity in terms of the new, smaller monetary unit requires a credit to the residual equity. Since no other asset or equity account can properly take the debit, the suspense account is needed again; debit it $15,000.

3. To record the genuine price level gain on net monetary equities, credit a gain account with the appropriate title. The debit, however, cannot be made in the accounts for monetary items, because they are already stated at the correct dollar amounts owed. The $5,000 debit may be recorded in the suspense account.

4. Close the price level gain on net monetary equities account to the residual equity by debiting the former and crediting the latter, $5,000.

5. Note how the suspense account has no balance after having served as a temporary haven for three entries that had no place to go. This account, with a dignified name and with places reserved for additional entries required when two of our initial assumptions are relaxed, appears as table 12. The entries explained above appear as entries (4), (6), and (5) respectively. Note, also, that the residual equity account, and statement, reflect the true effects of the price level change rather than the pseudo effect of the increase in the money value of the real assets. A simple debit to real assets and credit to the residual equity for $20,000 would result in the proper amounts for all items appearing on the Statement of Assets and Equities, but it would not provide a proper explanation of how those values came into being.

If real assets change in money value by exactly the same percentage as the general price level, the residual equity holders have neither lost nor gained by those changes in the prices of the real assets held. But such equivalence of price changes is not the usual experience. The price of any one commodity is likely to change either more or less than the average of all commodities and services. If a real asset held by the firm increases in money value by a smaller percentage than the increase in the general price level, the firm has suffered a loss on that asset. If the money value of the asset increases more than the increase in the general price level, the firm gains on it. Either of these changes could be recorded if real assets are measured at net realizable value or at replacement cost.

If all real net asset items are measured on an adjusted historical cost (or receipt) basis, the financial statements will indicate that there was neither a loss nor a gain on the real net asset items. On the other hand, if real items are valued at historical cost or historical receipt, even though the general price level rose, we are implicitly recording a loss from holding those real assets (and a gain on any real specific equities). This loss would have to be taken into consideration in reconciling the beginning and ending residual equity if the other price level effects (on net monetary equities or assets and on the initial residual equity) are explicitly recorded. For example, if the Mythical Corporation's real assets were stated at $200,000 on the December 31, 1960, Statement of Assets and Equities, the Residual Equity Statement would have to show a loss of $20,000 in order to reduce the residual equity from its converted value of $165,000 plus the $5,000 price level gain on net monetary equities to the $150,000 figure needed to balance the Statement of Assets and Equities. This $20,000 loss should be reported on the Residual Equity Statement as a "Loss from decrease in real value of real net asset items." On the Hypothetical Company Residual Equity Statement, it appears as a decrease of $4. This analysis emphasizes the fact that the failure of reported amounts of assets to vary with the price level implies a gain or loss on those assets. It therefore behooves the accountant to make certain that his measurement techniques are the best available so that the gains and losses he reports are as close to actual gains and losses as they can be.

At this stage of our discussion, a more complete review of the entries required to record the effects of these economic events may help the reader see the complete picture. Since the real effect upon the residual equity of a price level change is due to a change in net monetary items which is not recorded in accounts for monetary items, and since the real effect upon the residual equity of changes in the prices of individual real assets is not the amount of the price changes, it is easy to become confused on the mechanics of recording these phenomena.

The Price Level Changes Clearing Account in table 12 can serve as the focal point of the discussion. The amounts are taken from tables 10 and 11, and are based on the additional assumption that there was no turnover of real assets during the year.

TABLE 12

MYTHICAL CORPORATION PRICE LEVEL CHANGES CLEARING ACCOUNT, 1960

Debits		Credits	
(1) Write-downs of outgoing real assets which were charged to expense	$ o	(2) Write-ups of outgoing real assets which were charged to expense	$ o
(3) Write-downs of real assets on hand at end of year	o	(4) Write-ups of real assets on hand at end of year	20,000
(5) Gain on net monetary equities	5,000		
(6) Price level adjustment of beginning of year residual equity	15,000	(7) Balance—to residual equity	o
Total	$20,000	Total	$20,000

Entries (1), (2), (3), and (4) are offset by entries in real asset accounts which record changes in the money value of those assets, or by entries in the expense accounts to which the assets are being charged. These entries may record revaluations using the adjusted historical cost, replacement cost, or net realizable value methods of measurement, but they should not include any changes in valuations due to changes in valuation methods. If all real assets change in money value by the same percentage as the general price level changes, and if the total of the real assets does not change during the period, these four entries in the price level changes clearing account will exactly balance the entry (6) converting the beginning-of-year residual equity and the entry (5) recording the gain or loss on net monetary equities. In other words, if the money value of real assets changes at the same rate as the general price level, there is no balance in the clearing account to be transferred to the residual equity in entry (7), that is, there is no "Loss (or gain) from decrease (or increase) in real value of real net asset items."

Entries (1) and (2) relate to assets and parts of assets (amortization) which are disposed of during the period. (There are no dispositions in this example.) They record the differences between the valuation at the beginning of the period, or their cost if acquired during the period, and the valuation which would have been assigned to them at the time they were disposed of if a statement of assets and equities had been drawn up at that time. If these money value "gains" and "losses" are not isolated when the asset is assigned to expense, the amount so assigned will not be on a current basis comparable to the revenue being earned at that time. Failure to charge current costs to expense results in the difference between revenues and expenses reflecting the effects of price changes as well as the effects of "operations." Such a mixing of effects of separate economic events reduces the predictive value of the expense concept. The use of the price level changes clearing account for isolating gains and losses from price changes permits expenses to be reported more in accord with the definition set forth in chapter v.

The accountant should not be reluctant to attempt to separate price change effects and operating effects just because he cannot distinguish between them in every case. If a firm can accomplish current costing of expense for the most widely fluctuating costs and for those which are relatively large in amounts, the amount of price change effect that is allowed to affect expense will be reduced. In a typical manufacturing or trading concern, "costing out" the goods shipped to customers at replacement cost and computing depreciation on the replacement cost of a few major classes of plant assets would eliminate most of the price change effects from expense.

Entries (3) and (4) record the changes made at the end of the period in the amounts at which the real assets on hand at that time are presented on the statement of assets and equities. (In this example, all real assets increased in dollar amount by 10 per cent.) The offsetting credits and debits are recorded in the asset accounts, perhaps through a real asset revisions clearing account. This type of entry records, for assets which are on hand at the end of the period, the effect that price changes had upon their measurement at that time as compared to the amount at which they were stated at the time of their first measurement in the period—the beginning of the period or their acquisition date. The amount of such an entry may be determined by the difference in replacement or reproduction cost at the two dates or by the difference between adjusted historical cost at the two dates. If a long-life asset is measured at net realizable value, the difference between the valuation at two dates may have to be assigned partly to expense and partly to price change gain or loss, because part of the change in value may be related to use or age (depreciation).

Entry (5) records the improvement in the residual equity holders' position because of the lightening of the burden of the net monetary specific equities as the size of the measuring unit decreases. The offsetting entry is to a gain account which will be closed to the residual equity account and will appear on the residual equity statement.

Entry (6), like entry (5), could be omitted without impairing the balance of any asset or equity, but this would result in two reasons for the change in the reported dollar amount of the residual equity being reported as one. Failure to make this entry would cause a misstatement of the real asset gain or loss that is recorded in entry (7), and this error would offset a misstatement of the beginning residual equity.

The discussion in connection with tables 10 and 11 emphasized that the only gain or loss that can result from a uniform movement of prices is the gain or loss on net monetary equities or net monetary assets. The entries in the price level changes clearing account illustrate the recording mechanics of this fact. With uniform price movements, the only entry affecting the real value of the residual equity is entry (5) which records the gain on net monetary equities because of the price increase. Entries (1), (2), (3), and (4) adjust assets (and real liabilities, if any).[6] Entry (6)

---

[6] Only two of these types of entries will be made if prices change uniformly—(1) and (3) if prices decline; (2) and (4) if prices increase. Only one of these entries will be made if prices change uniformly and there is no turnover, as was assumed in the Mythical example.

adjusts the residual equity for the change in the measuring unit; it does not record a change in the real value of that equity. Entry (7) is unnecessary if prices change uniformly, because the net of entries (1), (2), (3), and (4) will balance the net of entries (5) and (6). The first four entries add up to an amount equal to the percentage change in the price level times the net real assets. Entry (5) is computed by multiplying the percentage change in the price level times the net monetary equities, and entry (6) is equal to the percentage change in the price level times the residual equity. Since net real assets equal net monetary equities plus residual equity, entries (1), (2), (3), and (4) equal entry (5) plus entry (6).

If the assumption that there was no turnover of real assets is omitted, part of the amount of entry (4) may be shifted to entry (2), but there will be no change in the total of the two entries. Then, if we assume that the dollar value of the real assets this firm holds increased by only 8 per cent, whereas the general price level increased by 10 per cent, entries (2) and (4) would add up to $16,000, and entry (7) would be for $4,000—a credit to the price level changes clearing account and a debit to the residual equity. In that case we could say that the position of the residual equity holders deteriorated because the money value of the real assets increased more slowly than the monetary unit shrank.

The balance of the price level changes clearing account after making the first six types of entries shown in the example is described properly as the real gain or loss from price changes on real net asset items (including any real specific equities which may be present) under certain conditions. These conditions are that all the entries described must be made completely and accurately, including the current pricing of all real assets part or all of which were disposed of during the period, and that there is no change in the residual equity during the period. For there to be no change in the residual equity during the period, there could be no difference between revenues and expense at any interim date, no transactions with residual equity holders, and no gains or losses—not even price change gains or losses.

Ideally, any changes in the residual equity that occur during the period should be adjusted to end-of-period dollars for presentation on the statement of changes in the residual equity, just as the beginning balance of the residual equity and all figures on last year's statement must be adjusted. For example the monthly revenues and expenses stated in current dollars at the time of occurrence could be adjusted to end-of-period dollars in order to determine the change in the residual equity from this source. The offsetting entry would be to the price level changes clearing account.

The adjustment of the current year's revenues and expenses for a change in the monetary unit may be helpful, but the adjustment of all changes in the residual equity may not provide any net advantage. One point to consider is that the adjustment of some of the items would result in variations from the original dollar amounts, which would be confusing to readers of the statement who have other sources of information about them. Thus, the residual equity holders probably would be better informed if the transactions between themselves and the firm that took place during the period were reported in original dollar terms. On the other hand, it must be recognized that failure to adjust every item on the residual equity statement with offsetting entries in the price level changes clearing account will make the balance of that account, which is closed to the residual equity, reflect something besides the difference between actual changes in prices of real net asset items and changes in those items equal to the percentage change in the general price level. The inaccuracy of that figure, however, is not very apt to mislead an investor because it is unlikely that much reliance will be placed upon this nonrecurring change when predicting future changes in the residual equity.

REVENUE AND EXPENSE STATEMENT

All changes in the residual equity are of interest to investors. In most periods of the life of a business firm, the largest change in the residual equity is that caused by the difference between total revenues and total expenses. This difference also is likely to be the best indication of future changes in the residual equity. For these reasons, the difference between revenues and expenses is of special interest to investors. They want detailed information about the phenomena contributing to that difference.

In view of the investor's concern with the difference between total revenues and total expenses, a short, convenient name for this concept is needed. "Income," "profit," and variations of these terms are used as names for closely related concepts. Profit, however, has such an important and definite meaning in economic theory, that there is some advantage in refraining from applying it to the concept in question. Income, too, is more generally used to indicate a broader concept that is very useful in taxation—a concept that is not restricted to recurring items. If the term "income" is to be applied to the excess of revenues over expenses, an adjective should be added to it. "Recurring income" may be the most suitable name.

The major objective of the revenue and expense statement is to provide information that can be used to help predict the change in the residual equity in the future due to recurring income. The statement also can be of value in predicting the firm's future money receipts. To be useful in making predictions, the statement must show revenues and expenses grouped on the basis of probable changeability. Different categories of revenues which are likely to change in the same direction and in the same proportion may be grouped together. Expenses may be grouped in the same way.

A likely basis for grouping revenues of a manufacturer is by products. Many large manufacturers produce a rather heterogeneous group of products. Neither the physical volumes nor the unit selling prices of these several lines are likely to vary together. If the investor is to predict the total revenue of the firm for the coming period, he must do it by predicting the amounts from specific sources. The only bases for predicting changes in revenues are expected changes in factors affecting physical volume or an expected change in unit price. Clearly, price changes are likely to be related to specific products or product lines. Also, a factor that affects the volume of sales of one product is likely to affect the sales of other products in a different proportion, if at all. For example, in forecasting the sales of a tobacco company, an analyst may take into consideration the effect upon the company's sales of publicity regarding a relation between smoking and several serious diseases. If this publicity is apt to affect sales of cigarettes more, less, or in a different direction than it affects sales of cigars, the analyst must know the firm's sales of cigarettes and its sales of cigars.

Division of revenues on the basis of products is only one possibility. Some firms, including some manufacturers, should distinguish between export sales and domestic sales. Other geographical breakdowns may be helpful. Types of customers and types of outlets are other possible bases for dividing revenues. It may even be worth while to employ two or more bases at the same time; to the analyst, more detail than is necessary is preferable to less.

Expenses must be assigned to the several classes of revenues so far as possible. This shows the profitability of the various classes of business. Furthermore, some expenses change because revenues change. In order to know the effect that a particular change in an underlying factor will have upon the residual equity, both the change in revenues and the change in expenses must be predicted. This means that expenses must be classified by variability with revenue as well as by revenues. There are, of course, all degrees of variability of expenses ranging from those that are more than proportionately variable with revenue or with physical volume to those that are completely fixed. Perhaps three categories, as illustrated in table 13, are sufficient for use on the revenue and expense statement.[7]

---

[7] The reader may wonder if the classification of expenses by behavior as activity varies implies "direct costing." It does not. The reader should have little difficulty in concluding that inventory measurement on the basis of variable costs is inconsistent with the argument of chapter iii. "Direct costing" is not acceptable for measuring assets, but detailed knowledge of cost behavior is essential in making investment and managerial decisions.

To provide the information needed for the revenue and expense statement illustrated, a system of accounting for product costs must provide for charging production with fixed indirect costs on the basis of a predetermined rate. Fixed, semivariable, and variable costs of production can be kept separate in the inventory and cost of goods sold accounts in order to provide information for separate reporting of these costs on the revenue and expense statement. Alternatively, the costs could be merged in the inventory accounts, but the cost of goods sold split on the basis of percentages derived from the subsidiary production cost accounts. A debit volume variance on fixed overhead would be charged to a loss account; it represents services disposed of during the period with no related benefit. A credit volume variance would be prorated to the inventory and cost of goods sold accounts. Note that the accounting period for overhead would be a year in order to provide an opportunity for the seasonal, calendar, volume, and erratic variations in costs to smooth out.

TABLE 13

HYPOTHETICAL CORPORATION REVENUE AND EXPENSE STATEMENT, 1960, 1959

	Product A	Product B	Other products	Miscellaneous and unassigned	Total 1960	Total 1959
Revenues						
Net realizable value of output......	$400				$400	
Sales of products................		$300	$100		$400	$690[a]
Furnishing of credit and miscellaneous.........................				$ 20	20	15
Total revenues................	$400	$300	$100	$ 20	$820	$705
Expenses excluding income taxes and interest						
Variable approximately in proportion to physical output or sales...	$200	$100	$ 19	$ 5	$324	$278
Partly or unevenly variable........	90	80	50	20	240	220
Substantially fixed over a likely range of output with present facilities......................	50	20	20	30	120	115
Total operating expenses........	$340	$200	$ 89	$ 55	$684	$613
Difference before income taxes and interest......................					$136	$ 92
Contributions to unassigned expenses and the residual equity..........	$ 60	$100	$ 11			
Taxes on income						
Federal income taxes.............				$ 60		$ 40
State income taxes...............				1		1
Foreign income taxes............				2		2
Total taxes on income..........				$ 63		$ 43
Cost of using capital						
Miscellaneous interest............				$ 9		$ 10
Bond interest...................				19		10
Dividends on preferred stock.......				30		32
Total capital costs.............				$ 58		$ 52
Less part assigned to specific areas				45		43
Interest expense................				$ 13		$ 9
Total income taxes and interest.......					$ 76	$ 52
Total unassigned expenses (operating, taxes, and interest)..............				$131		
Recurring income.................					$ 60	$ 40

[a] Adjusted figures for revenues and contributions to the residual equity of the three product classes in 1959 were, respectively: Product A, $300, $20; Product B, $320, $110; others, $70, $5. These and all other figures in the 1959 column have been converted to December 31, 1960 dollars by multiplying the original figures by 1.051.

A third basis for classification of expenses that would be helpful to investors is the natural description of the item, or what is commonly referred to as object of expenditure. Thus, labor, materials, depreciation, taxes, interest, and other descriptive groupings would enable the investor to improve upon his prediction of future expenses if he has any knowledge that a particular type of expense is likely to change in price per unit of material or service acquired. The objective of such a classification would be to distinguish between those purchased items the unit costs of which are likely to change independently of each other. Then, if the investor knows that the union contract will expire in six weeks and that most new labor contracts in this industry are being renewed at increases of from 4 to 5 per cent in gross hourly labor costs, he can take this change into consideration in making his prediction of future changes in the residual equity due to recurring income.

Classifying expenses on an object basis in addition to the revenue and variability bases would make the revenue and expense statement extremely complicated. Probably no more than two bases of classification of expenses can be used conveniently on one statement. It is suggested that a separate report be presented showing the firm's acquisitions of materials and services classified on an object basis. (See table 14.)

The *pro forma* revenue and expense statement in table 13 illustrates a breakdown of revenues to show those from sales of two main product lines, sales of other products, and miscellaneous revenues such as interest earned and sales of plant assets. Expenses of all degrees of variability are assigned to the three product classes as far as possible. Unassignable expenses are put into the fourth column; they are not deducted from revenues to arrive at a net figure in that column, because the resulting figure would not be very meaningful.

Income taxes are not allocated among the sources of revenue; such an allocation probably would result in more confusion than clarification. If the total tax were allocated on the basis of "contributions to unassigned expenses and the residual equity," the tax allocations would not be the product of the tax rate times the "contributions" (because of discrepancies between total contributions and total taxable income). If the average tax rate were applied to the contributions to unassigned expenses and the residual equity, a deduction would have to be made in the "miscellaneous and unassigned" column for the same reason. Neither of these approaches is satisfactory.

Part of the costs of capital may be capitalized in plant asset accounts and in other ways discussed in chapter v.[8] In order to provide full disclosure, the total of capital costs must be shown, followed by a deduction for the amounts capitalized or reported as expenses under other titles.

The reader may feel that in our desire to give useful information to investors we may also be giving useful information to the firm's competitors, suppliers, and other parties with which it deals. This problem is one which is frankly ignored here, because it is not subject to a generalized type of approach. It is a practical difficulty which must be handled according to the circumstances of the individual case.

PURCHASES STATEMENT

In the discussion of classification of expenses it was pointed out that it would be helpful to have expenses classified on the basis of object of expenditure in order to facilitate the prediction of changes in expenses. The revenue and expense statement cannot conveniently accommodate a third basis of classification, so a separate statement is needed.

The objective of the purchases statement is to report transactions involving monetary costs and real receipts (and perhaps income taxes) in such a way as to be of assistance in the prediction of future money flows and future expenses. For these purposes, we need to know the usage of the various items in the reporting period. Since purchases are likely to be easier to accumulate in the desired classifications than is usage, it is suggested that the purchase transactions be reported in terms of the monetary cost involved and that the approximate usage be indicated as a percentage of purchases.[9] Usage should be related to revenue, but

---

[8] See pp. 81-84.

[9] Since this statement is not directly tied to any other statement in the sense that the other four statements discussed in this chapter are, verifiable approximations are acceptable.

it may be substantially more convenient to consider production services and materials as used when applied to production rather than when the finished goods are sold. It may be noted that the *pro forma* statement shows a usage percentage even for land. This

TABLE 14

HYPOTHETICAL CORPORATION PURCHASES STATEMENT, 1960

Item	Usage as a percentage of purchases in 1960	Purchases in 1960	Totals
Labor services			
From members of ABC Union.............	100	$180	
From nonunion, nonmanagerial employees..	100	30	
From managerial employees..............	99	5	
Contribution to employees' pension fund....	100	15	$230
Materials and supplies			
Major item A..........................	80	$150	
Other materials in nearly raw form........	130	50	
Other substantially manufactured items.....	95	80	280
Taxes			
Property..............................	100	$ 40	
Payroll...............................	100	10	
Excise................................	100	7	
Income...............................	100	63	120
Transportation by common carriers			
By rail...............................	100	$ 12	
By other..............................	100	6	18
Utility services			
Electricity............................	100	$ 12	
Telephone.............................	100	5	
Gas..................................	100	6	
Water................................	100	7	30
Machinery, equipment, etc.			
Automobile vehicles....................	90	$ 7	
Machine tools.........................	50	15	
Sundry machinery, tools and apparatus.....	70	12	
Office machinery.......................	120	2	
Furniture, furnishings, and fixtures........	80	4	40
Real estate (including rent)			
Buildings.............................	65	$ 20	
Land.................................	92	4	24
Postage...............................	100		5
Insurance.............................	70		15
Interest...............................	100		58
Miscellaneous services.....................	100		20
Total...............................			$840

percentage may be zero if all land used by the firm is owned by it; but if land is rented, the contractual rent to which the firm committed itself for this period will be shown on this line, and the usage percentage will be something higher than zero.

Purchases should be classified on an object basis in sufficient detail to allow a separation of costs which are likely to fluctuate independently of others. For example, if all labor costs are expected to fluctuate in identical or nearly identical fashion, it is not necessary to subclassify them; but if the company deals with several different unions and each has a contract expiring at a different date, it may be necessary to show separately the labor costs under each of the several contracts in order to provide the most useful data for forecasting labor costs. This type of breakdown permits the analyst to take into consideration any information he has about an item of cost for use in conjunction with the revenue and expense statement in predicting future expenses.

FUNDS STATEMENT

The residual equity statement is an analysis of the causes of the net change in the residual equity between the dates of two statements of assets and equities. It is valuable to investors because it provides evidence for predicting the trend of an important but inaccurate item on the static statement. Money is another item on the statement of assets and equities that is important to investors—even more important, in many cases, than the residual equity. They would like to be able to make accurate predictions of future money balances. An analysis of past money flows may be helpful for this purpose.

There are two reasons, however, why a cash receipts and disbursements statement is not the most useful type of analysis for this purpose. One is that the money balance of the firm is too narrow a category to behave in a predictable way. Just as the changes in a particular bank account of a company with several accounts may be influenced by insignificant factors such as transfers between bank accounts, so may the total money balance of the firm be influenced by interpocket transfers. In this case the transfers would take the form of variations in the timing of money receipts and disbursements, perhaps for reasons that should not be permitted to affect predictions, such as whether the weekly payday falls on the last day of a month or the first of next month. A broadening of the category to be analyzed to include items that are near to cash receipts and items that are near to cash disbursements would reduce the influence of insignificant factors.

Another reason for not using a cash-flow statement as the dynamic analysis to aid in forecasting future money flows is that a more up-to-date analysis can be prepared on the basis of a broader category of monetary items. If the known near-term future cash receipts and disbursements are included in the money-flow concept the accountant reports, the analyst's projections can begin from a more advanced base. Changes in net short-term monetary assets seem to constitute the best type of money-flow data for use by the investor in predicting his future money receipts.

The net short-term monetary assets concept deserves a more careful description. Since many investors analyze the future by annual segments, and since a year seems to be the maximum period management is apt to consider when comparing cash balance with ability to pay low priority investors (e.g., when considering dividends), a one-year test seems appropriate for considering whether or not a monetary item is short term.[10] Net short-term monetary assets may be defined as money and all monetary items which are either due to affect money within a year or are available for influencing the money balance within a year. The phrase "available for influencing the money balance" is meant to include monetary assets such as temporary holdings of bonds which the management will not hesitate to dispose of when the need for money arises, and monetary specific equities

---

[10] The reader may recall that the classification of net asset items according to the amount of time that is expected to elapse before they affect the firm's cash balance was considered and rejected early in chapter iv. The monetary-real goods distinction was preferred as a basis for classifying net asset items. The present emphasis on the length of life of monetary assets and liabilities should not be thought inconsistent with the position taken in chapter iv. We are still relying upon the monetary-real goods distinction as the primary basis for classifying assets and specific equities; timing is used as a secondary basis of classification for those items that fall into the monetary pocket in the first sorting. This does not mean, however, that the funds statement is of secondary importance.

such as call loans, which the management must be prepared to pay at any time. Net short-term monetary assets may be given the short name, *funds*.

In order to predict future funds flows, the investor must analyze the past flows by causes, that is, by the types of events in which they occurred. This is significant because some types of events can be expected to continue happening, some are nonrepetitive, and some will continue but at a different rate. This is an important factor to keep in mind when designing funds statements. Also, the relative priority of the uses of funds in a going concern should be observed in determining the order in which they appear on the statement. Disbursements to different classes of investors must be clearly reported. When these factors are all considered, a statement similar to table 15 is the result.

TABLE 15

Hypothetical Company Funds Statements
1960 and 1959

	1960	1959[a]
Recurring events		
Receipts of funds from customers for products and services.....	$815	$700
Less, disbursements of funds to suppliers, employees, governments, etc. for materials, services, and taxes....................	641	595
Remainder, for investors and for reinvestment...............	$174	$105
Disbursements to senior investors for interest ($27) and preferred dividends ($30).......................................	57	48
Net recurring funds flow...............................	$117	$ 57
Nonrecurring events		
Funds invested in plant assets ($104) net of receipts from plant retirements ($9).......................................	(95)	(120)
Financing operations		
Issuance of common stock..............................	220	
Issuance of bonds.....................................		386
Long-term note approaching maturity or retired...........	(114)	(240)
Funds lost by decline in purchasing power of money........	(20)	–0–
Residual...	$108	$ 83
Dividends on common stock............................	28	19
Funds flow retained—increase in net short-term monetary assets	$ 80	$ 64

[a] The reader should not expect the amounts reported for 1959 to correspond with the amounts of these items reported in last year's funds statement. All figures on that statement have been multiplied by 1.051 to convert them to December 31, 1960 dollars.

The item "Funds lost by decline in purchasing power of money" may seem paradoxical when we remember that the residual equity statement showed a price level gain on net monetary equities. The latter item relates to net monetary equities when both short-term and long-term items are considered. Thirty-five dollars is the amount that was added to last year's net monetary equity figure to adjust for the change in the monetary unit. Referring to the comparative statement of assets and equities,[11] the $723 figure for net monetary specific equities shown for 1959 was $688 on last year's statement.

The $20 funds loss relates to the $415 net short-term monetary assets shown in the 1959 column on the statement of assets and equities. (In 1959 that item was shown as $395.) The purchasing power of this monetary fund shrank by twenty 1960 dollars between 1959 and 1960, from 415 to 395. However, this loss was more than offset by a gain of $55 on the long-term monetary specific equities, the net result being a price level gain on net monetary equities of $35.

The funds statement and the revenue and expense statement are used together to forecast funds movements.[12] The analyst may use the revenue and expense statement, the purchases statement, and miscellaneous information for preparing a forecast revenue and expense statement. Then he can deduct from the expenses estimated amounts for expenses that will not require funds. This latter data could be based largely upon last period's amortization as indicated by the purchases statement, or the revenue and expense statement could include a footnote indicating the approximate amount of depreciation that was included on each expense line.

---

[11] See p. 110.

[12] Although the revenue and expense statement may be used in conjunction with the funds statement for predicting future money flows, the latter report is likely to be the more useful for this purpose. But if a funds statement is not presented, the analyst will lean heavily upon the revenue and expense statement for forecasting money flows. In that situation, it may be necessary to limit revenues to inflows of short-term monetary assets. The use of a funds statement frees the revenue and expense statement of most of its responsibility for predicting near-term money flows, thus permitting it to concentrate on recurring changes in the residual equity. Revenue need not be limited to receipts of short-term monetary items.

Estimates of funds flows connected with plant assets and financing operations will require the use of data from the statement of assets and equities regarding maturities of debt as well as data from various nonaccounting sources.

A funds statement that distinguishes between recurring and nonrecurring funds movements provides valuable information to the analyst who is attempting to predict the firm's cash movements. The value of the funds statement is even greater if the accompanying revenue and expense statement is subject to substantial errors owing to the widespread use of historical cost measurements of real assets and the outflows of real assets that are reported as expenses. In those circumstances, the funds statement has the significant merit of being free of the material errors involved in measuring real assets, because it does not include any amounts that depend upon such measurements. This advantage, together with the logically close relation between funds flows and the investor's forecasting problem, suggests that the funds statement is fully as useful in accounting to investors as is the revenue and expense statement. The recurring income figure on the revenue and expense statement is invaluable as an indication of the direction and rate of change in the residual equity. The net recurring funds flow is equally useful as evidence of the direction and rate of change in the firm's ability to pay junior investors.

CONCLUSION

All of the accountant's work aimed at helping investors to make investment decisions is summarized in several financial statements presented at periodic intervals. The importance of the form and content of these statements cannot be overestimated. Of course, accurate information cannot be reported in these statements if it has not been accumulated in the accounts or in some other way. That is why the concepts dealing with what is to be measured and how it is to be measured have a logical priority over the design of statements. But upon going back a little further, we find that we must decide what to tell the investor before determining what to record and how to measure it. The information that is needed by the investor is, then, both the starting point and the finish line for the activity described as accounting to investors.

The investor must predict the future. Information about his money receipts from the firm on his investment contract is the investor's ultimate informational objective. Evidence of future returns is an intermediate objective. Future money movements of the firm and future residual equity changes are two of the most direct types of evidence. The statements presented here are designed to assist the investor-analyst in predicting money movements of the firm and changes in its residual equity, that is, they are designed to provide evidence of valuable evidence. Two or three of these statements may be omitted and the amount of detail on the others reduced if the accountant's and management's only objective is to present an easily digestible summary to satisfy the curiosity of the casual investor. This type of investor, however, should not set the standards for accounting to investors. Financial statements similar to the *pro forma* ones in this chapter would provide information of great value to the professional analysts who play such an important role in guiding capital in the current American economic system.

Maturity of the Theory:
The Nineteen-Seventies Edition

Commentary

The nineteen-sixties was a decade in which I gave little attention to decision-usefulness theory as such, although everything I wrote was based on it. After completing ATOATI in 1959, I turned my attention to a line of empirical work that followed from it. According to decision-usefulness theory, both changes in the residual equity and changes in cash (or some related pool of liquid funds) were relevant to cash flow-oriented decisions. But which historical data were the more relevant: cash flows or earnings flows? Which measure provided the better basis for choosing stocks for investment? With very little research literature to guide me, and with a minimal understanding of empirical research methods, I decided that I must find which measure was the more closely correlated with stock values. The accounting issue was: Does depreciation accounting contribute any information of incremental value for the investor—a serious challenge to depreciation accounting. Thus began seven pre-CRISP years of frustrating empirical research that yielded relatively little in the way of answers to that important question. Both cash flows and earnings flows were helpful in explaining stock prices. In the course of work on that issue, the data were moved from multicolumn "worksheets" and Marchant calculators to punched cards and an IBM 701. Other accounting questions that could be addressed with the same research approach were added. Results were reported in 1965a, 1967b, 1968d, and 1968e, the last one appearing more than nine years after the project began and the same year that Ball and Brown (1968) and Beaver (1968) published works setting a new quality standard for empirical work on relationships between accounting variables and securities prices (and premised on decision usefulness).

The second research topic that took a lot of my attention in the nineteen-sixties was activity costing, which was finished in the spring of 1970 (*Activity Costing and Input-Output Accounting*, 1971c). That work was another response to the decision-usefulness theory developed in the nineteen-fifties. ATOATI represented the application of the decision-usefulness approach to financial accounting. My interest in managerial accounting led me to turn to the heart of that field: cost accounting. "Activity costing" was the result. I am pleased to see that many academics and practitioners have become interested in that approach to cost accounting, even if it has not been as widely accepted as decision-usefulness theory. Neither theory has been applied to its potential.

My return to work on decision usefulness in financial accounting was stimulated by my association with Bob Sterling and Ray Chambers while on leave at the University of Kansas in the 1969-70 academic year. That was the heyday of the "Kansas Conferences," then organized by Bob Sterling, and he asked me to present a paper arguing the merits of measuring assets and liabilities by discounting their future cash flows, which was emphasized in ATOATI, for comparison with Ray Chambers' current cash equivalent view, Yuji Ijiri's justification for historical cost measurement, and Philip Bell's presentation of the Edwards and Bell current replacement cost reporting scheme. (See Sterling, 1971a.) The resulting lengthy paper was divided into two for publication (1970, 1971b).

In 1975, it seemed that so many extensions and repairs had been made to the decision-usefulness theory as I left it in the late fifties that a revised edition might be useful — one that could serve as a text for graduate theory courses. So I wrote a new book, starting from scratch, and including a list of additional readings and study questions at the end of each chapter as well as a substantial number of reprinted materials from other sources so as to give students both reinforcing ideas and alternatives. I gave a great deal of emphasis to the criteria approach to choosing among alternative accounting methods, so I gave the book the title *Making Accounting Decisions* (MAD, 1977c) although "making accounting choices" seemed equally good. MAD was finished and published during my term as Director of Research and Technical Activities at the Financial Accounting Standards Board (1976-78) — a time when the Board was deeply involved in its "conceptual framework" project which eventually completed the acceptance of the decision-usefulness theory by theory-oriented accountants in English-speaking countries. All but one of the reprinted materials in this Part have been selected from publications that appeared between 1970 and 1977 to show the development of the second stage of the theory. To my knowledge, no substantial changes in the theory have been made since that period. One later publication (1989a) is reprinted here because I believe it contributes to an understanding of why a few accounting scholars have been attracted by the ideas that "cash flow accounting" and emphasis on measurement of assets at their "as-is net realizable value" have more to offer to users than does emphasis on cash flow potential. My explanation is that those scholars are more concerned with reporting on enterprise liquidity than in reporting on enterprise wealth. Both are required by decision-usefulness theory. Standards setters appear never to have been impressed with such an emphasis on reporting on liquidity.

A word about the nineteen-sixties publication that did so much to publicize the decision-usefulness objective and thereby to stimulate interest in the development of decision-usefulness theory is appropriate here. In the nineteen-fifties and early sixties I seemed to be a lone voice for decision usefulness (excepting Supplementary Statement No. 8 of the AAA, on disclosure (1955)). Furthermore, ATOATI was not widely read in its early years. But then the American Accounting Association published the report of its Committee to Prepare a Statement of Basic Accounting Theory (ASOBAT) in 1966. I had no direct part in the work of that committee, but my colleague for fourteen years, the late L. L. Vance, was a member as was the very persuasive George Sorter from the University of Chicago who had reviewed ATOATI for *The Accounting Review* (1963). I was immensely pleased with the result, because it accepted and called attention to the decision-usefulness objective as the starting point for thinking about accounting issues and identified relevance as the primary "standard" for evaluating accounting methods. The committee could not have picked two features of decision-usefulness theory to emphasize that could have played bigger roles in the promotion of the whole theory than those two did. By then, the time apparently was ripe for theory-oriented academic accountants to think about objectives of accounting and criteria for making accounting choices. The result was instantaneous acceptance of the decision-usefulness objective by a substantial set of interested parties, especially academics and several members of the AICPA's Accounting Principles Board and its staff. It seemed that within a matter of months most of the research that related in any way to accounting theory either explicitly or implicitly incorporated decision usefulness as a premise. Completion of that prerequisite made subsequent acceptance of other features of decision-usefulness theory feasible, perhaps inevitable. The decision-usefulness objective became the nucleus of a snowball that, once it started to roll, picked up all of the other features of the theory. ASOBAT was followed by APB Statement No. 4 in 1970, and *The Objectives of Financial Statements* in 1973, each of which accepted several of the basic features of the decision-usefulness theory so can be said to have contributed to its eventual widespread acceptance. The final (to date) "official" document in that series was, of course, the FASB's "conceptual framework," starting with preliminary documents in December 1976 and concluding with concepts statement No. 5 in December 1984. That conceptual framework includes most of the features of decision-usefulness theory as I see it, so I call it a version of the theory. But without ASOBAT, who knows how long widespread acceptance would have taken?

Acceptance of Theory Features Emphasized in Nineteen-seventies Works — The multiple criteria approach to making decisions, and the set of criteria to be used, were not major features of my work on decision-usefulness theory until the nineteen-seventies. The exception was the emphasis on information *relevant to cash flow-oriented decisions* and mention of cost and bias in ATOATI. Several other academics published papers dealing with *criteria* in the nineteen-sixties. (See below.) My publications emphasizing this area started in 1970 and ended with 1977b. The big step towards acceptance of the multiple criteria approach in the broad community of accountants was made in APB Statement No. 4 (AICPA, 1970). After the FASB officially adopted the decision usefulness objective in its Statement of Financial Accounting Concepts No. 1(1978), it chose the multiple-criteria approach (without using that term) as the second building block of its conceptual framework. As FASB director of research and technical activities, I commissioned Professor David Solomons to prepare a groundwork document on qualitative characteristics of financial information for the Board in 1977. His work was well received by the Board and Solomons was asked to continue to advise the Board as it developed the exposure draft and Statement of Financial Accounting Concepts No. 2, *Qualitative Characteristics of Accounting Information.* (1980) The multiple criteria approach to making accounting choices was thus put into the official approach to standards setting in the U. S. in 1980, even though "criteria" terminology was not explicitly accepted and the effects-via-other-parties criterion was not addressed. Other differences between the Board's and my set of criteria in MAD were immaterial. Relevance was defined in different words, but the Board's meaning is similar to mine. The Board chose "materiality" instead of optimal quantity. I do not see either as important now. Costs of utilizing and producing information were merged and are to be compared with bemefits; no quarrel there. In general, this part of the decision-usefulness theory has been well accepted by neutral participants in standards setting.

Recognition of the alternative *measurement methods* has been a gradual process over many years, even decades, so no particular evidence of acceptance is noteworthy. The rankings of measurement methods on the relevance criterion, however, has neither been accepted nor rejected by authoritative bodies in accounting; they have not addressed the subject. The FASB tried to deal with it in the 1980s but the Board members could not reach agreement, although they did accept the idea of an array of measurement methods. Acceptance of the implications of decision-usefulness theory for *inflation accounting* has not been universal. In general, restatements of old measurements using a consumer price level index in inflationary environments has been accepted, so decision-usefulness thinking has prevailed there. On several other specific issues, however, the decision-usefulness approach has been rejected, as noted in the section on inflation accounting near the end of this part of the book.

Locations of Theory Features in the Nineteen-seventies Works.—The publications included in this part of the book represent a second look at decision-usefulness theory. Several features of the theory that are emphasized in the diagrammatic outline (p. x) were revisited or introduced in these materials. For the benefit of those readers who are looking for material on a particular feature, a few places to look are mentioned here.

The *decision-usefulness objective* was restated in the 1971 relevance paper, p. 42 (reprinted) and in MAD, Chapter II. *Investors' cash flow-oriented decisions* and information for them were addressed in the 1989 *Accounting and Business Research* (A&BR) paper, pp. 161-4. Alternative versions of *historical cash flows* were elucidated in the 1966 *Accounting Review* article and in the 1989 A&BR paper. Evidence of cash flow potential was discussed in the 1971 relevance paper, especially on pp. 48-50, and in the 1989 A&BR paper, pp. 166-8.

The criteria approach to accounting choices and the individual criteria were most fully developed in the 1976 A&BR article, with a further development of the effects-via-other-parties criterion in Chapter III of MAD and in the introduction to the FASB *Economic Consequences* volume. Descriptions and rationales for the ranking of *measurement methods* on the relevance criterion were addressed in depth in the 1971 relevance paper, pp. 50-62, and in Chapter VII of MAD. Relationships among the methods were also discussed in the 1989 A&BR paper, pp. 166-7. Finally, the *measuring unit* issue and other aspects of "inflation accounting" were attended to in MAD, Chapter IX.

The materials from the 1970s period that are reprinted in this Part emphasize only a few of the major features of the decision-usefulness theory, as outlined in the diagrammatic outline (page x). Explanations of other features of the theory, included in the nineteen-fifties materials, reprinted in Part I, were not improved significantly in the nineteen-seventies.

Criteria for Making
Accounting Choices

Introduction

The features of the decision-usefulness theory that serve as the more basic building blocks were born fully grown, so to speak. The early features of the theory — the decision-usefulness objective, the identification of users and uses, the focus on investors' cash flow-oriented decisions, and the value of accounting information that is relevant to those decisions — have remained unchanged in substance, although their exposition has been much improved. That was not true of the criteria for making accounting choices. They were developed over a long period, starting with ATOATI in the 1950s and concluding with MAD (1977) and with significant contributions by others. Those that impressed me the most are identified below.

My development of a set of criteria for making accounting choices appears in four major works. In ATOATI (p. 50), "two criteria for appraising measurement techniques" were recommended: "the relevance of the type of evidence utilized, to the problem of predicting future returns to investors; and the accessibility of the evidence, [including] such variables as the difficulties in making estimates and computations, fees to independent appraisers, and the risk that bias may reduce the reliability of the measurements." These three — relevance to investors' decisions, reliability, and cost, in today's terminology — constituted the first set of criteria I advocated for making accounting choices. In the University of Kansas lecture and the two publications (1970, 1971b) based on it, an attempt was made to develop a genuine multiple criteria approach to making accounting decisions. A set of four major criteria and eleven second level criteria were set out. Those criteria appeared in the *Abacus* article (1970), "Determinants of the Value of Accounting Procedures," which was entirely devoted to the case for using such a set of criteria. That paper marked my main development of the criteria. The multiple criteria article (1976a) was also devoted entirely to that topic, and was a superior presentation, so it is reprinted here. It included substantial enhancements of the case for the multiple criteria approach with a decision tree format and the addition of "effects via other parties," now called "unintended economic consequences," and "cost of utilizing information" as criteria. Essentially the same set of criteria appear in Chapter III of MAD, but with a significant improvement in the argument for the role of effects via other parties in the choices of some evaluators. The section on that criterion is included here. I consider the multiple criteria approach to making accounting choices as it was developed in those publications to be both descriptive and normative in character.

Developments pertaining to four of the criteria deserve special attention.

Relevance was not actually defined in ATOATI. The general usage of the word was accepted in the phrase "relevance of the type of evidence utilized to the problem of predicting future returns to investors" (p.50)—written as "relevance to cash flow-oriented decisions" in subsequent publications. In the University of Kansas lecture papers, the term was applied in choosing a property of an asset or liability — e.g., historical cost, contractual amount, or market value—to measure and report in financial statements. "A financial property is relevant to a decision if, given sufficient materiality, it has the power to affect the decision." By 1976 the FASB organization's use of "attribute" instead of property influenced my terminology, so I emphasized the value of knowledge of an attribute of an object or event in the decision process. With this usage, the relevance criterion is only applied in choices of attributes of assets and liabilities to measure, not in other choices, such as terminology or financial statement form. In FASB terminology, the alternative attributes of assets are: historical cost, current cost, current market value, net realizable value, and present value of future cash flows (1986, p. 209). In my post-1977 work on market simulation accounting (1985a and 1986) I have found little use for either the relevance criterion or the attribute concept in choosing measurement methods; close simulations of setting-specific market values cover that point.

Reliability was not defined in my work until the 1970 Kansas lecture, in the part published in 1970, when I related it to a measurement of a financial property: "that quality of a measurement that justifies dependence upon it as an accurate representation of the actual quantity of the property it purportedly measures." That emphasis on a measurement accomplishing what it *purports* to accomplish was intended clearly to distinguish reliability from relevance — a distinction that was not clear to many observers. For example, an historical cost measurement may, or may not, be highly reliable as a measurement of cost despite the low ranking of historical cost on the relevance criterion. In MAD (1977), "Reliability is that quality which permits users of a datum confidently to depend on it as an accurate representation of the specific phenomenon it purports to represent." That "purports-to-represent" view of reliability was accepted by the FASB in its conceptual framework (Concepts Statement 2).

Three types of *comparability* were identified in 1970. The major expansion of that analysis appeared in Part 2 (my part) of Kenley and Staubus (1972) and again in 1976a and 1977c. Consistency was included from 1970 on.

The least understood criterion that I have advocated must have been *effects via other parties*, which I now call *unintended economic consequences*. Its first appearance was in my presentation at the Southwest Regional Conference of the American Accounting Association in spring, 1976, subsequently published in *Accounting and Business Research* (1976) and in Chapter III of MAD. Further thoughts on the topic appeared in my introduction to the FASB book on economic consequences (1978). It was given more space in MAD than any of the other criteria for making accounting decisions. Not only is it a complex, often misunderstood criterion, but it might well be the most heavily weighted, though least acknowledged, criterion used by many respondents to standards setters' proposals for substantive changes in GAAP measurements. Indeed, a cynic might say that it has been the primary criterion in the minds of many respondents to discussion documents and exposure drafts as well as in the voting decisions of those standards setters who have "backed down" in the face of vehement opposition to proposals of standards that were viewed by some as in the ox-goring category. For these reasons, it needs more attention here than do other criteria.

When I arrived at the FASB in 1976, some form of unintended economic consequences argument was being used to oppose every major change in GAAP that the Board considered: immediate expensing of research and development costs, accounting for uninsured losses as they occurred instead of smoothing them, recognizing losses at the time of restructuring of weak loans, and successful efforts accounting for oil and gas exploration costs. I decided to invite people from all segments of the financial reporting community to submit research papers on the economic consequences issue and hold a conference at which the best papers would be presented. That conference was held on March 23, 1978. No researcher provided convincing evidence that material economic consequences ever occurred, nor did anyone participating in the discussion at the conference. I believe that that conference process substantially diffused the economic consequences issue. In subsequent arguments, reasonably neutral, well-informed observers tended to see through the economic consequences arguments. Fear of unintended economic consequences continued to play its role as a criterion for making accounting choices, but primarily in the minds of those who saw their own ox in danger of being gored. (Please see the discussion below in this section and the accompanying reprinted materials.) Five pages from the introduction that I wrote for the book (1978) that included the papers presented at the conference are reprinted here.

To an evaluator of an accounting method under consideration, the essence of the unintended economic consequences criterion is: "What will that accounting method do to or for me because of its effect or anticipated effect on someone else?" If I am an enterprise manager, a conservative accounting method might hurt me by impacting my earnings-based bonus or an evaluation of my performance by a superior or by my company's compensation committee. If I am a shareholder, it might affect me by impacting the price of the stock I own, either through effects on the decisions of other investors, or through decisions of my firm's managers. Note, however, that these effects depend upon the "other parties" relying just as heavily on the financial statements based on the old accounting method as on statements based on the new — that is, the effects in question depend on "market inefficiency." When adverse unintended economic consequences are feared, the evaluator may be so concerned about them that he/she underweights other criteria in judging the value to investors and other direct users of the information resulting from application of the proposed method. Also, in my experience at the FASB, potential favorable effects of a proposal to change an accounting standard were rarely mentioned. But respondents associated with companies whose financial statements were likely to be adversely affected foresaw catastrophic consequences from upsetting the status quo.

The popular term in the standards-setting world for unintended economic consequences has been "economic consequences," meaning adverse effects on prices of a firm's securities, or on its ability to raise capital, or the possibility of managers choosing suboptimal courses of action (for owners) because of fear of the effects of their choices on their performance as reported in the financial statements. If one wishes to recognize the positive and intended economic consequences of financial information — the basic

165

reason for accounting — then the consequences that typically have concerned opponents of more current and more risk-revealing accounting information might be called "economic side effects" to distinguish them from the fundamental positive effects of information on an economy. Reconsideration as I write this section has led me to a preference for the term "unintended economic consequences" to replace "effects via other parties" as a criterion for making accounting decisions. Unfortunately, both terms are awkward; I would welcome a more easily pronounced, descriptive alternative. "Economic consequences" has the serious disadvantage of not distinguishing the fundamental, intended, positive economic consequences of information from a special interest group's fear that its own ox would be gored by the required use of a certain accounting method.

Unintended economic consequences have not been recognized by the FASB as a criterion for making accounting choices—a "qualitative characteristic" of accounting information in the Board's jargon. Its recognition would raise the question of whether only other evaluators use such a criterion or if Board members, too, take it into consideration. Nevertheless, I believe that inclusion of unintended economic consequences as a criterion that an evaluator might use in making an accounting choice brings into the theory a factor that often dominates a person's accounting choices. What kind of a theory is it that does not explain the choices actually made in the high profile cases? More arguments for and against consideration of economic consequences in making accounting decisions were presented in 1995a, pp. 207-214. Additional recollections relating to this subject from my experiences at the FASB are included there.

Criteria for evaluating accounting methods (typically without the criteria label) began to show up elsewhere in the accounting literature in the 1960s. Especially helpful were Ijiri and Jaedicke (1966) who developed the mathematical versions of reliability, including objectivity and bias; Snavely's (1967) more complete set of criteria; and McDonald's (1967) work on feasibility criteria for assessment measures and prediction measures. The most influential work of that period was ASOBAT (1966), as noted above. Prior to that period, Chambers (1960) had emphasized the value, in a specific decision context, of information that is relevant to that decision. Subsequently, Sterling (1970) gave relevance a specific meaning in the context of decision models, and APB Statement No. 4 (1970) introduced the idea of qualities (relevance, understandability, verifiability, neutrality, timeliness, comparability, completeness) that make financial information useful. All of these works contributed to the development of the criteria for making accounting choices as a key feature of decision-usefulness theory and eventually contributed to the FASB's conceptual framework.

REFERENCES

Demski, Joel A. and Gerald A. Feltham, *Cost Determination: A Conceptual Framework* (Iowa State University Press), 1976.

Prakash, Prem and Alfred Rappaport, "Feedback Effects of Accounting," *Business Week*, January 12, 1976, p. 12.

The Multiple-Criteria Approach to Making Accounting Decisions[*]

George J. Staubus

This is a paper about making accounting decisions, i.e. choosing from among alternative methods of accounting for economic events affecting an entity. Accounting theory appears to be developing in the direction of a framework of concepts and procedures that can be used in making accounting choices. Surely the most elegant general form of such frameworks is that based on information economics and often referred to as the information evaluation approach (Feltham, 1972; Demski, 1972; Demski and Feltham, 1976). Unfortunately, difficulties of implementation limit its application, especially at the social, or public policy, level. Not only are economists unable to construct a social utility function but the measurement of private value of information is also not feasible except in special cases. Consequently, those making accounting decisions appear to be turning to a variety of frameworks consisting of one or two cost categories and a set of surrogates for the value of information (normative criteria of useful data). This latter approach to making accounting decisions is the subject of this paper.

The most direct antecedents of the present work are those which have concentrated on criteria for the evaluation of information or for choosing an accounting method, such as *A Statement of Basic Accounting Theory* (1966), Ijiri and Jaedicke (1966), Snavely (1967), McDonald (1967) and the American Accounting Association Committee on Concepts and Standards – Internal Planning and Control (1974). The development of the present author's framework can be traced from 1961 through 1967 and 1970 to Kenley and Staubus, 1972. Valuable contributions have also been made by authors concentrating on the measurement-of-cost-and-value approach, e.g. Feltham (1972) and Demski (1972). The main

objective of the present work is to consolidate these and other statements and to develop more fully the multiple-criteria approach to making accounting decisions.

The bulk of the paper consists of descriptions of the nine criteria that are proposed for use in evaluating accounting proposals: attribute relevance, reliability, comparability, effects via other parties, understandability and readability, timeliness, optimal quantity, cost of producing and cost of utilising. A new and more specific definition of relevance is proposed. The sources of unreliability are classified and a new measure of verifiability is suggested. The criterion 'effects via other parties' is introduced and its multifarious ramifications explored and exemplified. Hypothesised relationships between the frequency and lag measures of timeliness and the value of reported data are graphed and the interdependencies among the concepts of optimal quantity, materiality, disclosure, costs of producing financial data and costs of utilising data are discussed briefly.

Following the descriptions of the proposed criteria, the applicability of the approach is illustrated by suggesting, for each criterion, some accounting decisions for which that criterion is likely to play a major role in detecting differences between the alternative accounting proposals. Some suggestions regarding the development of decision-making techniques, or accounting decision models, are given in the final section.

Criteria for the evaluation of accounting methods

The interpretation of the proposed criteria may be easier if the reader agrees with two points which have been taken into consideration in their selection. One is that, in each case, a criterion may be partially met, or met to a degree. Attribute relevance, for example, is not a go, no-go criterion; there are degrees of relevance. Rarely will a criterion be met

[*]A paper presented in a plenary session of the Southwest Regional Meeting of the American Accounting Association at San Antonio, Texas, March 18, 1976 and adapted from chapter III of the author's book, *Making Accounting Decisions* (Scholars Book Co., forthcoming).

perfectly but complete failure on a criterion is also uncommon. As a consequence, tradeoffs must be made, as when a bit of relevance may be sacrificed for the sake of greater reliability, or lower cost of production. But, on the other hand, none of the seven benefit criteria can be completely absent; any accounting method which scores zero on any one criterion would be unacceptable. A minimum passing mark on each of the criteria is a necessary, but not a sufficient, condition for the acceptance of an accounting proposal. That is, in each case it is possible to imagine an appraisal on one criterion which would be so poor that it could not be offset by high ratings on other criteria.

Attribute Relevance

The first criterion of useful (valuable) accounting data is relevance of the attribute (of an object or event) being measured to the decisions of the user. An attribute (e.g. cost or market value) of an object or event is relevant to a decision if knowledge of its amount would help the decision-maker evaluate an outcome of one or more of the alternative courses of action under consideration. To make a decision is to choose, and a choice requires alternatives. The person using accounting data to choose among alternatives is trying to evaluate the consequences (outcomes, payoffs) associated with each alternative. The outcomes can only be in the future so prediction is required. Relevance does not guarantee that the particular datum (number) provided will be useful – its failure to meet one or more of the other criteria could make it useless – but only that the number pertain to an attribute in which the decision-maker is interested. An alternative view is that a relevant attribute is one called for by a decision model but we are not concerned with whether the decision process has been 'modelled' or not. We must remember that a model is an abstract representation of something; we are more concerned with the actual decision process, whether it has or can be modelled effectively or not. Please note that we are using the word 'relevant' in a specific way here. In a more general sense, everything we do in accounting should be relevant to accounting objectives. But we are limiting the relevance criterion to the relationship between an attribute being measured and a user's decision process. The emphasis this definition places on the necessity for accounting decision-makers becoming acquainted with the decision processes of users is as obvious as it is unavoidable if accountants do not wish to depend upon serendipity to make their products useful in decision-making.[1]

---

[1]For definitions of relevance which do not agree with the above, see Feltham (1972, p. 84) and Sterling (1972, p. 199).

The present usage of the term makes attribute relevance a large, but clearly bounded, subject; dropping it at this point would be inexcusable were not the space limitation so critical. We suggest, however, that the financial community's interest in predicting returns, which depend upon the entity's future capacity to pay and its cash flows, permits us to identify cash-flow-oriented decisions as the primary class of decisions for which people use entity financial statements. Within this context, economic analysis enables us to rank (on the attribute relevance criterion) the several attributes of assets and liabilities which we associate with the several measurement methods (Staubus, 1961, 1971, 1973). Other criteria must, of course, be considered in the selection of a measurement method for application in a specific case.

Reliability

Users of financial data prefer that it have a high degree of reliability. Reliability is that quality which permits users of a datum confidently to depend on it as an accurate representation of the specific phenomenon it purports to represent. But reliable information is not necessarily useful. A 1935 timetable may give reliable information about the time the first train of the day stopped at the local station in 1935, but that information may not be relevant to a commuter's decision as to when to leave his home on a 1975 morning. Or we may have reliable information about the price paid by another party for an asset in which we have no interest, or about some irrelevant attribute (or feature or property) of one of our assets. There is close 'correspondence' between such information and 'reality.' For example, if an asset is allegedly valued at historical cost, the amount shown is reliable if it truly represents the sum of the sacrifices made to acquire it. We do not consider such a valuation unreliable just because it does not represent the current market value of the asset. If market value is the attribute of which the decision-maker needs a measurement, historical cost is irrelevant to the decision at hand but it is not necessarily unreliable. An acceptable level of reliability is a necessary, but not a sufficient, condition for valuable information.

Reliability has so many facets that a review of the underlying sources and causes of unreliability may be helpful. The fundamental reason why financial statements often have unreliable components is that accountants make many choices, estimates and judgments in applying the various measurement and classification rules they choose to employ. The following categories come to mind; there may be others:

1. Predictions. These include lives, salvage values and service patterns of amortisable assets of all

kinds; failure of a debtor or other contracting party; worthlessness of assets. Different accountants will use different prediction techniques, involving different predictors and coefficients.

2. Allocations, i.e. splitting a sum into parts with the aid of a base that is not prefectly suited to the task. Examples are distribution of a cost among functional divisions, assignment of overhead to products, costing of joint products, amortisation of long-lived assets. Accountants make choices in connection with the selection of a base, accumulation of base data and calculations.

3. Predetermined overhead rates, standard costs, etc. The choice of using or not using such methods and the manner of their use, especially the disposition of variances, can make a considerable difference.

4. Selection of evidence in other cases. For example, when current market prices are being used there may be a choice of bid, asked, average or last sale; choice of market, source of the quotation, and so forth.

This listing, while not complete, should be sufficient to remind us of the multitude of opportunities for variation in the application of GAAP or any similar set of principles and rules. The results actually reported by the accountant in such cases will be influenced by a variety of circumstances such as the following:

1. Bias, e.g. conservatism; lack of objectivity, lack of independence on the part of the accountant or other party involved in these estimates and choices.

2. Habit, consistent use of established practices and rule-of-thumb approaches. These factors may either contribute to or detract from the reliability of the results.

3. Uncertainty, and the substitution of point estimates for probability distributions of future outcomes.

4. Errors in data supplied to the accountant which are used as predictors, price quotations, base data for allocations.

5. Weak association between predictors and attribute to be predicted; between basis of allocation and cost being allocated.

6. Prediction techniques; constants, variables and coefficients used.

Any user of accounting data who is thoroughly familiar with these many possible sources of unreliability will take them into consideration and avoid placing heavy reliance on any measurement made in circumstances which he believes to be conducive to bias or errors in predictors or requiring a choice from a wide range of possible outcomes, etc. The less knowledgeable user has a serious problem –

unless accountants give some clues (in their reports) as to the degree of reliability which should be attached to various financial statement items.

Now let us look at several parts of reliability which accountants have recognised. Verifiability and freedom from bias are two of the four accounting standards discussed in *A Statement of Basic Accounting Theory*. Verifiability and neutrality are identified as qualitative objectives in APB Statement No. 4. Ijiri and Jaedicke (1966) expressed reliability, objectivity and bias in mathematical terms while McKeown's (1971) measure of accuracy encompassed verifiability and bias. What do these various terms mean and how do they relate to reliability?

Verifiability. 'Verifiable financial accounting information provides results that would be substantially duplicated by independent measurers using the same measurement methods.' (APB, 1970, p. 37.) McKeown measures verifiability as:

$$v^{-2} = \frac{1}{n} \sum_{i=1}^{n} (x_i - \bar{x})^2 \quad \text{or}$$

$$v = \sqrt{\frac{n}{\sum_{i=1}^{n} (x_i - \bar{x})^2}} = \frac{1}{\sigma}$$

where σ is the standard deviation of x. x_i is the number arrived at by the ith measurer. It is assumed that n different measurers are measuring the same object by the same method but that they end up with different numbers. The distribution of the various measurements about their mean ($\bar{x}$) is described as *dispersion*. But note that it is not normally known in a practical setting because we normally do not have a sample of measurements of the same thing. Dispersion does not exist for one observation. However, experienced accountants working with a familiar problem, such as estimating uncollectible receivables for a department store, may be able to judge the dispersion that would result if a sample of accountants were to estimate those uncollectibles. Thus, experience is a basis for judging the verifiability of a measurement made by a relatively 'soft' method if the circumstances are known. Experimentation is another possible basis for judging verifiability, or dispersion. Variations in personal bias on the part of several individual measurers can contribute to dispersion as can any of the other variations in the circumstances of measurement as listed above in this subsection. Finally, we must remember that a highly verifiable measurement is not necessarily 'correct'. All it means is that other measurers would see it the same way; they may all be in error.

One difficulty with the McKeown measure of rifiability is that it is not expressed in a form that rmits comparison of the verifiability of a set of easurements of a high-value object and a set of easurements of a low-value object. For example, the standard deviation of several measurements of a asset is $20,000 and the mean of the measurements $1,000,000, the verifiability (per McKeown) of e set of measurements is 1/20,000, a very low gure. If, in another case, the mean is $100 and the andard deviation is $40, the verifiability, 1/40, is uch higher. It appears that it would be helpful to xpress these measurements in a comparable manner.

Adapting a suggestion made by Abdel-Khalik 1971, pp. 468–469),[2] we propose that the comple-

ent of the coefficient of variation, that is $1 - \left(\dfrac{\sigma_x}{\bar{x}} \right)$,

e used as a standard measure of verifiability. On is basis, the verifiability of the measurements of ne valuable asset mentioned above is $1 - 20,000/1,000,000) = \cdot98$, while the verifiability of ne measurements of the low-value asset is $1 - 40/100) = \cdot60$; the former has the higher degree of erifiability. If $\sigma_x > \bar{x}$, verifiability is negative – not n intuitively obvious interpretation but perhaps an cceptable one.

Bias. Freedom from bias, objectivity, neutrality nd independence are terms used for a state of mind hat permits an observer to perceive phenomena and ecord his perceptions without influence from his ersonal stake in the phenomena in question or the ses to which his record of those phenomena may be ut. An objective observer 'calls them as he sees hem' and he sees them as they are without con- ideration of who may be benefited or harmed as a esult. Bias can only occur when choices are made so t is found in association with the judgments listed bove in this subsection. Here we are concentrating n personal bias. The term 'bias' is also used in the iterature to mean systematic bias which is inherent n a measurement method and can be estimated and emoved by a correction technique.

Accuracy. McKeown defines accuracy as follows:

$$A^{-2} = \frac{1}{n} \sum_{i=1}^{n} (x_i - T)^2 \quad \text{or}$$

$$A = \sqrt{\frac{n}{\dfrac{n}{\sum\limits_{i=1}^{n} (x_i - T)^2}}}$$

where x_i is a set of n measurements of the same thing and T is the true measure. This makes accuracy a combination of verifiability and any difference between the mean of the sample of measurements and the true value. This latter difference is some- times called bias. Thus, according to McKeown, $A^{-2} = V^{-2} + (\bar{x} - T)^2 = V^{-2} + B^2$ where B is bias. Accuracy, in this meaning, is only applicable to predictions – which permit a subsequent determina- tion of T. The only reasonable meaning of T for a past event is $\bar{x}$, unless we are willing to say that one observer (e.g. the one who is most qualified or who is working under the most favourable con- ditions; see McDonald, 1967) has the truth while others do not. Consensus of qualified observers (lack of dispersion) is the final word on observations but not on predictions; for the latter, outcomes can be observed and accepted as truth for comparison with individual predictions or the mean of a sample of predictions – providing there is no dispersion among several observations of the outcome.

Comparability

In accounting, comparability has to do with relationships between accounting practices which contribute to the process of relating two or more financial data. Its importance depends heavily upon the almost universal need to compare data when using them; an isolated datum is rarely of much use. The information value of the data is enhanced by the application of similar accounting practices to similar events (but not, of course, by treating significantly different events as if they were similar). An accounting method ranks low on the comparability criterion if it permits identical objects or events to be reported as if they were different or different things to be reported as if they were identical.

Six types of comparability have been discussed in another publication (Kenley and Staubus, 1972, p. 55): interperiod, intercompany, interline and intraline comparability; comparability of lengths of reporting periods and *ex ante-ex post* comparability. Careful examination of these types of comparability may reveal that there is a good deal of overlap between them and the relevance and reliability criteria.

---

[2]'Unlike the Ijiri-Jaedicke model, it appears that *the complement of the coefficient of variation* would be a better measure of reliability than the variance. This preference, on my part, is due to several reasons. For one thing, the co- efficient of variation (and its complement, of course) is independent of the magnitude of the asset's or the transac- tion's value. Secondly, the complement of the coefficient of variation is more consistent with the intuitive assessment since the higher the complement of the coefficient or varia- tion, the higher the reliability.' This is not true of the Ijiri- Jaedicke (1966) measure although it is true of McKeown's.

Indeed, we could omit comparability as a separate criterion of valuable information and divide it between relevance and reliability. But this would dilute a concept which appears to deserve a lot of weight in the evaluation of accounting proposals; we prefer to apply it as an independent criterion.

Effects via Other Parties

Any person who is choosing among alternative accounting methods should take into consideration the effects the methods may have on his interests through the actions of other parties. A dramatic example was the 1971 controversy in the USA over the choice of the liberal 'flow through' method or the conservative 'deferral' method of accounting for the 'investment credit' permitted by the US Internal Revenue Code. The Accounting Principles Board apparently believed that the deferral method yielded data which were the more relevant to the decisions of investors but this view did not prevail. The US Treasury Department, which was interested in the investment credit's effects on the US economy, *via the decisions of businessmen,* argued for the liberal flow-through method. Corporate managers, who were interested in the effects the chosen method would have on themselves and their corporations *via the investment decisions and management appraisals of investors,* also preferred the flow-through method. Investors, as usual, exerted little influence but they, too, may well have been influenced by the prospective effects that the deferral method would have on the price of their securities via *the market actions of other investors.* It seems likely that effects via other parties was the key criterion in the ultimate decision, made by the US Congress (and President), not to prohibit any method. Most corporations have chosen the flow-through method.

Many other examples could be given of accounting decisions in which effects on an interested party via other parties could be a significant consideration. Several general categories of such cases are tabulated in Exhibit I. In addition to these widely recognised cases of 'ricochet effects', there is also the possibility of what might be called the 'two-cushion bank shot'. Consider the issue of whether uninsured fire and casualty losses should be reported as losses on the income statement in the period in which they occur or, alternatively, 'self-insurance reserves' should be established by regular periodic charges to expense in amounts similar to the insurance premiums which would have been paid if the risks had been insured against and actual losses charged to the reserve instead of against income. If (a) investors are believed to be averse to instability in reported earnings then (b) managers may be reluctant to report losses as they occur (unevenly) so may incur the cost of uneconomical insurance if self-insurance reserves are not permitted. As a result, (c), investors may prefer that the FASB permit self-insurance reserves in order to encourage managers to economise on insurance costs.

Understandability and Readability

This criterion (or set of criteria) focuses attention on the receiving phase of the communication process. Effectiveness and efficiency of communication are desirable attributes of financial reports. The strengths and limitations of the readers of financial statements must not be overlooked by any accountant who is seriously interested in communicating with users. If data are equated with facts, and if information depends upon someone being informed, then data are converted to information by the communication process. Different sets of financial statements may be needed to reach different classes of readers, each class of which may have different vocabularies and backgrounds in accounting and finance.

Timeliness

There are two types of timeliness. One is *frequency* of reporting, i.e. the length of the reporting period. Should it be a month, quarter, half-year or year? It is possible to report too frequently or too infrequently. If the period is too short, a report on operations may be too heavily influenced by random or seasonal variations in the firm's activities, with the result that the data are misleading or at least not worth the user's time. But if the reporting period is too long, the user is required to wait too long before obtaining and using the information included in the reports. This delay is related to the other type of timeliness – *lag* between the end of the reporting period and the date the financial statements are issued. The value of information is always related to the lag, or delay, in reporting because it is always used for prediction.[3]

Exhibit II illustrates the relationships between the net value of information and frequency and lag. The zero point on the time axis represents infinitely short reporting periods or immediate reporting after the end of the period. The negative segment of the frequency curve indicates costs of producing and utilising data in excess of the benefits. The shape of the lag curve in the negative lag range indicates that predictions are more valuable than *ex post* reporting, other things (including reliability) being equal.

Optimal Quantity

Several concepts that relate to the quantity of data supplied to users have been discussed in the literature.

---

[3]Gregory and Van Horne (1960, p. 349) emphasised *interval* and *delay* instead of frequency and lag.

EXHIBIT I

Examples of accounting decision situations in which effects upon an interested party via other parties may be significant

Interested Party	Accounting Choice	Other Party	Potential Effect	Probable Choice
Taxing authority	Treatment of tax incentives in accounting to investors	Managers of reporting entity	Effect on internal investment decisions	Flow through
Shareholders	Treatment of tax incentives in accounting to investors	Managers of reporting entity	Effect on internal investment decisions	Deferral
Managers	Treatment of tax incentives in accounting to investors	Shareholders	Effect on appraisals of managerial performance and on share investment decisions	Flow through
Shareholders	Asset and liability measurement methods (and 'instant earnings' and 'instant losses')	Managers	Decision to sell or hold an asset; decision to retire debt prematurely or not	Current value methods
Managers	Asset and liability measurement methods (and 'instant earnings' and 'instant losses')	Shareholders	Appraisals of managerial performance; share investment decisions	Historical cost
Shareholders	Capitalising or expensing research, development, exploration and 'human asset' costs	Managers	Expenditure decisions	Capitalisation of successful investments
Shareholders and managers	Choices affecting debt/ equity ratio, working capital, stability and level of earnings	Lenders	Extension of credit and terms	'Liberal' methods
Shareholders and managers	Inventory cost flow assumption	US Internal Revenue Service	Tax liability of entity	LIFO
Top managers and owners	Any choice of method of reporting results vs. plans	Any subordinate manager	Decisions by subordinates not in interests of owners	Methods providing congruence
Managers and shareholders	Any choice affecting reported earnings	Union representatives	Bargaining on labour contract	Conservative methods

The APB (1970, p. 38) included completeness as a qualitative objective: 'Complete financial accounting information includes all financial accounting data that reasonably fulfil the requirements of the other qualitative objectives.' Disclosure is given a great deal of emphasis in the traditional literature of accounting and in recent efforts of the SEC. For example, Moonitz (1961, p. 50) postulated that 'Accounting reports should disclose that which is necessary to make them not misleading'. Materiality has perplexed practitioners for decades. Significance and efficiency have also been advanced as criteria for the evaluation of information (Snavely, 1967). The literature of information economics stresses optimal partitioning and optimal aggregation, where partition-

ing refers to the fineness or coarseness of the classification scheme employed and aggregation involves merging separate events for reporting. The dangers of 'information overload' have also been recognised. Obviously all of these concepts are related to the quantity of data reported.

The issue is just how far to go in providing detailed data which appear to be borderline with respect to value in excess of cost of producing and utilising. Three segments of the issue come to mind. One is the extent to which such general categories as assets, liabilities, revenues and expenses, which are included in the accounts of the double-entry system, are broken down, or condensed, for presentation to users. Or, starting with the original events which the

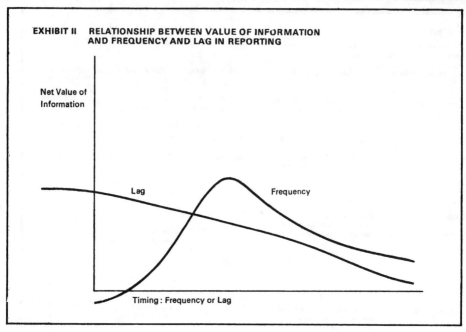

EXHIBIT II   RELATIONSHIP BETWEEN VALUE OF INFORMATION
AND FREQUENCY AND LAG IN REPORTING

Net Value of
Information

Lag   Frequency

Timing : Frequency or Lag

accountant records, the question is 'how much aggregation of events is appropriate prior to reporting them?' The second segment is the extent to which additional descriptive material, including captions, parenthetical comments and accompanying notes, are included in the financial reports. Finally, circumstances not included in the double entry system may be included in financial reports; examples are contingent liabilities and valuable attributes of the entity which do not meet the criteria for inclusion as an asset. While the term 'optimal quantity' of data is not ideal, it does appear to cover this related group of concerns satisfactorily, although the necessity for cost-benefit comparisons may cause some readers to prefer the merger of this criterion with the cost of utilisation and cost of production criteria.

Cost of Producing Accounting Data

The costs of performing accounting activities (salaries, depreciation or equipment rental, supplies, audit fees, etc.) are often neglected by people who emphasise maximisation of the value of information to users. But accounting costs are not negligible. American Telephone and Telegraph (1975), for example, showed accounting expenses of $786,802,000 on its 1975 income statement, an amount equal to 2·7 percent of its revenues. And the

entire revenues of the auditing branch of the accounting profession – perhaps two to three billion dollars annually in the USA – are accounting costs. One reason why the information evaluation approach to external financial reporting decisions has not been popular is that the parties who have the best feel for the costs (managers and owner-managers of firms) are not the same as the parties who enjoy the benefits (absentee investors, government agencies, and, in a sense, auditors), and most of the decisions have been made by the former. Such circumstances make cost-benefit efficient decisions very difficult. As an analogy, consider how a society made up of 100 university students and 100 childless adult taxpayers – don't ask what happened to the students' parents – might decide on how much money to spend on university education and what portion should be paid by the students in fees. The usual solution is to select policy makers (elected officials or members of the Financial Accounting Standards Board) and empower them to decide and impose their decision on the rest of us. The surprising aspect is not that it works poorly but that it works at all. However, we should recognise that shareholders bear the firm's accounting costs to the same extent that they bear other operating costs of the firm; managers do not pay these costs out of their own pockets. The final cidence of the cost presumably is on consumers of the firm's products and the benefits from better decisions by investors also tend to be diffused throughout the economy, in the long run. As we said in the introduction to this paper, implementation of the aggregate social welfare criterion of accounting systems is not feasible at the present time.

Even a straight comparison of internal accounting costs is difficult enough, especially when one of the methods under consideration is unfamiliar. The typical reaction of someone who is familiar with one procedure is that a proposed alternative is more difficult. This view may reflect his vision of 'first time through' performance; the 'learning curve' phenomenon is not as prominent in the first picture he sees. In addition, we must keep in mind that new services may become available (e.g. new price indexes, published price quotations) if a new method is widely adopted. Finally, we must not forget the role that computers can play in reducing the cost of what would be tedious calculations and retrieval of data by older methods.

We must be careful to avoid allowing a vague feeling of ignorance and 'difficulty' associated with a new technique to be converted into an unsupported argument that the new method is too costly. This is especially relevant to the evaluation of alternative asset measurement methods and general price level adjustments as the costs of these aspects of accounting are relatively small compared to the costs of the routine, high-volume procedures such as those pertaining to billing and receivables, disbursements, inventory quantities and payroll accounting. It seems quite unlikely that the total annual accounting costs of the average firm would be increased by more than two to four percent (after the first time through) by any choice from among the widely-discussed measurement methods (including historical cost adjusted for changes in a general price index). For example, a vice-president of AT & T estimated that only $10,000 of its $728,207,000 1974 accounting costs was spent on producing a rough set of general purchasing power financial statements.[4] The costs of accounting must be taken into consideration without using them as a club to beat down any proposal for change.

Cost of Utilising Accounting Data

This criterion is closely related to two of the criteria discussed above: understandability and readability and optimal quantity. If the financial state-

ments and accompanying material are not easily comprehended by the users; if they are poorly organised so that the user must spend time searching for data which he wants to consider together; if he must make his own additions, subtractions and divisions in order to obtain the sums, differences and ratios he needs; if he must plough through many pages of details in order to extract the data he needs – all of these circumstances add to the costs of utilising accounting data. These costs take the form of consumption of the user's own time, salaries of professional analysts and subscription fees for investment services. While the difference between the cost of using the data produced by one accounting method and the cost of using that produced by another method may seldom be material, we should keep it in mind for consideration in the minority of cases.

The relationship between the two cost criteria and the optimal quantity criterion is illustrated in Exhibit III. If the accountant starts with the most valuable data he can accumulate and report, then gradually adds data in order of incremental value, we can picture a declining curve of incremental value as the quantity of data increases. If the combined cost of producing and utilising data increases more than proportionately to the increase in quantity as the receiver's analysis chores multiply, a rising and convex cost curve may be superimposed on the same graph. Conceptually, the point (on the data volume scale) at which the incremental value equals the incremental cost is the optimal quantity of data to accumulate and report. We conclude that the optimal quantity criterion cannot be applied independently of the cost criteria.

Applicability of the Criteria

Decision-making is an exercise in differential analysis. 'What difference will it make whether we do this or that?' is the question. Events which are common to the alternative courses of action cannot help the decision-maker choose among them. This applies to accounting decisions as well as to other economic decisions. In many accounting decisions the evaluation procedure will disclose that there is no perceptible difference between method A and method B on several of the criteria but that differences are found on other criteria. For example, if the accounting issue is one of choosing the wording for a line item on the income statement, the alternatives may not differ on the criteria of attribute relevance, reliability, timeliness, optimal quantity, effects via other parties and cost of accounting but they may differ on understandability, cost of utilising and comparability. On the other hand, a choice between historical cost and current market value for valuation

---

[4]Warren Brown, in conversation with the author, 17th April 1975.

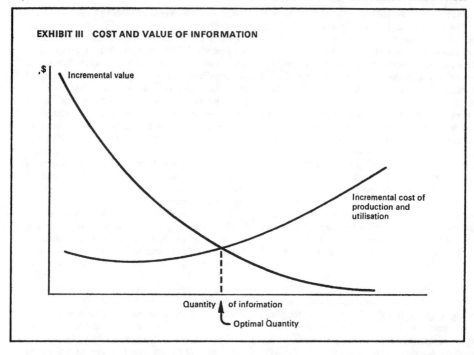

EXHIBIT III   COST AND VALUE OF INFORMATION

of a security owned may be made primarily on the criteria of attribute relevance, reliability, comparability and effects via other parties while the other criteria are insignificant. But each of the criteria has its role. The following list of criteria and accounting choices to which each criterion may be critical may convince the reader on this point:

Relevance of attribute being measured to the decisions of the user – any choice of a measurement method applicable to an asset or liability.

Reliability – many choices of a measurement method.

Comparability:

Interperiod comparability – any proposal to change an accounting method.

Intercompany and intracompany comparability – choices of classification schemes for reporting revenues and expenses.

Comparability of lengths of reporting periods – decision regarding changing length of reporting period.

Understandability and readability – choice of descriptive terms, format or presentation of a note.

Timeliness – choice of length of interim reporting period; choice between a procedure which keeps records up to date daily and a procedure which requires substantial end-of-period work.

Optimal quantity – many decisions regarding possible aggregation for external reporting of data kept in separate accounts for internal needs.

Effects via other parties – choices of measurement methods.

Costs of producing accounting data – choices of data processing equipment and procedures; choice of publishing forecasts or not.

Costs of utilising accounting data – format decisions; aggregation decisions; choice of publishing forecasts or not.

As we have pointed out before, these nine criteria are not mutually exclusive. One consideration in the decision to emphasise these particular criteria, in addition to the desire to provide full coverage of the factors that affect accounting decisions, is the fear that several criteria which could have been merged would be neglected if not set out separately. Otherwise the number might have been reduced to five or six. The several facets of comparability, for example, are fairly well covered by attribute relevance and reliability. Timeliness is closely related to optimal quantity and both are intimately involved with cost of production and cost of utilisation. In addition to these possibilities for shortening the list f criteria to be used, there are some candidates for addition to the list. Thus, the reliability criterion could be split into verifiability and lack of bias or timeliness could be broken down into frequency and lag. Another criterion which some empirical researchers would favour is predictive power. It is omitted here only because it cuts across relevance, reliability and sometimes one or two other criteria rather than taking a place alongside them; it appears to have important applications.

Patterns for making accounting decisions

Most major decisions are based on a mixture of objective evidence and subjective opinion, although the mix varies. Some choices of accounting methods, e.g. in several areas in which choices are made for reporting to taxing authorities, are heavily influenced by measurable economic considerations. But many choices in external reporting must be made primarily on the basis of subjective judgments of the consequences of the choice. This does not, of course, mean that an organised technique of decision-making is impossible. In fact, this paper is based on the premise that accounting decision-making can be more 'systematic and rational' than it has been in the past (to our knowledge).

We have all seen lists of steps involved in rational decision-making – but not in the accounting literature. Perhaps such a listing would be helpful in establishing a possible systematic pattern for making accounting decisions:

1. Identify the accounting problem to be solved.

2. Identify two or more possible solutions – the alternative accounting methods (information systems) to be evaluated.

3. Identify the users and nonusers affected by the choice.

4. Identify each user's uses and method of use, e.g. decision techniques, and the nature of the effects on nonusers. Intragroup differences must not be overlooked.

5. For one user group and one criterion, rate the alternative accounting methods for each use and then combine the ratings for all uses by that user group. Repeat for each criterion and each user group.

6. Combine the ratings on the various criteria to obtain a user group's choice. Repeat for each user group.

7. Combine the choices of the various user groups to obtain a final choice of accounting method (if the decision-maker must consider the wishes of more than one user group).

Exhibit IV illustrates steps five to seven of this list, moving from the right to the left of the diagram. (The Exhibit is incomplete due to the space limitation but blank lines are left to indicate that the basic approach permits variation in the numbers of user groups and criteria.) Frequently, only one significant use by a user group need be considered and the analysis leading to the choice of method by one user group on a particular criterion may serve equally well as the basis for another group's choice if one evaluator is representing more than one group, as in the case of the FASB or SEC. When the technique is applied by a particular user, or user group, step 7 (and one level of the diagram) is eliminated. (The general approach appears to be applicable to the making of accounting decisions at any level: society, industry, entity or segment.)

Two serious limitations of this approach to making accounting decisions may be recognised. One is the clarification of users' decision-making techniques that is required by step 4. To some accountants, this is a serious roadblock which requires a major detour. To those who are oriented towards decision usefulness, it is a challenge which must be faced; to expect to be helpful to users without understanding their needs is fanciful. Any partial accomplishment of this requirement is to be preferred to sidestepping it as we can only hope to hit users' needs by chance if we do not even take aim on the target.

The other serious limitation of this approach is the lack of quantification of the preferences that must be identified, compared and combined in steps 5, 6 and 7. Some readers may be tempted to use a point scoring system to convert preferences to numbers. For example, 100 points could be divided among the nine criteria in a particular fashion to represent the maximum significance of each criterion to a particular user group. Then the rating of an accounting method on a criterion would be expressed in a number between zero and the maximum permitted for that criterion. And/or weights could be assigned to several user groups in order to permit aggregation of the preferences of some groups for a particular accounting method for comparison with the preferences of other groups for another method. But how could the weights assigned to groups, or to criteria, or the score given to any accounting method on one criterion by one user group, be defended? If I give method A nine points on the relevance criterion and you give it only five points, how can either of us justify our scoring?

Exhibit V illustrates how a weighting scheme might be reflected in a scoring sheet and shows hypothetical results of its use by two decision-makers who were faced with the necessity of choosing between the

EXHIBIT IV
Criteria approach to accounting decisions

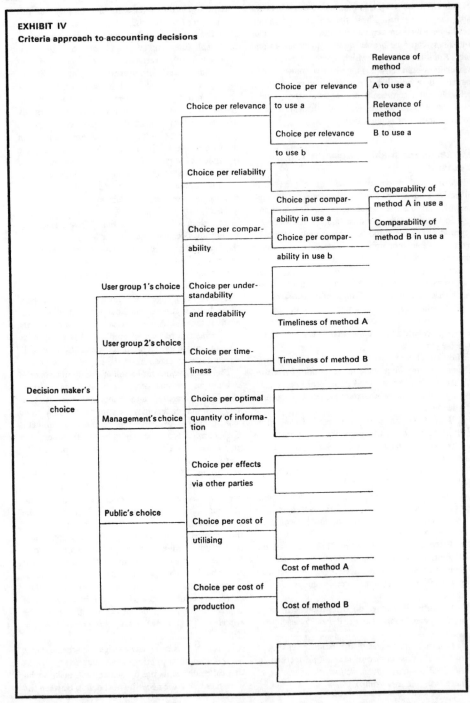

ᵗferral-amortisation and the immediate expensing ᵗethods of accounting for research and development ᵗsts. The particular scheme illustrated here is ᵗsed on the assumptions that the decision-maker ᵗust recognise the rights of several interested groups ᵗd that the ratings on all of the criteria except ᵗlevance do not vary across groups. For example, ᵗᵗe deferral-amortisation method gets the same rating ᵗᵗ the cost-of-production criterion by all groups of ᵗterested parties – an assumption that appears ᵗnable if one independent party is doing the rating ᵗut would not be reasonable if each group were ᵗting the methods as it saw them. (Note that the ᵗlatively low weight assigned to the effects via other ᵗarties criterion reflects the tendency of the effects

recognised by different groups to cancel each other ont except for the managerial suboptimisation effect which is a net disadvantage to society. Weights assigned to this criterion may well be higher on scoring sheets designed for partisan use, e.g. by managers only or employees only.)

The example in Exhibit V is designed to show that the use of a point scoring system cannot overcome the subjectivity of the decision-makers' preferences. Even though the two individuals, DM_1 and DM_2, are in perfect ordinal agreement, i.e. they have no disagreements as to the rankings of the two accounting methods on any criterion for any interested group, they still disagree on the final choice. The source of their disagreement is differences in the strengths of

---

EXHIBIT V

Example of accounting decision scoring sheet applied by two decision makers to the case of accounting for research and development costs

	Maximum Scores	Defer and Amortise		Expense Immediately	
		DM_1	DM_2	DM_1	DM_2
Relevance	40	30	25	5	15
To Owners	20				
To Long-term Creditors	9				
To Short-term Creditors	5				
To Managers	2				
To Employees	2				
To Public	2				
Reliability	20	8	3	18	20
Comparability	12	3	3	8	8
Effects via Other Parties	6	4	4	1	1
Understandability	6	3	3	5	5
Timeliness	4	3	3	3	3
Optimal Quantity	4	2	2	3	3
Cost of Production	4	3	3	4	4
Cost of Utilisation	4	3	3	4	4
Total Scores	100	59	49	51	63

DM_1 and DM_2 are two hypothetical individuals who have the responsibility of choosing between the deferral-amortisation and the immediate expensing methods of accounting for research and development costs.

their preferences for the deferral-amortisation method on the relevance criterion and for the immediate expensing method on the reliability criterion. (Incidentally, the ratings by DM_2 may be interpreted as the author's guess as to the FASB's views which led to its choice of the immediate expensing method.) Generally speaking, scoring sheets may serve as check lists, as an aid to an individual in organising his analysis and as a basis for identifying the locus of disagreement among members of a decision-making group.

It is important that we recognise that all of the numbers on the scoring sheet, or on any similar scoring sheet, are lacking in objectivity, with the possible exception of those in the four decision-maker columns on the cost of production line (where it is possible to obtain some data on which independent observers would agree). The development of 'public models' for rating accounting methods on the other criteria and for weighting the criteria and the interest groups is a prerequisite to the objective application of this approach to accounting choices. The subjective selection of numbers to represent personal opinions (private models) and subsequent arithmetic operations on those numbers do not make the procedure objective, and while the literature of multi-attribute decision-making (e.g. Cochrane and Zeleny, 1973 and Green and Wind, 1973) is relevant to the multiple-criteria approach to accounting choices, it does not have a solution to this problem. This does not mean that a decision-making procedure that calls for the recognition of uses, users, alternatives and criteria cannot be helpful; it only means that it cannot be shown to yield an unequivocally correct answer. When an objective (and otherwise suitable) procedure becomes available, the one suggested here should be set aside. In the meantime, the multiple-criteria approach to accounting decisions may play a useful role.

Conclusion

Maximisation of social welfare is as appropriate a goal of decision-making in the areas of external financial reporting as it is in any other public policy area but, unfortunately, it is also almost as difficult to approach in quantitative terms in the former domain as in others. Until such a time, if it ever arrives, when a mathematical model of the social welfare approach becomes operational, those who are faced with accounting choices may be able to improve their decision-making techniques by identifying and applying a set of criteria of desirable accounting methods. The purpose of this paper has been to

describe such a set of criteria and to suggest some techniques for its use in making accounting decisions.

Bibliography

Abdel-Khalik, A. Rashad, 'User Preference Ordering Value: A Model', *Accounting Review* (July 1971), pp. 457–471.
American Accounting Association, Committee on Concepts and Standards – Internal Planning and Control, 'Report of the Committee on Concepts and Standards – Internal Planning and Control,' *Accounting Review* (Supplement 1974), pp. 79–96.
American Accounting Association, Committee to Prepare a Statement of Basic Accounting Theory, *A Statement of Basic Accounting Theory* (1966).
American Institute of Certified Public Accountants, Accounting Principles Board, 'Basic Concepts and Accounting Principles Underlying Financial Statements of Business Enterprises,' *Statement of the Accounting Principles Board No. 4* (1970).
American Telephone and Telegraph Company, *Annual Report* (1974).
Cochrane, James L. and Zeleny, Milan (eds.), *Multiple Criteria Decision Making* (University of South Carolina Press, 1973).
Demski, Joel S., *Information Analysis* (Addison-Wesley, (1972).
Demski, Joel S. and Feltham, Gerald A., *Cost Determination: A Conceptual Approach* (Iowa State University Press, 1976).
Feltham, Gerald A., 'Information Evaluation,' *Studies in Accounting Research*, No. 5, (American Accounting Association, 1972).
Green, Paul E. and Wind, Yoram, *Multiattribute Decisions in Marketing: A Measurement Approach* (Dryden Press, 1973).
Gregory, Robert K. and Van Horne, Richard L., *Automatic Data Processing Systems* (Wadsworth Publishing Co. Inc. 1960).
Ijiri, Yuji and Jaedicke, Robert K., 'Reliability and Objectivity of Accounting Measurements,' *Accounting Review* (July 1966), pp. 474–483.
Kenley, W. John and Staubus, George J., *Objectives and Concepts of Financial Statements* (Australian Accountancy Research Foundation, 1972).
McDonald, Daniel L. 'Feasibility Criteria for Accounting Measures,' *Accounting Review*, (October 1967), pp. 662–679.
McKeown, James C., 'An Empirical Test of a Model Proposed by Chambers,' *Accounting Review* (January 1971, pp. 12–29).
Moonitz, Maurice, 'The Basic Postulates of Accounting,' *Accounting Research Study No. 1* (American Institute of Certified Public Accountants, 1961).
Snavely, Howard J., 'Accounting Information Criteria,' *Accounting Review* (April 1967), pp. 223–232.
Staubus, George J., *A Theory of Accounting to Investors* (University of California Press, 1961; Scholars Book Co. 1971).
Staubus, George J., 'Current Cash Equivalent: A Dissent,' *Accounting Review* (October 1967), pp. 650–661.
Staubus, George J., 'Determinants of the Value of Accounting Procedures', *Abacus* (December 1970), pp. 105–119.
Staubus, George J., 'The Relevance of Evidence of Cash Flows', in R. Sterling (ed.), *Asset Valuation and Income Determination* (Scholars Book Co. 1971), pp. 42–69.
Staubus, George J., 'The Measurement of Assets and Liabilities', *Accounting and Business Research* (Summer 1973), pp. 243–262.

Effects via Other Parties

Any person who chooses among alternative accounting methods should consider the effects of each method on his own interests through the actions of other parties. A dramatic example was the 1971 controversy over the choice of the liberal "flow-through" method or the conservative "deferral" method of accounting for the "investment credit" permitted by the U.S. Internal Revenue Code. The APB apparently believed that the deferral method yielded data that were more *relevant* to the decisions of investors, but its view did not prevail. U.S. Treasury Department officials, who intended that the investment credit spur investment in plant and equipment, argued for the liberal flow-through method because they thought that the credit would have a more favorable impact on the economy, *via the decisions of business managers,* if its contribution to income could be reported immediately. Corporate managers, who were interested in the effects that the chosen method would have on themselves and their corporations *via the investment decisions and management appraisals of investors,* also preferred the flow-through method. Although investors, as usual, exerted little influence, they may well have been influenced by the prospective effects that the deferral method would have on the price of their securities *through the market actions of other investors.* It seems likely that the effects via other parties criterion was the key criterion in the ultimate decision, made by the U.S. Congress (and President), not to prohibit any method. Most corporations have chosen the flow-through method.

EXHIBIT III-3 illustrates the process by which an evaluator's choice of an accounting method can affect his interests via other parties. An accounting method chosen by an evaluator may influence another party either through the latter's use of accounting data yielded by the method chosen, or through his anticipation of the way the method would report his prospective actions. The Treasury officials' concern with managers' response to the method used to account for the investment credit illustrates the second type of influence; managers presumably would be more likely to purchase fixed assets if they knew that the flow-through method were being used. It was the influence of actual accounting outputs on investors, however, that managers (as evaluators) had in mind when they expressed a preference for the flow-through method.

When *company managers* evaluate alternative accounting methods for internal reporting, they give a great deal of attention to the methods' effects on their own interests via others—especially

EXHIBIT III-3

EFFECT OF AN ACCOUNTING METHOD ON AN EVALUATOR'S INTERESTS VIA OTHER
PARTIES

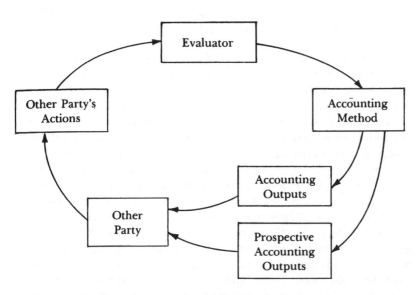

Note: The EXHIBIT indicates why Henry Cuevas has suggested
the term "boomerang effect" in conversation with the author.

subordinates. The effect of performance reports on the motivation
of subordinates is one of the prime considerations in the selection
of internal performance-reporting methods. Managers' interests
in external reporting, which is generally considered separable from
internal reporting, are also directed towards the effects the reports
will have on others. In this case, the "others" are primarily investors
(creditors and owners). Managers appear to prefer those accounting
methods which result in or permit relative stability of reported
earnings, because it is believed that investors interpret stability
as evidence of lack of risk; the lower the risk in an investment,
the lower the required rate of return. Thus, managers believe
that using accounting methods that yield stable reported earnings
lowers the firm's cost of both debt and equity capital (and raises
the price of the firm's stock). Similarly, managers appear to prefer

accounting methods that yield higher reported earnings. Their preference is based on the "bottom line fixation" view mentioned in chapter I, in which investors tend to apply the same price/earnings multiple to the reported earnings regardless of the accounting methods used, so that higher reported earnings are translated into higher stock prices. On the other hand, managers may opt for the more conservative method if they are concerned about the use of the firm's financial statements by union leaders in formulating bargaining goals. In all of these cases managers are concerned about the effects that the accounting data will have on their interests by way of the actions of others; they may give this factor great weight when they choose an accounting method.

Shareholders' evaluation of accounting methods may also be affected by their perception of the effects the methods would have on others. For example, the effects that the reported earnings may have on union negotiators, mentioned above, may be of concern to shareholders, too. Another example is owners' likely preference for financial statements that help the firm obtain credit on favorable terms.[9] But the "other" group that might well be most important in this connection is management; shareholders must be concerned about the effects that external reporting methods can have on management decisions. When managers face a difficult problem, they perceive that one solution to it will be reported in the financial statements in a manner that makes them look bad, while another possible solution will make them look good, at least in the short-run; managers' perception of this difference may well influence the decision—to the detriment of shareholders.

More simply, if good decisions will reduce the reported earnings and bad decisions will increase them, managers may be motivated to make bad decisions. In such a case, goals are not congruent; when managers meet a major goal—high short-run earnings, for

---

[9]A peculiarly American case in which investors must consider the effects on them via other parties is the choice between LIFO and another cost flow assumption in an inventory. Regardless of which method gives the most useful information for investment decisions, investors must consider that if LIFO is not used for external reporting it may not be used for computing taxable income. The effect on investors via the Internal Revenue Service may be material.

instance—then a goal of shareholders—high value of the firm, which depends upon discounted long-run earnings—may be neglected. Any accounting method that contributes to a lack of congruence (to disharmony) of managers' and shareholders' goals has a strike against it in the eyes of the shareholders. Actions that are good for the shareholders must be reported as good for the shareholders; management actions that are detrimental to shareholders' goals should be reported as detrimental. Poor measurements of income and wealth lead to poor evaluations of managers' performance which, in turn, lead to poor decisions by managers. An accounting method's contribution to the harmony of managerial and shareholder goals is one element of "effects via other parties"—an important criterion for the evaluation of accounting methods.[10]

The basis for "disharmony" in an accounting system is failure to measure assets and liabilities at their ideal economic values to shareholders. The problem encompasses the whole area of accounting measurement; a few examples will serve to illustrate it.

1. Over- and undervaluation of any asset or liability may affect a decision regarding its retention or disposition. Undervalued assets are excellent sources of instant earnings, as are overvalued liabilities. In his desire to meet an earnings target, a manager may sell an asset or pay off a liability on terms that are actually unfavorable to the owners. Similarly, a manager may fail to dispose of an asset or a liability on favorable terms because he is unwilling to "take the loss" that would be reported on the income statement. When assets or liabilities are carried at out-of-date values, wise dispositions easily can be reported as loss transactions and unwise dispositions can be reported as successes.

2. Managerial planning and decision making frequently involve careful calculations (and use of decision models) such

---

[10] Demski and Feltham (1976) use the term "decision influencing" in connection with the effects subsequent reporting can have on the decisions of managers. Another descriptive term is "ex ante effects of accounting choices on managerial decisions." Prakash and Rappaport (1976) emphasize the "feedback effects" of accounting on management decisions and the economy.

as discounted cash flow analyses and economic order quantity calculations. It is possible, under some accepted accounting practices, that a decision-making analysis may indicate the wisdom of a particular course of action and that subsequent events may occur exactly as predicted, but that the financial statements may indicate that poor results were achieved. For example, if a discounted cash flow analysis of an investment project that yields a constant cash flow over its life indicates a rate of return of 12 percent, the financial statements based on customary straight-line depreciation will show a return on net investment that is much lower than 12 percent in the first year of the project's life and much higher than 12 percent in the last year—even if the predictions on which the discounted cash flow analysis is based were perfect. Straight-line depreciation in these circumstances scores low on the harmony criterion.

3. The use of the completed contracts method of accounting for long-term construction projects instead of the percentage-of-completion method can bias a manager in favor of short contracts if he feels the need to report more profit in the short-run; a less profitable but shorter job may be ranked over the more profitable, long-term contract.

4. Failure to capitalize costs that are expected to yield future benefits may discourage many desirable activities, e.g., research and development, training, preventive maintenance, holding of land or securities that yield little or no "income" in the short-run, and introduction of new products or development of new markets.

5. Omission from the accounts of the detrimental effects of management actions on "human assets," of public attitudes towards the firm, or of possible class action suits on behalf of customers, employees, or neighbors may cause managers to give insufficient weight to such factors in making their decisions.[11]

6. There is also the possibility of what might be called the two-cushion bank shot. Consider the issue of whether uninsured fire and casualty losses should be reported as

---

[11] Note that the inclusion in the overall evaluation framework of the views of all interested parties, including the general public, recognizes the "externalities" pertaining to entity operations.

losses on the income statement in the period in which they occur. Alternatively, "self-insurance reserves" may be established by regular periodic charges to expense in amounts similar to the insurance premiums that would have been paid if the risks had been insured against and actual losses charged to the reserve instead of against income. If investors are believed to be averse to instability in reported earnings, then managers may be reluctant to report losses as they occur (unevenly), and they may incur the cost of uneconomical insurance if self-insurance reserves are not permitted. As a result, investors may prefer that the FASB permit self-insurance reserves in order to encourage managers to economize on insurance costs.

It should be clear that these examples do not represent endorsements of any particular accounting method, because only one of the nine criteria included in our scheme for evaluating alternative accounting proposals has been considered here. Consideration of other criteria, especially reliability, may cause shareholders and others to reject the methods that contribute the most to harmony of goals.

When a broadly based *policy-making body such as the FASB* makes accounting decisions on behalf of the society as a whole, it may take into consideration the possible *economic side effects* of accounting standards, that is, the effects that accounting data might have on the economy other than those due to the data being used by decision makers in the intended ways. Examples of economic side effects are included in EXHIBIT III-4 (excluding the third and seventh cases which illustrate primary effects). Other examples are competitor's use of publicly reported data, effects on management bonuses based on reported earnings, imposition of price controls or excess profits tax based on indicated profitability of business in general or a particular industry, risks of liability on behalf of auditors and managers, and costs of producing and using accounting information.

EXHIBIT III-5 illustrates the mechanism of economic side effects as viewed from the perspective of a policy-making body. The reader is urged to give special attention to notes (D) and (F) accompanying that EXHIBIT. We suggest that the market's perceptiveness, or ability to perceive the underlying economic

EXHIBIT III-5

EFFECTS VIA OTHER PARTIES: THE FASB AND ECONOMIC SIDE EFFECTS

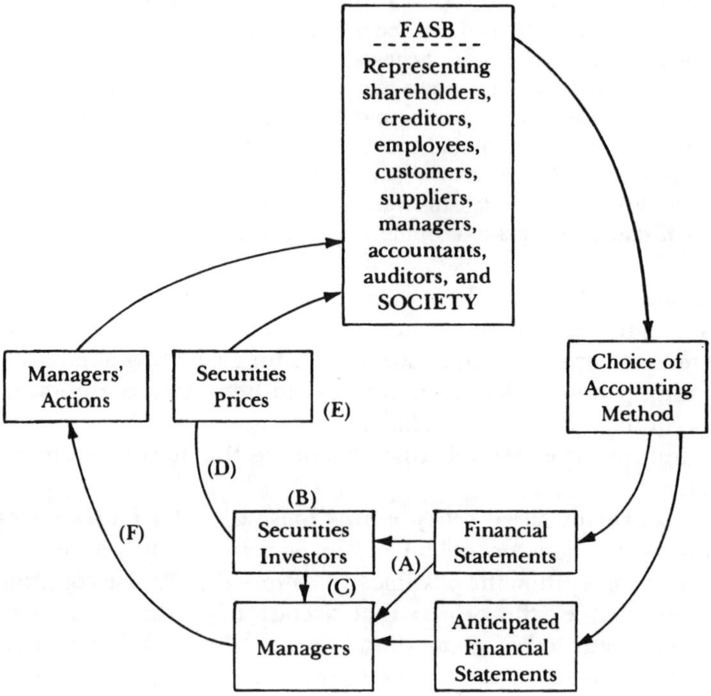

(A)   Computations of managers' bonuses may be based on reported earnings.

(B)   More broadly, the parties whose perceptions could be of concern to managers
       might include depositors, union officials, legislators, and others whose use
       of company financial statements could affect the company or its managers.

(C)   Securities investors exercise varying degrees of control over managers.

(D)   This effect depends on investors being influenced by the choice of accounting
       method, sometimes called bottom line fixation, market inefficiency, or market
       misperception.

(E)   If (B) is not a security investor, (E) is not a security price, but may be
       deposit levels, wages, legislation, or something else.

(F)   This influence depends on managers believing in (A), (C), or (D).

phenomena regardless of which accounting method is used for reporting those phenomena, together with managers' belief or lack of belief in market perceptiveness, is critical to a policy-making body that is concerned with how much weight to give to potential economic side effects of a change in accounting standards.

Finally, a note about the rights of nonusers of financial reports is in order in this section. An example is the chart-oriented securities trader who does not read financial statements or data derived from financial statements. His welfare may be influenced by the effects of financial statements on the actions of others who trade in the market, and thereby affect the price of the security and the nonuser's profits. Needless to say, he is not likely to have much to say to the FASB (or a similar body), and the FASB is even less likely to give significant weight to his problem. Other nonusers (the general public) who are indirectly affected by financial statements through managers' and investors' actions that influence the general level of economic activity would appear to merit more consideration.

Economic Consequences of Financial Accounting Standards

Selected Papers

July 1978

Financial Accounting Standards Board
of the Financial Accounting Foundation
HIGH RIDGE PARK, STAMFORD, CONNECTICUT 06905

*   *   *   *   *

A substantial number of empirical research studies support the conclusion that the employment of alternative accounting methods has no statistically significant impact on the prices of listed securities of reporting entities. Some observers have questioned the importance of the standard-setting function in an "efficient market" setting such as this. On the other hand, the papers in this volume and other research reports provide evidence that financial accounting standards can and do have economic consequences of the "side-effects" variety. Does the evidence really conflict, or do differing circumstances provide explanations? What conclusions should the FASB draw? A few nonconclusive comments on these matters are offered in the following paragraphs.

It seems likely that users, and user groups, vary in their understanding of financial reporting issues and in their capacity to discern underlying economic phenomena under adverse circumstances such as (a) lack of comparability of accounting information among enterprises, (b) lack of consistency of accounting methods used by an enterprise over time, and (c) less than full disclosure of relevant economic events in the financial statements. At one extreme, full-time, well-educated, experienced, highly motivated analysts, as a group, may obtain a clear view of historical events despite these and other handicaps; the market for an institutional favorite listed on the New York Stock Exchange may be highly efficient. At the other extreme, John Q. Public may "hear" that Company X is earning high profits and, as a result, form a conclusion about X's ability to hold down product prices, raise wages, or absorb the costs of pollution abatement on the basis of that "bottom line rumor." Other users of financial data may fall between these two extreme positions on the "scale of perceptiveness," as illustrated below. (The five categories listed at the right end of the scale are intended to represent only the "lay" members of those groups, not those with above average backgrounds in fields related to financial reporting.)

SCALE OF USER PERCEPTIVENESS REGARDING UNDERLYING ECONOMIC EVENTS AND CONDITIONS NOT CLEARLY, CONSISTENTLY, OR UNIFORMLY REPORTED IN FINANCIAL STATEMENTS

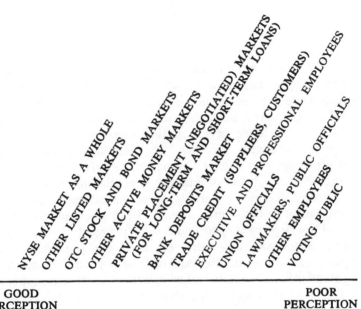

| GOOD PERCEPTION | POOR PERCEPTION |

In addition to variations among users on the scale of perceptiveness, it also seems reasonable to recognize variations in the complexity of the financial data processing and interpretation problems that users face. The analyst, if he so chooses, may quickly and accurately eliminate goodwill and its amortization from the financial statements of one company to make them comparable with those of another, but the conversion of the financial statements of an inveterate acquirer of companies from a pooling basis to a purchase basis, or vice versa, is quite another problem. Analysts' ability to cope with financial statement interpretation problems may also vary as a particular type of transaction and the reporting of it becomes more familiar. Thus, it has been said that accounting for the leasing of computers (to others) and for franchising were not well understood when those types of activities were novel, but that analysts learned (sometimes the hard way) as time went by. In this vein, one could argue that by the time an accounting issue has received the public attention associated with the FASB's due process, professional users of financial statements are unlikely to be misled by subsequent financial reports regardless of the solution chosen by the Board.

In any event, it seems safe to say that the obstacles users encounter in their quest for an understanding of an enterprise's economic circumstances vary in scope and magnitude. When these variations are associated with variations in the perceptiveness of users, and when both the obstacles to understanding and users' perceptiveness are unstable, the question of whether a choice of accounting methods may have economic consequences becomes very complicated indeed. But that is not the whole story. Managers' beliefs concerning "the market's" perceptiveness and the potential for managers to take costly action to avoid prospective adverse market responses must be considered as well. In these circumstances we should not be surprised to find a wide range of views, varying across issues and observers, on both the prospective and experienced economic consequences of a change in accounting standards. The studies of economic consequences reported in this volume reflect and provide support for that range of views.

Under circumstances such as these, to what extent should those who establish accounting standards take potential economic consequences into consideration in choosing among alternative proposals? The reader who expects the six research studies presented in this volume to answer that question or even yield substantial clues may be disappointed. Although the studies provide modest evidence that economic consequences can occur, they give little, if any, insight as to whether or how the Board should treat potential economic consequences as a criterion in choosing an accounting method. Nevertheless, the FASB's 1977-1978 drive for understanding of the economic consequences issue has raised several questions to which one concerned with that issue might well give some thought:

1. Can accounting standard-setting bodies determine, either before or after a standard is issued, which financial reporting methods yield the greatest benefits to society?

2. Under what circumstances can the Board count on "market efficiency," or user perceptiveness, to prevent any drastic economic consequences that might result from changes in financial reporting practices that it mandates? Is it important that managers believe in user perceptiveness?

3. Can financial reporting contribute to the effective allocation of resources without affecting anyone's decisions? Without affecting securities prices? Does adverse impact on the securities of an industry count as a favorable or unfavorable economic impact? If an accounting standard causes capital to shift out of one industry, can we assume that that capital moves into another industry where it makes an equal or greater contribution to society? How is the standard setter to determine if that shift is desirable or undesirable?

4. If the elimination of a previously available accounting alternative is found to affect the securities prices of those enterprises who were forced to change their practices, should that effect be treated as evidence of users' previous inability to cope with noncomparable financial statements?

5. Should the macroeconomic impact of accounting standards through the decisions of public policy-makers be given separate consideration by the standard setters? Or should the uses of externally reported accounting data in making public policy decisions be considered, along with uses by investors and creditors, when the relevance test is applied to a proposed change in accounting standards?

6. How can a standard-setting body charged with responsibility for acting in the public interest specify those economic consequences of its decisions that it should consider and those it may freely ignore when making those deci-

sions? Is the Board directly responsible for maximizing social welfare, or is its responsibility more limited, e.g., restricted to improving the quality of information available to decision-makers and policy-makers?

7. Should accounting standard setters choose whom to favor —other than the users of financial data?

8. Should accounting standard setters deliberately mandate what they believe to be an otherwise inferior accounting method in order to better achieve the public policy objectives (a) they perceive or (b) someone else perceives? If the latter, whose perceptions should count? Is it proper, in a democratic society, to bias the information system in favor of the majority's, or a minority's, objectives?

I encourage the reader of this volume to reflect on the above questions as he or she reviews the six papers that follow and the general subject of the economic consequences of financial accounting standards.

Stamford, Connecticut

July 1978   GEORGE J. STAUBUS

The Evidential Approach to Measurement of Cash Flow Potential

Introduction

Clarification of the concept of cash flow potential came slowly in the decision-usefulness literature. It still is not widely recognized as playing the critical role that I see it playing. My early treatments of it certainly left much to be desired. In ATOATI, investors' interest in cash flows to themselves and, therefore, in future cash flows to and from the enterprise were given a great deal of emphasis. That was carried into a discussion of alternative general approaches to the measurement of net asset items. "If future cash receipts and future cash disbursements of the firm are of primary importance to investors, perhaps we should attempt to determine the amount of cash that will flow into the firm because of the existence of the particular asset being measured." (p. 30) That undiscounted future cash flows approach was discarded in favor of a present value approach, with the objective of estimating the present value of the residual equity. The timing of a cash flow matters. The remainder of that chapter (III) presented the original ranking of asset measurement methods on the criterion of relevance to cash flow-oriented decisions, showing the linkages between them: (1) counting money, (2) discounted future money movements, (3) best-use net realizable value, (4) current replacement cost, (5) adjusted historical cost (constant dollar HC), and (6) original money cost. In the case of marketable debt securities, contractual future cash flows discounted at the appropriate risky rate equals current market value, which approximates best-use net realizable value. In the case of assets held for use, best-use NRV typically is "completed-cycle NRV," but occasionally it is "as-is NRV." (MAD, pp. 177-83)

Later, as the theory of finance developed and I got acquainted with the concepts of complete markets and perfect markets, I recognized that market value under those conditions was the ideal measure of an asset's or liability's cash flow potential. That ideal, of course, is not practically available — such prices are not observable in the real world — so all accounting measurements of noncash assets and liabilities are based on imperfect, observable surrogates for, or estimates of that ideal. The accountant's choice of surrogate is a circumstantial one, based on all of the criteria for choice that he/she considers important. (1989a, pp. 166-8) All of the measurement methods that I had earlier identified have places in such a view, and their rankings on the criterion of relevance to cash flow-oriented decisions remains unchanged.

Accounting theorists' interest in measurement was strong in the 1960s and early 1970s. I especially admired the work of Ray Chambers (e.g. 1966) and Bob Sterling (e.g. 1971). The level of their reasoning was well above that of most of their predecessors and it certainly stimulated me to reexamine my own, and to find better ways to explain it. My 1970s publications included various explanations supporting the ATOATI ranking of measurement methods on the criterion of relevance to cash flow-oriented decisions. One of the most difficult links for some students to see was that between net realizable value and replacement cost. The 1967 article disagreeing with Professor Chambers' emphasis on current cash equivalent (1967c, not reprinted here) included the "gap chart" (see 1971b, p. 56, reprinted herein). It showed that the buildup of costs of production of a commodity via careful current cost accounting differs from its net realizable value only by pure economic profit or loss (the gap), which is zero in competitive equilibrium. Thus, economic reasoning tells us that current replacement cost is a reasonable (imperfect) surrogate for net realizable value in typical circumstances. Although that point was made in ATOATI, the gap chart was a substantial improvement in exposition.

The relevance of replacement cost to future cash flows in the case of assets held for use was developed from another angle, independent of net realizable value, viz., the incremental effect on future cash flows that an existing stock of a resource can have. I called it the supply adjustment analysis of an asset's incremental effect on future cash flows. I argued that the most common incremental effect on the residual equity from holding a stock of a commodity for future use is that it reduces future purchases. Current (replacement) cost is a logical surrogate for a future purchase cost saved. (Other possibilities were included in the analysis.) This argument appeared first in 1967c and was improved in 1971b, 1971c, and 1977b. Support for the point that a current market price is a good surrogate for a future market price subsequently was gathered through empirical research reported in 1977b, pp. 173-4. The correlation between a sample of commodity prices at date A with the prices of those same commodities at date B was found to be high, thus showing that a current buying price can serve as a surrogate for a future buying price, and that a recent price paid can serve as a surrogate for a current buying price and, therefore, for a future buying price. The longer the time lapse, the lower the correlation, so the older the historical cost, the weaker the surrogacy relationship. The impossibility of a perfect measurement of the incremental effect of one asset on the current value of the residual equity in the face of multiple assets working together to produce future cash flows was not allowed to inhibit apparent progress. The incremental approach was accepted as imperfectly useful.

"Additivity" was a topic of considerable interest to accounting theorists in the 1960s and 1970s. One view was that the attempt to add the historical cost of one asset to the net realizable value of another and the present value of the future cash flows expected from a third, and so on, resulted in a meaningless number. Two apples plus three oranges do not add to five of anything. My view was, and is, that the use of several different ways of estimating a net asset item's incremental effect on the present value of the firm's future cash flows does not invalidate the result. A common property — incremental effect on the firm's future cash flows — could be estimated in various ways with useful results. Those who insisted on use of only one measurement method up and down both sides of the balance sheet, regardless of reliability, cost, and other criteria of good accounting, were not able to convince me or very many practically-oriented accountants.

Viewing the measurement process as the selection and gathering of the most appropriate types of evidence began in ATOATI, Chapter III (reprinted in Part I, above). "The selection of a measurement technique is a selection of the most appropriate type of evidence." (p. 50) The idea of judging the value of evidence on the basis of multiple criteria, starting with relevance, began in that same paragraph. That led to the title of 1971b: "The Relevance of Evidence of Cash Flows." (Reprinted in this section.) A summary of the more fully developed reasoning from MAD (1977c) is also reprinted here. The "surrogate chain" (pp.190-1) clarifies the linkages between the measurement methods and shows that each of the nine methods is connected to the asset's or liability's cash flow potential. My best presentation of the general philosophy of accounting measurement of wealth may be in 1989a (reprinted in the next section, below), especially the summary in Exhibit I. "Cash flow potential" had become the clear-cut focal point of efforts to measure enterprise wealth; historical cash flows and "as-is" net realizable values were vital information for assessing enterprise liquidity. A case designed to help students focus on the timing of changes in the amounts of liabilities

ASSET VALUATION

AND

INCOME DETERMINATION

A Consideration of the Alternatives

Papers Given at a Symposium
Held at the
School of Business
University of Kansas
May 1970

Edited by Robert R. Sterling

SCHOLARS BOOK CO.
P.O. Box 3344
Lawrence, Kansas 66044
1971

3

The Relevance of Evidence of Cash Flows

by GEORGE J. STAUBUS
UNIVERSITY OF KANSAS
on leave from UNIVERSITY OF CALIFORNIA, BERKELEY

THIS paper deals with the relevance, to investors and managers, of several measures of assets that utilize various types of evidence of future cash flows. Net realizable value, discounted future cash flows, replacement costs and historical cost are examples of the measures with which we shall concern ourselves. The most familiar types of evidence considered are contracts, market prices and "physical observation." In the interest of efficiency, the background material is presented in the form of the following series of premises:

I. The proper objective of accounting is to provide quantitative economic information to assist decision makers. This objective can be met more satisfactorily if accountants explicitly recognize the major users of accounting data and familiarize themselves with users' problems.

II. We recognize entity personnel and external investors as the primary users of the data accumulated in an entity's accounting system—for the purposes of this discussion.

III. Managers and other entity personnel use the products of the double entry system in making many decisions. Benefits and costs associated with limited categories of activities are of particular importance to managers.

IV. Investors do not have sources of information about amounts of net asset items that are superior to a balance sheet. They rely upon balance sheets for information as to the current amounts of net asset items and upon income statements for explanations of the changes in net assets from operations.

V. The future of accounting depends upon its ability to produce information that is worth more than it costs. The following framework may help accountants judge the net value of a proposed accounting procedure:

A. Determinants of gross value

 1. Relevance of the measure employed to the decisions to be made by users

 2. Reliability of the specific measurement
  a. Lack of dispersion
  b. Lack of displacement
  c. Comparability of components of a flow measure

 3. Effectiveness of communication
  a. Comparability (contextual reliability)
   i. Intertemporal
   ii. Intracompany
   iii. Intercompany
  b. Understandability
  c. Timeliness
   i. Frequency
   ii. Lag
  d. Optimal disclosure
   i. Sufficient detail—all material items
   ii. Not excessive
  e. Good format: headings, classifications, net figures, juxtaposition

B. Cost of providing information

VI. Accountants should find, select, accumulate and report evidence of valuations made by others.

I. Relevance

The primary criterion of the usefulness of measures of financial properties is their *relevance* to *decisions*. A *financial property is relevant to a decision if, given sufficient materiality, it has the power to affect the decision.* In the economic order quantity decision model, EOQ = $\sqrt{2AP/S}$, S is the total cost of holding a unit of the commodity for a year. Any component of this total, and the total itself, is relevant to the EOQ decision if the decision-maker uses this model. An economic property may be considered *directly relevant* to a decision if a perfect measurement of that property would fill the specific need perfectly, i.e., as well as we could possibly desire. This does not mean that a reliable measurement of a relevant property is the only information needed about one alternative, but it does provide perfect information about one variable in the decision model. Unfortunately, reliable measurements of perfectly relevant properties are rarely available.

A property that is closely related to a relevant property may serve as a *surrogate* for a relevant property and may be said to be *indirectly relevant* to a decision. In the EOQ model, future holding costs are directly relevant; past holding costs are likely to be indirectly relevant because they are closely related to future costs.

Several typical qualities of relevance can be identified. A measure or property may lack any one of these qualities and, thereby, fail to qualify as a directly relevant property or measure. The crucial quality is *activity relevance*, meaning that the measure must reflect an activity that is of concern to the decision-maker. S in the EOQ model must reflect the costs of holding the commodity over time; receiving and issuing costs are not relevant at this point. To take another example, the external investor relies upon financial statements to help him predict aspects of the firm's future activities, e.g., earnings and dividends; the property of assets that he needs to know must have some relation to what will happen to the asset; the asset's past itinerary or a future course it could—but will not—take are activities that are not directly relevant to the investor's decision. His alternatives are to buy, not buy, sell or hold the firm's security; the company's financial statements must help him see what his returns will be if he buys or holds, not whether the firm should sell or hold a specific asset.[1] An accountant would be guilty of reporting an irrelevant asset amount if he were to show to investors nothing but the scrap value of a two-year-old ship if he found no evidence of early scrapping.

For a measure to be relevant to the managerial decision of holding an asset "as is" or disposing of it either by use or sale, it must tell the manager either the net advantages to be enjoyed by holding (and sacrificed by disposition) or the net advantages to be enjoyed by disposition (and sacrificed by holding). The manager needs to know both to make the decision; he will be fortunate if his accounting staff can help him with either. The accountant may be able to justify reporting (to the manager) the net realizable value of the asset, because it is a close surrogate for the cash flow to be enjoyed by disposition without further processing and it is relevant to the activity of selling the asset. The manager should compare it with the cash flow to be enjoyed by retaining the asset, if he can obtain this information.

When the managerial decision to be made is whether or not to do something that requires the use of an existing asset, such as using raw materials or plant assets in production, the advantages and disadvantages may be outlined as follows:

Advantage—the net realizable value of the resulting product, i.e., the gross value less other costs.

Disadvantage—the sacrifice resulting from using the asset in question. If we are to calculate this sacrifice, we must know the consequences of using the asset. What undesirable event will occur, or what desirable event will not occur, because the asset is used in production? Putting it another way, what will be the supply adjustment? Where will the incremental consumption of the asset "come from"? Exhibit I illustrates the possibilities.

We believe that the most common method of adjusting the supply of assets that is typically used internally is by changing future

---

[1] Occasionally an investor does have the opportunity to play a role in a decision regarding the sale or retention of firm assets, but we classify such a role as a managerial activity. Owner-managers, including stockholder-directors, need information that will help them make sell-or-hold decisions about entity assets but the typical stockholder, or bondholder, in a publicly held corporation is more concerned with sell-or-hold decisions for his security, and this requires knowledge of what is most likely to happen to the firm's assets.

Exhibit I

RELATIONSHIPS BETWEEN POSSIBLE SUPPLY ADJUSTMENTS
AND COST OF USING AN ASSET

Supply Adjustment	Financial Consequence	Possible Reliable Surrogate
I. Reduce another use of the asset.		
A. An internal use, e.g., in a second product.	Loss of value in second use.	?
B. An external use, i.e., sale.	Loss of future net realizable value.	Present net realizable value.
II. Increase future acquisitions of assets of the same type.		
A. Acquisition by production.	Future production cost.	Current production cost.
B. Acquisition by purchase.	Future purchase cost.	Current purchase cost.

production or purchase schedules for such assets. If so, the most common financial consequence of using more of an asset is adding to future acquisition costs; so future acquisition cost has activity relevance. Present replacement cost may be the best reliable surrogate for future acquisition cost. If, on the other hand, using more of the asset will result in selling less, then net realizable value by sale has activity relevance to the decision regarding use. Similarly, if using more for one product means robbing another production process, the value of the asset for use in the other production process has activity relevance.

Entity relevance requires that the measure be related to the entity whose asset is being measured. If we need replacement cost, we must find the price in the market in which this entity buys and add fringe costs that must be paid by this entity. If net realizable value is needed, we must refer to the market in which this entity sells. Estimates of asset lives must relate to the environment of the owner.

Place relevance requires that the measure take into consideration the location of the asset. Transportation costs between the place of a market quotation and the physical location of an asset must be considered in obtaining net realizable value, replacement cost or historical cost.

Time relevance requires that a measure reflect the existence of the property at the time the action being considered by the decision-maker will take place. Measures reflecting service potential at a time earlier than the present are rarely directly relevant, because decisions cannot be made in the past; future service potential is more commonly needed.

These qualities of relevance are related to the traditionally recognized ways of creating utility. Activity relevance reflects functional utility based on the form of a good. Entity relevance is related to possession utility; a good may have different values in the hands of different owners. Place relevance is necessary because transportation may create utility. Time relevance takes into consideration the effect of time on the utility of a good; holding may create or destroy utility.

One other quality of relevance should be noted here. *Completeness* is necessary for any specified measure to be of maximum usefulness. This requires that no material item of cost be omitted in a measure of cost; that the net part of net realizable value not be overlooked; that the probability of collection be considered in stating future cash inflows.

All of these qualities of relevance must be present if a measure is to be directly relevant to a decision. Omission of any one quality, however, does not necessarily make the measure completely irrelevant or useless, but it does make it indirectly, or imperfectly, relevant. Whether it is still useful depends upon its degree of correspondence with the perfectly relevant measure, the extent to which it meets other criteria of valuable information and upon the availability of alternative measures.[2]

Relevance is the primary criterion of valuable accounting data. In the next section, we appraise common asset measurement methods using the relevance criterion. To place that discussion in the proper setting, the reader should remember that while reliability, effectiveness of communication and cost of accounting are additional criteria

---

[2] The absence of one of these features of relevance may have a tendency to produce a bias in the measure in question. For example, omission of fringe costs may result in a routine understatement of costs or use of old prices may result in understatement in a period of rising prices. If this type of procedural bias is measurable, the decision-maker may be able to adjust for it and minimize the harmful consequences.

to be met by any accounting procedure that is adopted, the present paper focuses on relevance.

II. The Relevance of Cash Flows

We hypothesize that the property of an asset or a liability that is most frequently relevant to the decisions for which accounting data are helpful is the difference in the present value of the firm's future cash flows that will result from the existence of the asset or liability. We do not intend to prove this hypothesis at this point, but we do feel obligated to provide enough support to assure its credibility.

First, let us consider the needs of *securities investors*. At least since Irving Fisher wrote, in 1906, that "the value of any capital-good, either of wealth or of property-rights, assuming that all future income is foreknown, is the discounted value of that income,"[3] the present value concept of securities values has been recognized by students of finance.[4] We believe that this view is now generally accepted among finance theorists. "The fundamental proposition of capital theory is that the value of an asset is the future payments it provides discounted at the appropriate rate."[5] More recently, the work of the American Accounting Association's Committee on External Reporting suggests that not only is the present value view of securities widely accepted but its implications for investors' interest in the firm's future cash flows can no longer be avoided. The Committee's dividend prediction model emphasized the firm's future cash flows from continued operations and from changes in its asset and liability positions to the virtual exclusion of all other attributes of net assets.[6] This work provides welcome support for a view that we have held for some fifteen years: the present value of the future cash flows resulting from the presence of an asset or liability is the property that is most *relevant* to securities investment decisions.

[3] Irving Fisher, *The Nature of Capital and Income* (New York: The Macmillan Company, 1906), p. 223.

[4] See Robert F. Wiese, "Investing for True Values," *Barron's*, September 8, 1930 and John Burr Williams, *The Theory of Investment Value* (Cambridge, Massachusetts: Harvard University Press, 1938), p. 6.

[5] Myron Gordon, *The Investment, Financing and Valuation of the Corporation* (Homewood, Illinois: Richard D. Irwin, Inc., 1962), p. 3.

[6] American Accounting Association, "An Evaluation of External Reporting Practices—A Report of the 1966–68 Committee on External Reporting," *The Accounting Review*, Supplement to XLIV (1969), pp. 79–123.

One of the major concerns of *managers* in most entities is to satisfy their employers, the owners (if the managers are not themselves the owners). Their measure of success is the same as owners'. In current jargon, the firm's objective function is generally recognized as maximizing either its present value or its market value. A measure of success, other than the change in the market value of the firm's securities, must be closely related to a measurement of a change in the present value of the firm over time. This requires the measurement of the firm's present value at two points in time which, in turn, requires the measurement of the various components of the firm's present value—assets and liabilities—if accounting is to have a role in it at all.

The broad spectrum of *management decisions*, surely, is as important a use of accounting data as any. Decisions that require information as to asset amounts generally involve possible changes from present plans; the alternative courses of action include at least (a) no change from present plans and (b) an alternative "use" or future course for the asset. The possible alternatives encompassed in (b) are, of course, numerous. Some of them are immediate sale of the asset (1) for scrap or (2) for a more typical use of the asset, leasing the asset to another party, switching it to a different use in its present location and changing both its use and its location within the firm. It is obvious that the accountant would have a hard time trying to provide asset amounts relevant to these alternatives as a matter of routine reporting. But, what is more important, the presently planned use is more likely to be an alternative in any managerial decision than is any single alternative use, so it is more likely to have *activity relevance* for managers.

This is a good time to remind ourselves of the role of present values of future cash flows in the analysis of capital investment opportunities. "Capital budgeting" models typically focus on the objective of investing in projects with positive net present values. If the decision is made primarily on the basis of an anticipated rate of return in excess of the cost of capital, the projects that are accepted have positive net present values. If the analysis focuses directly on the net present value of future cash flows discounted at the cost of capital rate, again projects with net present values are accepted. Finding and investing in projects with net present values is the logical managerial approach to specific asset purchase decisions and to maximizing the present value of the firm.

This section can now be summarized by saying that the present value of future cash flows resulting from assets and liabilities is the property that is most frequently relevant to financial decisions. The present value of future cash flows is the essence of securities values, the property of existing assets and liabilities that is most commonly relevant to the decisions of external investors and managers, and is the objective of the search for investment projects. In other words, the present value view of assets and liabilities is consistent with the most widely accepted ex ante approach to assets and with the generally accepted view of securities value. Accordingly, *we believe that the most useful meaning of asset and liability quantities is the item's incremental effect upon the net discounted amount of the entity's future cash flows.* This is what we seek to measure.

III. Measures of Asset Amounts

Having defined the amount of an asset or liability as its incremental effect upon the net discounted amount of the firm's future cash flows, we must now turn to the implementation of this concept. How can we ascertain the amount of an asset or a liability? Accountants do not rely heavily on their own opinions of asset values, but they do rely upon their own judgments of various types of evidence of value. If the accountant has any area of expertise pertaining to value, it is in the field of evidence of value. The professional accountant uses his greatest skill, his most professional judgment, when he selects the types of evidence on which he will rely in ascertaining the amount of a specific asset or liability. The outline in Exhibit II gives explicit recognition to a variety of types of evidence of asset and liability amounts; we believe it includes the major categories that have a direct relation to the accountant's work. Note that the types of documents and communications media used to transmit the information to the accountant, such as invoices, price lists and newspapers, are ignored.

The amount of an asset may depend upon its physical quantity and the unit price attached to it. For example, measurements of commodity stocks and plant assets typically require measures of these two factors. The outline provides for evidence of both. Categories I and

Exhibit II

TYPES OF EVIDENCE OF ASSET VALUE

I. Face or Nominal amount of a cash item

II. Contractual evidence

III. Market prices
   A. Exit prices
      1. Current
         a. Entity participated in establishing price
         b. Entity did not participate
      2. Past
         a. Entity participated in establishing price
         b. Entity did not participate
   B. Entry prices
      1. Current
         a. Entity participated in establishing price
         b. Entity did not participate
      2. Past
         a. Entity participated in establishing price
         b. Entity did not participate
   C. Price Indexes
      1. Specific (narrow) index (current entry prices)
      2. General (broad) measuring unit index

IV. Physical observation and count of quantities
   A. By entity personnel
   B. By external personnel as reported to entity

V. Miscellaneous statistical evidence
   A. Provided by entity personnel
   B. From external sources

II apply mostly to assets that have no separable quantity and price factors involved in their measurement. Category III includes prices only; categories IV and V relate primarily to unpriced quantities. Receiving reports and physical inventory sheets are examples of documents that transmit type IV-A evidence to accountants. Statements from brokers and independent warehousemen may reflect type IV-B evidence. Type V-A evidence provides much of the basis for estimates of bad debts and lives of amortizable assets. Type V-B evidence from appraisers or trade associations may also be used by accountants in connection with asset lives.

We contend that these types of evidence constitute the building blocks from which measurement methods are constructed. In accounting, a *measurement method* is a procedure for utilizing one or more types of evidence in ascertaining the amount of an asset or liability or the change in the amount of an asset or a liability. A *measurement* is both the act of measuring and the specific number resulting from the application of a measurement method to an object (asset or liability) in a particular case. A *measure* is the general result of applying a measurement method. The phrases used to identify measures (and variations thereof) listed in Exhibit III may also be used as short symbols for the related measurement methods. Thus, net realizable value is a common measure of asset amounts and is a measurement method that requires evidence of the physical quantity of goods on hand, the current entry prices for services required to sell those goods and the current exit price of the commodity. If an accountant finds evidence of 1,000 units of a commodity on hand, an exit market price of $8 and costs of selling of 50¢ per unit and makes the calculation $1,000(\$8 - .50) = \$7,500$, his measurement method is net realizable value and $7,500 is his measurement of the stock of this commodity. Net realizable value is also the measure of asset amount the accountant has chosen to use. Exhibit III outlines some of the more likely measures of assets (and measurement methods).

The next step in our inquiry is to examine the relationships among the measurement methods we have recognized and between the resulting measures and our concept of value. Determining the amount of an asset by *counting the face value of cash items* is a highly relevant measurement method. These cash items are currently available to pay investors or to use in other ways that may appear more desirable and involve no material probability of loss. All noncash assets involve significant measurement problems. In the case of receivables, measurements of *future cash flows* involve a tradeoff between relevance and reliability. To achieve the highest degree of relevance in one figure, we must sacrifice at least a little reliability. We must either ignore the probability that the promised future cash flow will not materialize (and, thus, report claims to cash instead of the future cash flows decision-makers need to know) or estimate uncollectibles (and report

Exhibit III

MEASURES OF ASSETS AND TYPES OF EVIDENCE UTILIZED

Measures		Types of Evidence Utilized
1. Face value	I.	Face or nominal amount
2. Future cash flows	II.	Contractual evidence of future cash flow
a. Subject to recognized uncertainties	V.	Miscellaneous statistical evidence
b. Discounted	III-B-1.	Market price for use of money
3. Net realizable value	III-A-1.	Current exit price
	III-B-1.	Current entry price for services required to sell
	IV.	Physical observation and count of quantities
4. Replacement cost	IV.	
a. Based on specific market prices	III-B-1.	Current entry price
i. Amortized	V.	Miscellaneous statistical evidence of quantities
ii. Not amortized		
b. Based on a specific price index	III-C-1.	Specific price index
i. Amortized	IV, V.	
ii. Not amortized		
5. Adjusted historical cost	III-B-2-a.	Past entry price involving the firm
	III-C-2.	General measuring unit index
	IV.	
	V.	
6. Original historical cost	III-B-2-a.	
a. Amortized	IV.	
b. Not amortized	V.	

a net amount that cannot be relied upon as the true amount of future collections). Then, we must either select a discount rate (which is probably not quite correct) or we must fail to discount (thereby omitting the information available on the timing of the future cash flows). Accountants typically assume that they can improve upon the contractual amount of the future cash flow as a measure of asset amount by adjusting for uncertainty (uncollectibles). We believe that they can also improve their future cash flow measurements by discounting if the waiting period is material; a delay in a cash flow reduces its asset amount by a quantity that can be calculated with useful accuracy. Furthermore, the addition of undiscounted amounts due at different times yields a sum that has no definite meaning at a point in time.

Now, let us consider measurements at the *net realizable value* of an asset on a market in which it is expected to be sold. The current price in a highly developed and competitive market, less a current calculation of minor selling costs, can be expected to be a useful surrogate for the present value of the future cash flows that will be produced by this asset. The most likely defects in such a net realizable value arise from limitations in market quotations as single-valued and independent representations of the market price, probable changes in the market price prior to sale, a change in the sale plan, the absence of a discount factor and errors in the calculation of the costs to be deducted from the current selling price. By reference to these defects, we can see that net realizable value is a better surrogate for discounted future cash flows if the market is active and competitive,[7] the probable asset holding period is short and the remaining costs involved in converting the asset to cash are minor.

Replacement cost of an inventory item is an alternative to net realizable value. Full replacement cost, including all holding costs such as cost of capital, is equal to net realizable value (net of holding costs) in competitive equilibrium. This relationship is shown by

---

[7] The importance of the competitive feature is obvious when we note that a sloping demand curve yields marginal revenue less than the selling price. This suggests that a beginning inventory may contribute an incremental future cash flow less than the average future selling price, especially if the inventory is greater than is needed to avoid loss of sales. In many cases, this may weaken the relevance of net realizable value to the point that replacement cost would be the preferable measurement method.

Exhibit IV, which illustrates both the cost accumulation view of inventories in a manufacturing firm (starting at the lower left) and the receipt offset view (starting at upper right). If the two approaches fail to meet, a pure profit or loss is involved. The chart reflects the various stages in the operating cycle and relates to a product that meets the qualifications for measurement at net realizable value in its finished good stage. In traditional terminology, the accountant is said to "recognize revenue" when he elects to "jump the gap" between the two measurement approaches. Note that the gap is likely to be positive if some items of cost, such as cost of capital and general administrative costs, are completely omitted from the cost categories listed at the right-hand edge of the chart.[8] Under these circumstances, the gap would not represent pure profit.

The preceding discussion of the relationship between future cash flows, net realizable value and replacement cost pertains to stocks of commodities involved in the operating cycle of manufacturing or merchandising firms. In the case of necessary inventories of stock-in-trade, net realizable value appears to be more closely related to future cash flows than is replacement cost. Net realizable value is also closely related to future cash flows in the cases of securities and plant assets held for sale rather than use (e.g., a retired machine). In this latter case, replacement cost seems to be particularly irrelevant.

In another set of cases, replacement cost appears to be more directly related to the asset's effect upon future cash flows. If the absence of an asset would not affect future sales but would only require greater future acquisitions (by production or purchase), its differential cash flow effect appears to be equal to future acquisition cost. Present acquisition cost may be viewed as a good surrogate for future acquisition cost. Net realizable value presumably is not a good candidate in these cases if the presence or absence of the asset will not affect future sales. We believe this situation is typical of raw materials inventories and nonobsolete, fully utilized plant assets. The incremental effect on future cash flows from having one more or one fewer units on hand would be the cash effect of acquiring one fewer or one more unit in

---

[8] The usual reason for omitting the cost of any necessary input from product costs to be compared with product revenues is inability to associate the input with specific products with useful accuracy.

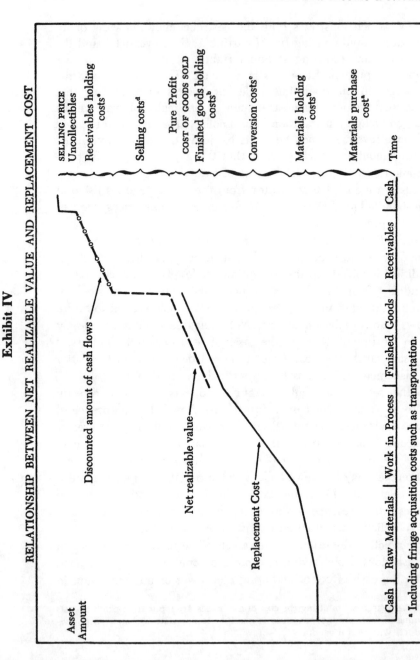

Exhibit IV

RELATIONSHIP BETWEEN NET REALIZABLE VALUE AND REPLACEMENT COST

Asset Amount

Discounted amount of cash flows

Net realizable value

Replacement Cost

| Cash | Raw Materials | Work in Process | Finished Goods | Receivables | Cash |

SELLING PRICE
Uncollectibles
Receivables holding costs[a]

Selling costs[d]

Pure Profit
COST OF GOODS SOLD
Finished goods holding costs[b]

Conversion costs[c]

Materials holding costs[b]

Materials purchase cost[a]

Time

[a] Including fringe acquisition costs such as transportation.
[b] Cost of capital, insurance, storage space, etc.
[c] Including holding costs during conversion.
[d] All costs are assumed to be allocable to one or more of the categories shown.
[e] Especially cost of capital.

the future. We have applied this sort of "disappearing asset" approach to a few other cases with the results appearing in Exhibit V.

The other two major measurement methods listed in Exhibit III—adjusted historical cost and historical cost—may be admitted to the accountant's tool kit because of their relationship to replacement cost. Adjusted historical cost differs from current replacement cost by the change in the real price of the asset, while historical cost (unadjusted) differs by the change in the money price. (Adjusted historical cost is historical cost adjusted by the percentage change in an index reflecting changes in the size of the monetary unit between acquisition date and the measurement date.) Since the money price of assets typically changes more than the real price, we consider adjusted historical cost to be more closely related to replacement cost than is historical cost. We should also recognize that the cost-based measurement methods may be justified as reflections of minimum value judgments by the management. Replacement cost is relevant on this basis if the management is purchasing similar assets relatively currently. Adjusted historical cost reflected a minimum value judgment at acquisition date. Exhibit VI summarizes the foregoing discussion of relationships between measurement methods.

We conclude that measurement methods can be ranked in order of relevance and that the array of Exhibit III is generally the proper rank order. The major exception involves nonmonetary assets held for "operating" purposes but whose absence would not result in a loss of operating revenues. A differential analysis indicates that replacement cost frequently is more relevant than net realizable value for such assets.

Several caveats should be recorded before we move on. The inclusion of net realizable value as a highly relevant measurement method for external reporting is dependent upon the interpretation that it must be based on a market in which the firm expects to sell the asset. Possible but improbable sources of net realizable values do not deserve such high ranking. (In fact, they would seem to have no place at all in a single-valued, external reporting system.) Furthermore, neither the order of the Exhibit III listing nor the right-hand column of Exhibit V is meant as a recommended application of any measurement method. Only relevance has been considered; the other major criterion—reliability—has not been considered in ranking the methods.

Exhibit V

REVIEW OF SOME POSSIBLE DIFFERENTIAL EFFECTS UPON A FIRM IF A SPECIFIED TYPE OF ASSET DISAPPEARED

Asset Held	Possible Activity Effects of Disappearance	Possible Financial Effects	One Possible Surrogate Measurement Method
Receivables	Less payoff to investors More external financing Reduced scope of operations	Difference in future cash flow to or from investors	Discounting "expected value" of future cash flows
Marketable securities	Same as above	Same as above	Discounting future cash flows or net realizable value

"Real" assets needed to maintain operations	A. Reduce usage
	  1. Internal use
	    a. Substitute another input
	    b. Reduce output and sales
	  2. External use (sales)
	
	B. Delay usage and increase future acquisitions
	  1. Internal use
	    a. Increase future production
	    b. Increase future purchases
	  2. External use (sales)
	    a. Increase future production
	    b. Increase future purchases
		Incur higher cost of substitute
		Loss of future net realizable value
		Loss of future net realizable value
		
		Disruption costs and future production costs
		Disruption costs and future acquisition costs
		Goodwill loss and future production costs
		Goodwill loss and future acquisition costs
			Present replacement cost of asset held
			Present net realizable value
			Present net realizable value
			
			Present replacement cost by production
			Present replacement cost by purchase
			Present replacement cost by production
			Present replacement cost by purchase

"Real" assets not needed to maintain operations	A. Reduce sale of "excess" B. Increase future acquisitions	Loss of future net realizable value Future replacement cost less holding costs saved	Present net realizable value Present replacement cost

Exhibit VI

RELATIONSHIPS BETWEEN ASSET VALUE AND
ASSET MEASUREMENT METHODS

Measurement Method	Relationship Justifying Its Use	Incremental Error versus Previous Method
Counting cash items.	Direct component of entity value.	
Future cash flows with allowances for failures and time.	Direct component of entity value marred only slightly by errors in estimating failures and in selecting proper discount rate.	Inaccurate estimate of uncollectibles, discount rate probably unsuitable.
Net realizable value in market in which asset is to be sold.	Current price in a highly developed market, less a current estimate of minor future costs, is a good surrogate for net future cash flows.	Inaccurate estimate of future costs, choice from range of market prices, firm's effect on market, change in price or costs prior to sale.
Replacement cost:		
A. If absence of asset would reduce future sales.	Full replacement cost (including cost of capital) equals NRV (net of COC) in competitive equilibrium.*	Pure profit ($\pm$) due to imperfect competition or disequilibrium.
B. If absence of asset would increase future acquisitions.	Good surrogate for future cash outflows avoided by presence of asset and for cost of using asset (needed for cost minimization decisions).*	Not comparable.
Historical cost adjusted for change in measuring unit.	Surrogate for replacement cost, difference depending upon real price changes.*	Differs from replacement cost if real price has changed.
Historical cost stated in original number of monetary units.	Surrogate for replacement cost, difference depending upon real price changes and change in measuring unit, i.e., money price changes.*	Ignores fluctuations in the size of the measuring unit.

* Cost-based methods may also be defended on the ground that management
has judged the asset to be worth more than its cost.

We should also note that Exhibit V is not complete; it merely illustrates the nature of activity relevance of measurement methods.

One final observation about a relationship between measurement methods may be made here. In the case of receivables, net realizable value in the normal course of operations (rather than by quick sale or assignment) is, from a practical point of view, essentially the same as the discounted amount of future cash flows. If the net realizable value of receivables is net of carrying costs (mainly cost of capital) and uncollectibles, and if discounted future cash flows omit uncollectibles, the only conceptual difference would seem to be between cost of capital and discount—a difference which may disappear in practice.

This review of relationships among measurement methods and asset values reveals two practical views of relevant asset amounts, both based on the concept of present values of future cash flows. In an idealized decision-making environment, future cash inflows are assets, and future cash outflows are equities. If the decision-maker knows the times and amounts of the future cash inflows an asset will produce in each use under consideration, he has all the information he is likely to need about that asset. The times and amounts of future cash flows are the principals for some managerial decisions involving an asset, such as the sell-or-hold decision. The expression of the time and amount in one figure for each asset and the addition of such assets to one meaningful sum requires discounting. The discounted value of the future cash flows pertaining to an asset may be thought of as either an excellent surrogate for the times and amounts of those flows or a single-valued principal. Reliable discounted values are valuable data for use in the decisions of secondary beneficiaries of entity asset values, i.e., investors in the entity's securities. The accountant must seek reliable evidence of such discounted values. Such evidence may be found in contracts and in prices in markets in which assets are expected to be sold. Backward-looking measurements, such as replacement cost, adjusted historical cost and historical cost are poor surrogates for discounted values of future cash inflows. Where we have been is of interest only if it gives us our best clue as to where we are going; it is a pale substitute for reliable evidence of what is likely to happen.

The other view of relevant asset amounts picks up where the first leaves off. In the cases of many assets held for internal use, reliable evidence of their contributions to future cash inflows is unavailable. Furthermore, accountants encounter substantial practical difficulties in associating future selling, administrative and manufacturing overhead costs with specific assets in order to make the deductions necessary to obtain net realizable value. Net realizable values of many assets, such as supplies, minor raw materials and depreciable assets, via use in operations are not useful in current managerial processes because of formidable conceptual and practical difficulties; managers do not and cannot use them. Net realizable value of such assets via immediate sale, if immediate sale is improbable, is not likely to be a valuable output of the accounting system for use by managers and is not likely to represent a useful statement to the stockholder of what his share of stock represents. Another view of asset value appears to be more useful in such cases.

The contribution to a firm's future cash position that will be made by most assets held for internal use is by way of reducing future cash outflows, not by increasing future cash inflows. While it is possible for a stock of raw materials or a machine to make a distinct difference in the firm's future sales, many production operations have sufficient routing flexibility (alternative methods) and timing flexibility through "built-in holds" (inventories) to permit the firm to achieve the same future cash inflows regardless of the presence or absence of a specific input stock at a specific date. The differential effect of the presence or absence of the asset will show up in future acquisition costs, not in future revenues. The value of a stock of early-stage inputs comes from their contribution to the maintenance of operations with lower future cash outflows than would otherwise be required. The accountant should work towards reporting such a value, or a reliable surrogate, to investors rather than engage in the futile exercise of attempting to find direct evidence of future cash flows or the irrelevant exercise of reporting liquidation values of assets held for use.

But more importantly, recognition that assets held for use will affect the firm's future cash position by reducing future cash outflows leads us to the close surrogate—present replacement cost—which can make a great contribution to *costing* and to *cost minimization decisions*. A unit of a needed raw material, supply or machine that is on hand is a unit that need not be purchased in the future. When a manager wants to know the cost of using a unit of a regularly-used, scarce resource, he wants to know what difference it will make if he uses more or less of it. Since more or less use typically means more or less will be acquired in the future, future replacement cost is the relevant environmental variable; present replacement cost is a good surrogate. We believe that the most important use of measurements of the amounts of nonobsolete assets held for use is in cost minimization and other decisions requiring knowledge of the cost of using resources. We believe that replacement cost is by far the most reliable surrogate for the true cost of using such a resource. For this reason, we do not lament the unavailability of a reliable discounted value or a relevant and reliable net realizable value. If a penny saved is as good as a penny earned and if a cash outflow avoided is as good as a cash inflow, replacement cost of an asset held for use is as relevant as net realizable value of an asset held for sale in its existing form.

We conclude that the order in which the measurement methods are listed in Exhibit III is their order of relevance to the general run of managerial decisions and decisions of external investors but that the list begins with replacement cost when it is applied to that major class of nonmonetary resources held for "internal use" rather than for direct sale.

IV. On Additivity and Subjectivity

The property we seek to measure is the differential effect of an asset or liability on the present value of the firm's future cash flows. Recognizing that direct measurements of this property are seldom feasible, we accept a variety of types of evidence of the target property. Some of the amounts thus selected are relatively accurate indicators of the target property; some are quite inaccurate. We intend, of course, to omit those that are not usefully accurate. We cannot expect the sum to have a smaller absolute error than that in the least accurate component, although offsetting errors may yield a smaller net error (but cumulative errors may yield a very large net error). We cannot hope for perfection in the measurement of the present value of a business enterprise any more than space scientists can hope for perfection in measuring the density of the moon's surface at a point chosen for a future landing, but in both cases, we can hope for a degree of accuracy that makes the measurements useful. While we may be able to make a more accurate measure of another property, such as the proceeds from a near future liquidation of the firm or the density of the moon's surface at the point of a past landing, we may well conclude that a rough measure of a relevant property is more useful than a precise measure of an irrelevant property.[9]

Several of the procedures that we have called measurement methods (e.g., net realizable value, historical cost) yield what might be called surrogate measures of an asset's discounted value. The use of surrogate measures in accounting almost assures imperfect representation of the principal. The addition of amounts derived from several different surrogate measures is an additional blemish, because it makes adjustment for systematic bias (in a surrogate as a representation of a principal) more difficult. But ". . . the fact that a representation is imperfect does not necessarily mean that it is totally useless. . . . This is fortunate for those who design accounting information systems since if an imperfect representation were totally useless, it would be virtually impossible to develop any workable accounting information system."[10] Additivity can be overemphasized at the cost of reduced relevance or reliability. While it is true that adding the replacement cost of one asset to the net realizable value of another yields neither a total replacement cost nor a total net realizable value, this observation is of limited assistance to an accountant who has no reliable data on the replacement cost of certain assets and no reliable data on the net realizable value of others. Furthermore, for a myriad of specific managerial decisions, all useful data that it is feasible to accumulate in the accounts may be based on only one measurement method despite a mixed balance sheet; to pass up the most relevant data in such cases because of the additivity argument would indeed be foolish. Furthermore, those of us who believe that "consistency in objective is to be preferred to consistency in method"[11] can argue that imperfect measures of a common property—present value—arrived at by different

---

[9] Or as Sterling puts it, "A guess at a relevant figure is infinitely more valuable than a precise and objective irrelevancy." Robert R. Sterling, "Conservatism: The Fundamental Principle of Valuation in Traditional Accounting," *Abacus* (December 1967), p. 131.

[10] Yuji Ijiri, *The Foundations of Accounting Measurement* (New York: Prentice-Hall, 1967), p. 13 .

[11] Raymond J. Chambers, *Accounting, Evaluation and Economic Behavior* (New York: Prentice-Hall, 1966), p. 260.

methods meet the technical requirements for additivity. Various degrees of imperfection in the individual measurements do not render their sum completely meaningless or useless.

Perhaps an analogy will help. Suppose a person is planning a motor trip from San Francisco to Colon, Panama and wants to know the distance to help him judge the driving time and the gasoline consumption. Suppose that on the Sunday that he is making these judgments, the information available to him is limited and varied but he is able to accumulate the following data:

(1) The distance from San Francisco to the Mexican border at Tijuana, according to an oil company map he had in his car is   530 miles

(2) A friend who recently had driven from Tijuana to Mexicali said that he recorded the distance as 125 miles on his odometer.   125 miles

(3) A Mexican-American friend who once was traffic manager for a Mexican bus company had an old fare schedule showing a fare of 600 pesos for the trip from Mexicali to Mexico City. He said that the company set its fares on the basis of 25 centavos per kilometer and then rounded it off to the nearest peso. On this basis he thought the distance from Mexicali to Mexico City was 2,400 kilometers. At roughly .62 miles per kilometer this came to   1,488 miles

(4) The Mexican-American friend also had an old map of southern Mexico. The distance figures from town to town were very difficult to read, but from what could be read plus a few guesses at last digits it appeared to be 968 kilometers from Mexico City to the Guatemala border.[12] Multiplied by .62 this came to approximately   600 miles

(5) A banana company executive said that when he was stationed in Costa Rica and had his own plane he once flew from San Jose, Costa Rica to Guatemala City in 4 hours. He was confident that he had

---

[12] The friend said a new road saves "a few kilometers" on one stretch.

maintained a constant air speed of 200 miles per
hour and thought there was only a slight breeze
off his left wing-tip.   800 miles

(6) An atlas with a scale of miles showing 100 miles per
inch revealed that it was one inch from the Mexico-
Guatemala border to Guatemala City and ¾ inch
from San Jose to the Panama border.   175 miles

(7) A call to the Panamanian Consul General's home
brought forth the belief that the distance from the
Costa Rica-Panama border to Colon was between
200 and 250 miles. The atlas map showed 1.9
inches.   225 miles

    Total   3,943 miles

(8) A globe showed the distance from San Francisco to
Los Angeles to be 400 nautical miles and the distance from Los Angeles to Colon as 2,600 miles,
for a total by sea of 3,000 nautical miles. At 1.13
land miles per nautical mile this amounts to 3,390
miles.

The 3,943 miles is a measure of the road mileage from San Francisco
to Colon that is unlikely to be correct to the nearest mile, but it may
be more useful for making decisions about driving from one city to
the other than the measure of sea mileage, despite the latter's neatness.
We believe that balance sheet and income statement sums and differences based on the evidential approach are likely to be more useful
to decision-makers than would similar figures consistently based on
a historical cost, adjusted historical cost, replacement cost or net
realizable value method of measurement.

Some readers may feel that measuring an asset or a liability by
reference to the expected future cash flow related to the item places
too much reliance on future events. But in what sense does it rely
on the future? It relies upon the same type of evidence as does net
realizable value, viz., a past transaction price, so surely, it cannot be
said to be any less objective than net realizable value. The fact of
the matter is that the *usefulness* of all accounting measurements is

227

dependent upon future events. If the debtor fails to pay, if the cash box is stolen, or if the inventory is burned, the asset amount based on contractual evidence of future cash flows, counting cash, or current market value will turn out to be a poor basis for an investor's predictions. Net realizable value of an inventory is not useful information unless it can be relied upon as an indication of what will or could happen. It is useful as a surrogate for future cash flows that will or could happen; it is not useful because the manager or investor must know net realizable value. Similarly, when product costing is done on the basis of replacement cost, the information is only useful if it is a good surrogate for the future cash disbursement that is caused by using the resource in question today. Even historical cost is a surrogate for future cash flows; we certainly do not need to know historical cost per se. The usefulness of all of these measurements is dependent upon future events; their basis is factual information from the past.

If the value of accounting measurements is dependent upon future events, by how much do we reduce their value by explicitly making use of reliable evidence of what will happen rather than regarding such evidence as tainted and unfit for user consumption? We certainly would look foolish refusing to utilize evidence of what will happen in connection with receivables and payables, telling thousands of stockholders around the world that only they are in a position to make such predictions, that we accountants can only report the December 31 net realizable value (via factoring?) or historical cost (including allocated selling and administrative costs?) of receivables and historical receipt of, say, wages payable. There is nothing about measurement, accounting, economics, finance or management that rules out reliance on evidence of future events in making accounting measurements.

Nor can accountants reasonably omit judgments made by parties within the firm, e.g., estimates of uncollectible receivables or of depreciable lives. Our much-admired market values reflect judgments of sacrifices, alternatives and utility. There is no fundamental difference between judgments made by accountants and judgments made by buyers and sellers, at least none that says one is objective and the other subjective. Either may be biased. The only objective aspect of a market price is that a transaction did occur at that price. The price itself, which is the measure in which we are interested, is not even an explicit opinion of the worth of the good; the buyer thinks it is worth more than the price; the seller, less. The relationship between the judge(s) and the entity does not, by itself, determine which judgments are useful and which useless. The accounting process of selecting useful valuations must be based on assessments of relevance and reliability after considering a number of environmental conditions, including, but not limited to, the relation of the evaluator to the entity. How much risk of bias and how much subjectivity can be accepted is partly dependent upon the alternatives that are available. If the alternative is replacement or retirement accounting, internal estimates of asset lives may (or may not) be useful; their acceptability must be decided in the light of the attendant circumstances. Whether or not estimating asset lives is an accounting function is of little concern to us. We urge those who have a narrow view of the accounting function to be less concerned about overstepping the boundaries of that function and more concerned with providing useful information. "Any attempt to cope with the difficulties of measuring a property known to be relevant is preferable to any attempt to measure an entirely different property instead, unless the measure of a different property is the closest possible approximation to the measure of the desired property."[13]

The practical import of our argument may be elucidated by considering the following problem. You have been asked to prepare a balance sheet for the Company for use in determining the sale price of an ownership interest. Owner A has agreed to sell his 40% interest to Owner B, who already has a 15% interest, at its "book value based on sensible, but not necessarily generally accepted, principles of accounting." Mr. A and Mr. B are two of your best friends. You have been able to gather the data shown in Exhibit VII.

We believe that you would minimize the risk of losing a friend if you make use of several different measurement methods. We specifically recommend that you use the present value of future cash flows (discounted at 8%) for the notes receivable, undiscounted future cash flows for the cotton (based on the contract to sell), net realizable value for the cottonseed, replacement cost for the dress shop inventory

---

[13] Chambers, p. 231.

Exhibit VII

Company
Balance Sheet
December 31, 1969

Cash .... $40,000   Current Liabilities $100,000

Notes Receivable (See Note 1)   Long-term Debt   200,000

Cotton (See Note 2)   Total Liabilities   300,000

Cottonseed (See Note 3)

Dress Shop Inventory (See Note 4)   Owners' Equity

Land (See Note 5)

Total Assets .... $_____   Total Equities ....$_____

NOTE 1.   During the year the company sold a portion of its land for a cash amount and a mortgage note calling for payment of $20,000 per year each January 1 for 15 years. The state agriculture department's record of average interest rates on farm mortgages stands at 8%. The land had cost $22,000 when purchased in 1939. (See Note 5).

NOTE 2.   The company operates a cotton farm and a gin for separating cotton fiber from the seeds. The company has contracted to sell the entire 1969 crop, consisting of 1,000,000 pounds, at a price of $.30 per pound for delivery to the buyer's loading and trucking crew at the company's gin between January 1 and January 15, 1970. This grade of cotton is quoted at $.28 per pound at the nearest wholesale market and the company would have to pay a trucker $2 per ton to haul it to market. The cost of growing and ginning the year's crop was $240,000.

NOTE 3.   The cottonseed inventory of 600 tons consists of the entire year's crop (see Note 2). The local seed processing mill is currently paying $60 per ton and will pick it up at the seller's gin.

NOTE 4.   The company operates a dress shop, Alice's Store, which caters to the local high school and college girls. The inventory has current marked prices amounting to $25,000. The historical cost of the inventory on a specific identification basis was $14,000; due to several markdowns by suppliers, the replacement cost of the goods is $13,000. Operating expenses have varied between 39 and 45% of sales in recent months.

NOTE 5.   The company's land was acquired for $50,000 in 1939 when the county index of crop land prices was one-third of its present level.

and replacement cost computed with the aid of the land price index for the land. In the absence of the specific price index, we would have chosen adjusted historical cost in preference to historical cost.

V. Conclusion

Measurement of net asset items is still the fundamental problem underlying most of the controversies in accounting. The profession's refusal to face up to this problem has unnecessarily prolonged the disastrous diversity of inventory practices in similar circumstances; it has driven security analysts to cash flow; it has split the business community over the purchase-pooling issue.

We believe that a careful analysis of the needs of users of accounting data will disclose that the property of noncash assets that is most relevant to most decisions of investors and managers is their incremental effect upon the present value of the firm's future cash flows. Other measurement methods can be ranked behind discounting on the criterion of relevance. With these rankings in mind, the accountant can compare his assessment of the reliability with which several measures can be applied in the specific case against their relevance rankings and choose that measure which he believes will provide the most useful information.

The preceding analyses of the relevance of measurement methods to cash-flow-oriented decisions is summarized in EXHIBIT VII-7. Consolidating the partial conclusions reached in relation to assets held for sale, assets held for use, and assets held as investments results in some discontinuities. For example, current market price is ranked above best-use NRV for application to investments that are bought and sold in the same market, but it defies ranking for application to assets held for sale because of variations in the significance of deductible costs. And the equity method ranks between current market value and restated historical cost for equity investments, but it is not applicable to any other asset category. In the case of up-to-date assets held for use, the first five methods are unlikely to be reliable enough even to be thought of as possibilities. In sum, while EXHIBIT VII-7 is only a rough guide to the relevance of measurement methods for application to assets in general, it is intended to illustrate the linkages that are the heart of the surrogate chain. These linkages may be summarized in a series of brief statements as follows:

1. The measurement of cash items at their face value is assumed to be the ultimate in the measurement of financial attributes relevant to cash-flow-oriented decisions.
2. We assume that the amounts and times of cash flows promised by or to the entity can be combined with the aid of a discount rate to yield the most relevant measure of cash flow potential for noncash assets. Undiscounted future cash flows can, if the waiting period is short, yield a close surrogate for discounted future cash flows.
3. NRV—the net proceeds that could be obtained by selling a unit of the asset (a) in its "best use" and (b) employing market prices prevailing at the measurement date—is a close surrogate for the present value of the flow that will be realized if the market is competitive and well informed.
4. The tendency of full cost to equal selling price in a competitive market makes replacement cost a close surrogate for NRV in many cases.
5. Restated historical cost—an old market price adjusted by the average change in market prices during the holding

EXHIBIT VII-7

MEASUREMENT METHODS RANKED BY RELEVANCE TO CASH-FLOW-ORIENTED DECISIONS (THE SURROGATE CHAIN)

Measurement Method	Relationship Justifying Use	Variance from Related Method
1. Face value of cash	Direct measurement of cash flow potential	
2. Discounted future cash flows		Vs. cash, uncertainties introduced: timing, amount, discount rate
3. Future cash flows, if short term	Direct measurement of quantity dimension of cash flow potential	Ignores timing of flow
4. Current market price of single-market assets	Competitive market price is based on actors' judgments of present value of future cash flows from asset. Current price≈future cash flow from sale	Imperfections in market
5. Best-use NRV	Good surrogate for discounted future cash flows per (4) above	Vs. discounted future cash flow, imperfections in market; uncertainty of costs deducted

6. Current replacement cost		
a. If incremental unit affects sales	Surrogate for (5): full replacement cost equals NRV in competitive equilibrium	Pure profit (±) due to market imperfections
b. If incremental unit affects future acquisitions	Surrogate for incremental future cash flows via reduced future purchases	Vs. discounted future cash flow, imperfections in market
7. Equity method	Improves upon cost methods by updating per investee's accounting methods	Vs. market, all limitations of investee's accounting. Vs. cost, recorded value changes since acquisition
8. Restated historical cost	Estimate of replacement cost	Differs from replacement cost by real price change
9. Historical cost	Surrogate for replacement cost or restated historical cost	Differs from replacement cost by nominal price change

period to date—is a reasonable surrogate for replacement cost—an old market price adjusted by the change in the price of the specific commodity.

6. Historical cost is the equivalent of restated historical cost expressed in a different (older) measuring unit. If the change in the measuring unit between the two measurement dates has not been great, historical cost may be an acceptable surrogate for restated historical cost. Historical cost is also a surrogate for replacement cost, the only source of difference being in the timing of the entry market prices used.

7. A set of statements similar to 2 through 6 above can be written so as to apply to liabilities.

The reader must see clearly that the ranked list presented here is not a full guide to the choice of a measurement method because it reflects only one criterion—relevance. It does, however, provide a basis for stating our general procedure for choosing a measurement method for application in circumstances calling for information relevant to cash-flow-oriented decisions. *Starting at the top of the list in EXHIBIT VII–7, evaluate each measurement method on the basis of the other eight criteria presented in chapter III (especially reliability, effects via other parties, and cost of production) until a method is found which is acceptable on those other criteria. Choose that method.*

Another way of reviewing the relationships between measurement methods is to start with historical cost and consider its weaknesses and how to improve upon it. Following this pattern, we can step on up the ladder to discounted future cash flows as follows:

1. The first readily available measure of a newly acquired noncash asset is its acquisition cost, or *historical cost*—its market price at acquisition date. But with the passage of time and changes in the purchasing power of the monetary unit, the sacrifice made to acquire an asset may be communicated more effectively if we state it in the current measuring unit.

2. This leads us to *restated historical cost,* which permits us to add the costs of all assets in terms of the same measuring unit.

3. But rather than measure the asset at its old entry market price (expressed in current measuring units), why not

update the measurement to current entry market price—
current replacement cost—including fringe acquisition costs,
of course? Of all the past market prices that are available
for use, the most recent one is the most relevant to
future-oriented decisions.

4. If the asset is available for sale and its NRV in the market
in which it is likely to be sold can be calculated, we should
make use of this evidence of the cash flow that could be
received at the date of the measurement by committing
the asset to its most valuable use. Current price in an exit
market is more future-oriented than current price in an
entry market if the asset's presence is expected to affect
future sales.

5. The only measure of an asset that is more relevant to
cash-flow-oriented decisions than the cash flow that could
be enjoyed at the measurement date is direct contractual
evidence of the cash flow that will occur. Considering the
waiting period, or financing cost during the holding period,
discounted future cash flow is the ultimate relevant measurement of a noncash asset.

This chapter has dealt with the relevance of measurement
methods to cash-flow-oriented decisions. We have attempted to
explain those linkages between measurement methods that provide
the economic basis for acceptance of surrogates for discounted
future cash flows. If this approach seems complicated, you can
fall back on two simple tests of the relevance of financial information:

(a) If you were a partner in a business and had an agreement
to either buy your partner's interest or sell your interest
to him at book value according to the balance sheet, which
measurement method would you consider most equitable
for application to any particular asset? Your sense of equity
will rarely lead you to an irrelevant measurement method.

(b) If you were the manager of the business for the current
period only, which measurement method should be used
for determining the beginning and ending values on which
the calculation of income is based, assuming that your
performance is appraised on the basis of reported income
and that you are honest?

In the next chapter, the discussion of measurement method

choices will be expanded to take into consideration criteria other
than relevance.

The Magnate-Financio Case

Once upon a time male twins were born to a famous merchandising magnate. As they reached manhood their father refused to take them into the business because they quarrelled incessantly. So I. Magnate and J. Magnate each, independently, decided to start their own businesses. The similarity of their backgrounds resulted in their making identical decisions in forming and operating their businesses except that I. Magnate selected "Shorty" Financio as his financial vice-president while J. hired "Slim" Financio. Shorty talked I. into a major one-year bank loan at 6% because he thought interest rates would fall, while Slim convinced J. that the issuance of 20-year bonds at 6% was the way to go because interest rates were going to rise.

Lo and behold! Interest rates rose and Shorty issued 8%, 19-year bonds at the end of the year to replace his 6% bank loan.

Query 1: Which financial manager was most successful in year 1? How should this be reflected in the financial statements just before Shorty's refinancing?

Query 2: Immediately after Shorty's refinancing, is there a difference in the obligations of the two companies? If so, how should it be reflected?

Historical Cash Flows

Introduction

Information regarding the past typically is consulted by those concerned with the future. Thus, as investors seek to predict both cash flows from the firm to themselves and cash flows to the firm (at least to their particular investment horizon, if they have one), information regarding the firm's past cash flows is sought. To the extent that an enterprise's activities tend to continue beyond the reporting date, the past has relevance to the future. Investors' interest in past cash flows becomes apparent to anyone thinking about accounting to investors, so it was a charter feature of decision-usefulness theory. In addition, investors may be concerned with their firm's liquidity; it must survive in the short run to provide pay-offs in the long run. This is another reason for investors' interest in historical cash flows.

A long-standing issue involving the reporting of historical cash flows is the choice of breadth of the net asset pool on which to focus. Prior to the increase in interest in the subject in the 1960s, "funds statements," or statements of sources and uses of funds, that appeared in corporate annual reports and text books usually focused on net working capital. In ATOATI, however, I chose net short-term monetary assets as the focal pool. In 1966, after finding a disappointing level of understanding of the nature and significance of "funds flows," among my students, I tried to show the possible roles and limitations of alternative concepts of asset flows from operations (1966). There I defined cash flow, quick flow (net quick assets), working flow (net working capital), and earnings (net assets) and argued that information related to the broader funds concepts was more *relevant* to the decisions of those investors concerned with stocks and flows of wealth but that statements based on the narrower concepts provided more *reliable* information because they avoided the more difficult measurement problems. For example, measurements of nonmonetary assets do not affect quick flow; measurements of plant assets do not affect working flow. In Chapter XII of MAD, I added subjective earnings and called attention to the susceptibility of each of the flow concepts to operating manipulation and accounting manipulation.

The date of the 1989 article reprinted here falls outside the period in which the decision-usefulness theory was developed, but I have chosen to include it because I think it contributes something to the issue of the respective roles of cash flow accounting and wealth accounting. In Chapter XII of MAD, I had developed the idea that cash flow accounting was relevant to users' assessments of firm liquidity and the

245

risk of encountering a period of illiquidity. In the 1989 article, I sought to distinguish between the roles of cash flow accounting and "as-is exit values" of net asset items in elucidating liquidity and the role of accounting for cash flow potential by the evidential approach in measuring wealth and income.

The Accounting Review

| VOL. XLI | JULY 1966 | No. 3 |

Alternative Asset Flow Concepts

George J. Staubus

THE purposes of this paper are to clarify the relationships between several asset flow concepts and to explore their potential uses. The concepts discussed are earnings, the working capital concept of funds flow from operations, the net quick asset version of funds flow from operations, and a literal cash flow from operations. We shall commence with an elementary exposition of the four concepts and illustrations of the related financial statements. This presentation also serves to explain the conceptual advantages of each step in the conversion of a cash statement to an earnings statement in an attempt to satisfy the fundamental curiosity of owners about their enterprise. A more technical explanation of the four concepts and their differences, with emphasis on the balance sheet items that need not be measured as the concept is narrowed from earnings back to cash flow, follows. Next, we turn our attention to selected decision situations in which one or more of the four types of flow data may be helpful. Finally, we focus attention on the problems of measurement and lack of comparability that affect the more refined flow concepts.

THE DEVELOPMENT OF FLOW STATEMENTS

The relationships between several asset flow concepts may be visualized by thinking of the development of an accounting system by a businessman who has had no training in accounting. The necessity for remaining solvent and his acquaintance with the value of money are likely to lead such an individual to maintain some kind of records of cash receipts and disbursements. The separation of receipts and disbursements and some breakdowns of both follow from the above considerations; a statement similar to Exhibit I could be the culmination of the businessman's first efforts at accounting.

George J. Staubus is Associate Professor of Accounting in the School of Business Administration, University of California, Berkeley.

247

EXHIBIT I
HYPOTHETICAL COMPANY
Cash Receipts and Disbursements
1966

EXHIBIT I
HYPOTHETICAL COMPANY
Cash Receipts and Disbursements
1966

Receipts:

Cash sales and collections from customers. . .	$11,600
Collections of interest, etc.	450
Investments by creditors and owners.	2,000
Sales of unneeded plant and other facilities. .	500
Total cash receipts.	$14,550

Disbursements:

For merchandise.	$8,400
For selling and administrative costs.	1,400
Interest.	400
Income taxes.	500
Capital expenditures for new plant facilities	2,300
Repayments to creditors.	600
Dividends.	350
Total cash disbursements.	$13,950
Net change in cash balance.	$ 600
Cash balance, January 1.	500
Cash balance, December 31.	$ 1,100

After some experience with the cash receipts and disbursements statements, the fledgling businessman may begin to see some relationships between cash movements other than their direction. As he, and perhaps his banker, attempt to foresee the

results of operations, he may feel the need to distinguish between those cash transactions that tend to follow patterns, even though somewhat roughly, and those that show little tendency to recur. He may see that some categories of transactions keep happening over and over in sufficiently regular patterns that they can be used as indications of what is going to happen in the future. Such events may be distinguished, in the summary cash statement, from the non-recurring cash transactions. Also, inflows and outflows of cash in financing transactions could be paired on the statement as could receipts and disbursements in the sales and purchases of property other than the stock-in-trade of the business, especially long-lived items used in conducting the major activities of the organization. Such pairings would help the reader to comprehend the impact of financing activities and capital expenditures on the firm. Consideration of these points could easily lead to a report similar to Exhibit II.

Working with cash flow statements may

EXHIBIT II
HYPOTHETICAL COMPANY
Cash Flow Statement
1966

Routine operations:
Inflows:

Cash sales and collections from customers.	$11,600	
Collections of interest, etc.	450	$12,050

Outflows:

Cash disbursements for merchandise.	8,400	
Selling and administrative costs.	1,400	
Interest paid. . . . . :	400	
Income taxes paid.	500	10,700
Net recurring cash flow.		$ 1,350
Dividends paid.		350
Net recurring cash flow retained.		$ 1,000

Financing transactions:

Cash invested by creditors and owners.	$ 2,000	
Repayments to creditors.	600	1,400

Capital expenditures, net of cash receipts from dispositions of unneeded facilities ($500)   (1,800)

Net change in cash balance.		$ 600
Balance January 1.		500
Balance December 31.		$ 1,100

EXHIBIT III
HYPOTHETICAL COMPANY
Quick Asset Flow Statement
1966

Routine operations:		
Inflows:		
Sales of merchandise and related services....................................	$12,000	
Interest accrued on investments, etc.......................................	400	$12,400
Outflows:		
Purchases of merchandise..	$ 8,700	
Routine purchases of supplies and services................................	1,600	
Interest cost accrued...	400	
Income taxes for the year...	600	11,300
Net recurring quick asset flow...		$ 1,100
Dividends declared...		300
Net recurring quick asset flow retained..................................		$ 800
Financing transactions:		
Long-term investments by creditors and owners............................	$ 2,000	
Current maturities and premature retirements of debts......................	600	1,400
Capital expenditures, net of receipts from sales of unneeded facilities ($500).............		(1,800)
Net change in net quick assets..		$ 400
Net quick asset balance January 1 (credit)................................		(100)
Net quick asset balance December 31.....................................		$ 300

give the businessman ideas for further improvements. If, for example, someone asks him how business was last month he may find himself answering, "Not bad, according to our cash flow statement, but I'm not happy with the month's operations." "Why not?" "Well, I'm afraid our sales took a beating. Traffic in the store was light and goods piled up in the reserve stocks. This month's cash collections on account may be way down, but we won't know until we make up the cash flow statement at the end of the month." A few situations like this could give our potential accountant the idea that he could record both the inflows relating to sales and the outflows needed to produce the sales more promptly if he did not wait for the cash movements to occur.

The advantages of knowing more about what his customers owe him and what he owes suppliers could provide additional incentive to convert to an accrual basis of accounting. Sales, whether the sale price has been collected or not, would replace cash receipts; purchases of goods and services would be recognized as the major offsetting group of transactions. The budding accountant may not think of it this way, but he would be recognizing increases in net quick assets as favorable flows and decreases in net quick assets as unfavorable flows. Exhibit III reflects this approach to the reporting of asset flows.

Further experience with asset flow statements as representations of the firm's operations may disclose deficiencies in the quick flow statement. A few cases of substantial changes in inventories, which reflect poor matching of receipts of purchased goods with shipments of goods sold, may suggest the need for a change in the procedure for accounting for the cost of merchandise. Despite steady sales and steady prices, heavy purchasing could result in a negative net recurring quick flow in a short period, or slow purchasing could result in a bulge in the net recurring flow.

The alert manager-accountant might see that his flow statement would give a better indication of operating success if it in-

EXHIBIT IV
HYPOTHETICAL COMPANY
Working Capital Flow Statement
1966

Routine operations:
Inflows:

Sales of merchandise and related services	$12,000	
Interest accrued on investments, etc.	400	$12,400
Outflows:		
Cost of goods sold	$ 8,000	
Selling and administrative costs	1,600	
Interest cost accrued	400	
Income taxes for the year	600	10,600
Net recurring working capital flow		$ 1,800
Dividends declared		300
Net recurring working capital flow retained		$ 1,500

Financing transactions:

Long-term investment by creditors and owners	$ 2,000	
Current maturities and premature retirements of debt	600	1,400
Capital expenditures, net of receipts from sale of unneeded facilities ($500)		(1,800)
Net change in working capital		$ 1,100
Working capital balance January 1		2,400
Working capital balance December 31		$ 3,500

cluded deductions from sales for the cost of those goods sold rather than those purchased. He might also recognize a similar, although less significant, improvement from spreading the cost of such things as insurance coverage evenly over the periods rather than deducting them when purchased. If his business operations involved frequent cases of collections from customers prior to the provisions of goods or services to those customers, he may feel that he is not entitled to report the favorable flow until the related unfavorable flows can be matched with it; the deferral of credits to revenue may be appropriate. The merits of matching costs with revenues in these ways might have sufficient appeal to entice the recordkeeper to adopt the deferral technique of accounting for inventories of merchandise, short-term prepayments of routine operating costs, and precollections from customers.

To defer the reporting of such transactions until some time after the cash movement permits a more logical cause-and-

effect matching on the working flow statement than on the previous flow statements. This is shown in Exhibit IV above.

The adoption of the accrual and deferral techniques of accounting for short-lived assets has resulted in an asset flow statement that appears to have important advantages over the cash statements of Exhibits I and II, but the stockholders and other readers of these statements may feel that the net recurring working capital flow could be converted to a figure that would provide a better indication of the management's success in serving the owners' objectives if it took into account the consumption of long-lived assets. While the working flow statement shows the application of working capital to acquire plant assets, it does not include those transactions in the computation of net recurring working capital flow and it does not give any indication of whether the acquisitions were greater or less than the consumption of such properties by use or wastage during the reporting period. A measure of the

EXHIBIT V
HYPOTHETICAL COMPANY
Earnings and Net Worth Statement
1966

Revenues:		
Sales of merchandise and related services..	$12,000	
Interest and miscellaneous earnings..	400	
Total revenues..		$12,400
Expenses:		
Cost of goods sold..	$ 8,000	
Selling expenses..	1,000	
Administrative expenses..	1,400	
Income taxes..	700	
Interest expenses..	500	
Total expenses..		11,600
NET EARNINGS...		$ 800
Extraordinary charges and credits:		
Loss on sale of real property..	$ (400)	
Gain on premature retirement of debt..	300	(100)
Dividends declared..		(300)
Proceeds of stock issue...		2,000
Net change in stockholders' equity...		$ 2,400
Stockholders' equity January 1...		10,000
Stockholders' equity December 31...		$12,400

consumption and loss of service potential embodied in long-lived assets would seem to be an appropriate deduction from revenues in the computation of a net recurring flow to be used as an indicator of the effects of routine operations on the owners' interests.

While this may seem to be a more difficult accounting task than the previous requirements (we assume have been adopted), the accountant may feel that he can improve the statement if he simply deducts from the revenues of each period during which a long-lived asset is expected to be used a systematically computed portion of the acquisition cost of that asset. The accountant who has worked out such a refined system may also see the need for recognizing some costs that have not yet been paid for and do not require payment in the near future. Some types of pension plans and gimmicks permitting postponement of income for taxing purposes are relevant examples. When such factors have been taken into consideration a net asset flow statement, or earnings statement, reflecting greater use of the accrual and deferral techniques, may be prepared as in Exhibit V immediately above.

FOUR RECURRING ASSET FLOW CONCEPTS

Exhibits II through V are organized so as to distinguish between recurring and non-recurring flows. The reflection of such a distinction on the statement implies that the accountant believes that some categories of transactions can be projected more reliably than others. The analyst who is interested in predicting these transactions is likely to start with historical data on the amounts of such transactions and make such adjustments as he sees fit in order to estimate the future amounts. Nonrecurring transactions, on the other hand, are not so accurately predicted by this approach. Instead of projecting from historical data, the analyst is more likely to make an independent estimate based upon evidence relating specifically to the future, such as contractual debt maturities and capital expenditure budgets, rather than start with last year's amounts and adjust them for anticipated changes. This is not a black and white distinction, of course, but it may well be a usefully realistic distinction.

Recurring events exclude financing transactions involving principal amounts as well as purchases and sales of noncurrent assets and marketable securities. Recurring flows typically should include charges for income taxes and for interest on debt as well as dividends on preferred stock. Financial credits, such as interest and dividends on investment securities, are also included in the recurring operations category. This leaves the analyst with figures that are relevant to the common stockholder: earnings to the common equity and other asset flow figures that are comparable in this respect. The concept of income as a return on owners' investment is not emphasized in this approach, although it would be the same as earnings if there were no preferred shares outstanding. Nor is the broader concept of income as a return on all long-term capital featured.

This may be a good stage in our discussion at which to pause to define the four concepts we have been developing.

1. *Earnings* is the term for the net change in net assets (assets less liabilities) produced by recurring operations.
2. *Working flow*, or current flow, is the net change in net current assets, or working capital, in recurring operations.
3. *Quick flow* is the net change in net short-term monetary assets, or net quick assets, from recurring operations.
4. *Cash flow*, or literal cash flow, is the net change in cash from recurring operations.

Now let us examine the technical features of these concepts.

Earnings is the broadest of the group. If one were to condense all of the double-entry system into two accounts, one for net-asset items (assets and liabilities) and one for net worth, earnings would be the net change in either of these accounts from recurring operations. Transactions such as dividends on common stock, issue and acquisition by the corporation of its own stock, catastrophic losses, windfall gains, and so on would change these two accounts but would not be included in the earnings concept because they do not tend to recur in a reliable pattern. We could say that earnings occur in transactions that change net assets, or we could say earnings involve transactions that change the net worth. However, for comparison with the alternative asset flow concepts, we can define earnings as the changes in net assets from recurring operations.

Working flow (or perhaps current flow) deals with a portion of the balance sheet that is narrower than net assets. Current assets or current liabilities must be involved in working flows, and, as in the case of earnings, the transaction must affect the net of the category. Offsetting debits and credits within the category, such as collections of accounts receivable, are not working flows; nor are transactions recorded by offsetting debits and credits entirely outside the working capital area, such as depreciation expense. Neither the debit to depreciation expense, which will end up in retained earnings, nor the offsetting credit to the contra fixed asset account affects working capital. This also holds for expenses credited to accounts such as allowance for depletion, unamortized bond discount, deferred income tax liability, and estimated long-term pension liability.

To state this point more concisely, no expense credited to a noncurrent account affects the working flow, and no revenue debited to a noncurrent account affects the working flow.[1] As a corollary of the preceding statement, we may say that the degree of accuracy or error involved in entries recording expenses credited to noncurrent balance sheet accounts does not affect the working flow figure. Stated in terms of balance sheet accounts, the measurement of noncurrent assets and liabilities does not affect the working flow.

Quick flow is the term suggested for the net change in net short-term monetary assets (net quick assets) from recurring operations. Monetary assets include cash and claims to cash such as various types of receivables and bonds owned. Monetary liabilities are obligations to pay cash at some future time. The amount of net short-term monetary assets is the excess of current monetary assets over current monetary liabilities, sometimes called net quick assets; this amount is frequently negative. The most common items included in working capital but excluded from net quick assets are inventories of commodities, short-term prepayments and, among the liabilities, deferred credits to revenue, such as unearned rentals received in advance. Looking at related transactions, we can see that purchases of merchandise do not affect net current assets (working capital), so they are not a component of working flows; but they do affect net quick assets (by credits to accounts payable or cash), so they are negative quick flows.

The shipment of goods to customers, on the other hand, affects working capital and working flows, as well as earnings; but since it does not affect net quick assets, it is not a quick flow. Likewise, prepaying insurance is a quick-flow transaction but not a working-flow transaction; the expiration of prepared insurance is a working-flow transaction but not a quick-flow transaction. Also, collecting rent in advance affects net quick assets but not working capital; earning the precollected rent affects working flow but not quick flow. All of this means that the measurement of the balance-sheet quantities of inventories, prepayments, and deferred credits to revenue affect working flow and earnings but not quick flow. To the extent that we are dissatisfied with inventory measurements in accounting we may lean towards the quick-flow concept rather than working flow. (Measurements of prepayments and short-term deferred credits to revenue are rarely cause for concern.)

Cash flow should be used to refer to changes in cash from recurring operations. It is a recurring asset flow concept comparable to quick flow, working flow, and earnings. Cash flow differs from quick flow in that collections of receivables that were created in revenue transactions are cash flows, while the creation of those receivables were quick flows. Likewise, payments of payables are negative cash flows, while the creation of payables through purchases and many expense transactions are negative quick flows. The most difficult common measurement that affects quick flows that is bypassed by switching to the cash-flow concept is the estimation of uncollectible accounts receivable. The normal adjusting entry to provide for uncollectibles records a quick-asset transaction but not a cash transaction.

[1] Similarly, any portion of a recurring credit to a current account that is offset by a charge to a noncurrent asset or liability account is a negative working flow item just like most expenses and any portion of a recurring charge to a current account that is offset by a credit to a noncurrent asset or liability is a positive working flow item, although this is a rare type of transaction. A good example of the former is the accrual of income tax payable in the later years of the life of an asset depreciated on a straight-line basis on the books but on a diminishing charge basis for tax returns by a firm practicing inter-period taxal location. The journal entry follows:

Dr. Federal income tax expense. . . . $2,500
Dr. Deferred Federal income tax
    liability.   500
    Cr. Federal income tax payable. $3,000

The entire $3,000 is a negative fund flow, not merely the amount of the expense.

EXHIBIT VI
HYPOTHETICAL COMPANY
Asset Flow Statements
1966

	Earnings	Working Flow	Quick Flow	Cash Flow
Inflows:				
From customers				
Sales..	$12,000	$12,000	$12,000	
Collections...................................				$11,600
On investments				
Accrued.....................................	400	400	400	
Collected....................................				450
Total inflows...........................	$12,400	$12,400	$12,400	$12,050
Outflows:				
Merchandise:				
Cost of merchandise sold......................	$ 8,000	$ 8,000		
Purchases....................................			$ 8,700	
Paid to suppliers.............................				$ 8,400
Depreciation..................................	600			
Pensions				
Funded......................................	600	600	600	600
Additional...................................	200			
Other operating costs..........................	1,000	1,000	1,000	800
Interest				
Nominal.....................................	400	400	400	400
Amortization of discount and issue expense.......	100			
Income taxes				
Per returns..................................	600	600	600	
Deferred....................................	100			
Paid..				500
Total outflows...........................	$11,600	$10,600	$11,300	$10,700
Net inflows..............................	$ 800	$ 1,800	$ 1,100	$ 1,350

Further elucidation of the four concepts may result from the juxtaposition of the flow statements of Exhibits II through V as shown in Exhibit VI above.

Inherent in these four definitions and the accompanying analysis of them are the reasons why earnings may not be the one and only useful asset flow concept. The measurement of the revenues and expenses that are offset in the calculation of earnings requires measurement of net assets (net worth), i.e. all assets and liabilities. Of all the measurement problems encountered by the accountant who is attempting to calculate earnings, those pertaining to noncurrent nonmonetary assets and noncurrent liabilities resulting from deferred payment of such expenses as pensions and income taxes are the most difficult.

Rather than undertake a digression to support this assertion, we will proceed on the assumption that the reader agrees that depreciation, depletion, amortization of leaseholds and intangible assets, income-tax allocation, and pension expenses constitute a package of problems that accountants would be very happy to avoid. Many users of the income statement would be just as pleased to be free of the uncertainties injected into the earnings figure by this group of measurement problems. Their yearning for an earnings concept that is free of the measurement errors and intercompany inconsistencies relating to noncurrent assets and liabilities may be so strong as to attract analysts to a working flow concept that is free of such defects. Unfortunately, the price of freedom from serious errors of measurement is loss of relevance to stockholders' interests. To accountants, this appears to be a classic case of throwing out the baby with the bath water; but to some readers of our statements it is a case of ranking reliability of calculation over conceptual relevance— a priority system with which adherents to historical cost ought to be sympathetic.

Just as the basic technical argument for relying upon working flow as opposed earnings is that working flow is free of the worst measurement errors and inconsistencies that affect earnings, one could also argue that quick flow is based on more reliable measurements than is working flow. Working flow is the net change in net current assets from recurring operations, while quick flow is the net change in net short-term monetary assets from recurring operations. Since the major items included in net current assets that are excluded in the computation of net quick assets are inventories, prepayments, and deferred credits to revenue, the switch from working flow to quick flow avoids the measurement problems pertaining to these specified items. If we feel that inventory valuation (or, less likely, the measurement of prepayments or deferred credits to revenue) is such a weak component of working flow accounting that it seriously limits the usefulness of the net recurring working flow, we might be just as happy to substitute the quick-flow concept.

Having side-stepped the problems of depreciation, depletion, amortization, and provisions for deferred tax and pension liabilities, etc., as well as the inventory valuation problem (by substituting quick flow for working flow), we have made the problems of calculating a net recurring flow a great deal more manageable. The most serious ones that remain are the estimation of such contra receivable items as uncollectibles, collection costs, and cash discounts to be taken by customers.

While these may not be cause for much concern in the typical case, firms that do a a great deal of installment-sales business may find that there is a considerable difference in the reliability of quick flows as compared with cash flows. Under such circumstances, the analyst may seriously consider switching from quick flow to cash flow (in the literal sense) as the starting point for his analysis.

The technical advantages and disadvantages of the several flow concepts may be summarized in a series of comparative statements.

1. If we substitute working flow for earnings we may gain by omitting our crude measurements of depreciation, depletion, amortization, and provisions for deferred liabilities; but we must recognize the disadvantage of completely ignoring capital consumption costs and the portions of pensions, income taxes, etc. that are not paid currently.

2. If we substitute quick flow for working flow, we may gain by eliminating dependence upon the valuation of inventories, prepayments, and deferred credits to revenue, but we expose the resulting net flow figure to the problems of mismatching of costs with revenues by failure to defer them when appropriate.

3. If we substitute cash flow for quick flow we may gain by avoiding the problems of valuation of receivables, but we lose the contribution to matching resulting from the use of the accrual method of recognizing revenues and costs.

4. To reverse the substitution, if we switch from cash flow to quick flow we gain better matching of costs and revenues through the use of the accrual technique, but must accept the problems of valuation of receivables.

5. If we substitute the more refined concept of working flow for quick flow, we gain the better matching contributed by short-term deferrals of merchandise costs,

prepayments of services, and revenue received in advance, but we take on the measurement difficulties relating to these deferrals, especially inventory valuation.

6. If we switch to earnings from working flow, we improve the relevance of the flow concept to investor's interests by providing for consumption of long-lived assets and for long-term delays in payment of some costs, but we must face up to the related measurement problems, especially depreciation.

From the point of view of the accountant who is considering the development of an accounting system by making improvements on a cash receipts and disbursements system, which refinements are worthwhile depend upon (1) the availability of the information needed to make the refinements, such as bases for estimating bad debts, collection costs and discounts to be taken by customers, and the service flow lives and patterns of depreciable assets; (2) the time (cost) required to make the refinements; and (3) the materiality of the differences between the refined flow concept (and related balance sheet data) and the cruder concept.

USES OF ASSET FLOW DATA

In this section we turn our attention to the uses of asset flow data. We shall relate the alternative asset flow concepts to several types of decisions frequently encountered by investors and managers. The discussion will focus on *conceptual relevance* of the data to the decision, or prediction, that has to be made without regard to the measurement problems associated with the calculation of the flows.

One broad category of decisions that are made partly on the basis of financial statement data is external investment decisions. Those deciding to invest or to refrain from investing, to sell or to hold their investment positions—any of these investors or prospective investors may be interested in the asset flows of the firm that is the object of their attention. One explanation of their interest utilizes the residual-equity point of view. The residual equity in a corporation is normally held by the common stockholders. It is the residual interest in assets remaining after deducting all prior claims, including those of preferred stockholders. Common stockholders, it may be argued, are vitally interested in their equity in the firm and in recent changes in that equity.

A measure of the recurring changes in the residual equity in the recent past is useful in predicting changes in the future. Earnings is such a measure. Further, the amount of the residual equity and the rate and direction of change in it are of great interest to other investors because the residual equity represents a buffer of assets available as a margin of safety protecting the senior investor. Preferred stockholders and creditors, also, are concerned about the amount and fluctuations in this buffer equity.

From this residual equity point of view, changes in all net asset items are significant. The most significant distinction, aside from direction of change, is between recurring and non-recurring changes. The form of an asset and the anticipated timing of its contributions to the cash balance are of lesser importance. Thus, the monetary-nonmonetary dichotomy and the current-noncurrent distinction need not be emphasized. Even the difference between assets and liabilities may be played down once we recognize the difference in mathematical sign applicable to them when they are merged into the net asset concept. A reduction in the service potential of patents or buildings owned is just as undesirable to the residual equityholders (in the long run) as a relinquishment of inventory or the incurrence of an obligation to pay cash. The net change in net assets produced by recurring operations, i.e. earnings, is the most relevant concept of recurring asset flows.

A quite different view emphasizes the investor's interest in his own cash receipts from the firm. If the investor expects cash transfers from the firm, he must predict the firm's cash balance (a useful measure of capacity to pay) at the future date or dates in which he is interested. Since a future cash balance at any particular date is determined by the present cash balance and cash receipts and disbursements between now and the future date, investors are interested in predicting the firm's future cash flows. Past recurring cash flows provide a starting point for predicting future recurring cash flows. (A capital expenditures plan and a balance sheet disclosing the due dates of major monetary assets and liabilities, particularly those involving nonrecurring cash movements, are additional indications of future cash flows.) We may conclude that a cash flow statement can be of help to investors.

Which of these views is more useful? One simple answer is that the residual equity point of view is more relevant to long-term investment decisions and that the cash view is more suitable for short-term analyses. In the long run all costs have to be covered, including depreciation; profitability is vital. The short-term investor, on the other hand, may do very well despite losses by the company if it can maintain its liquidity.

The Common Stockholder

Let us turn to the specific problem of the common-stock investor and his decision. Despite his interest in predicting cash dividends from the company, he may have relatively little interest in recent cash flows. The value of common stock typically depends upon a long view of the future. While the investor will not be able to enjoy the long-run benefits of holding the stock if the corporation does not survive the short run, the firm's inability to pay one quarterly dividend or even a bond interest payment, because of a liquidity deficiency, is not likely to threaten its survival if its earnings hold up.

The common-stock investor is almost certain to be more interested in predicting profitability than liquidity, and an accurate earnings statement is likely to be far more important to him than a cash flow statement or even a working flow or quick flow statement.

Investors in Fixed Income Securities

The purchaser of fixed income securities must give more attention to corporate liquidity than the common stock investor, because he presumably is more dependent upon steady income. The fixed income security analyst must give a great deal of attention to predicting the probability of the issuer's failing to make the regular income payments or the maturity payment (in the case of a security with a maturity date). Anticipated improvements in either profitability or liquidity are of much less interest than are potential reverses, particularly in liquidity. But it is also true that a temporary lack of liquidity is not likely to precipitate the ultimate financial disaster (business failure) as long as earnings are respectable. Both profitability and liquidity are of concern to the fixed income security analyst.

A popular test of the safety of a fixed income security is the times-interest-earned test. This measure gives the analyst an idea of the extent to which earnings could decline and still cover the periodic interest payments to the bond holder. A good case can be made for calculating the relationship between the net recurring working flow before interest, preferred dividends, and income taxes, and the bond interest cost—the number of times bond interest is covered by working flow. The major consideration in bond analysis is to judge the firm's ability to meet its fixed obligations under the *worst* conditions that the firm is likely to face during the life of the bonds or as far ahead as the analyst cares to look. Since poor operating results usually involve a reduction in the volume of business, replacement of fixed assets can probably be drastically cut back temporarily under such conditions; very little or no provision for consumption of fixed assets need be made in calculating the flow of assets available to meet the fixed charges. The analyst is not so concerned about the firm's ability to replace its plant assets as he is about meeting the current operating costs requiring working capital. Under these circumstances, depreciation is a distinctly lower-ranking cost.

The Preferred Stockholder

A similar approach may be taken to preferred stock dividend coverage. The number of times that the dividend is covered by working flow is perhaps as relevant a test as the number of times that the dividend is earned. Both of these tests may be used because both liquidity and profitability are required if the preferred dividend is to be safe. Of course, the preferred dividend may be paid even if not earned, but the fixed income investor can not count on such an attitude on the part of the board of directors. We conclude that both working flow and earnings are relevant to the fixed income security investment decision.

The Short-Term Creditor

The short-term creditor is much more interested in forecasting the liquidity of the firm than its profitability. He must attempt to predict the firm's capacity to pay at a specific time in the near future. Such a prediction may be based on short-term balance sheet items and the rate of

net recurring flow of net short-term assets. Working flow, quick flow or cash flow is almost certain to be more relevant than earnings. For example, the analyst may compute the firm's quick ratio and its net quick assets. If the latter is negative, it might be related to the monthly net recurring quick flow to determine the number of months required to pay off the net quick liabilities if the rate of quick flow were to continue (and if no nonrecurring quick flows occur). Or the analyst may prefer to relate the net quick liabilities to the rate of working flow in order to allow for the "normalization" of purchases. If there is, or is likely to be, an unusually wide discrepancy between quick flows and cash flows, the latter may be of considerable interest instead of, or in addition to, working flow or quick flow. Earnings is unlikely to be the flow concept most relevant to the short-term credit decision, although it should not be ignored.

The Corporate Point of View

These discussions of the relevance of alternative flow concepts to investment decisions suggest that no one of the concepts is always the most relevant; any one of them may be the first choice of the investment analyst, depending upon the circumstances surrounding the decision. While the discussion emphasized the point of view of the external analyst, we should recognize that the corporate treasurer must make a very similar analysis. What is bad for the investor is likely to be bad for the corporation. For example, the corporate management is no more eager to issue bonds that it cannot service than an investor is to buy them. A satisfactory financing arrangement must be satisfactory to both parties. However, we should keep in mind the nature of the financial position that requires the issuance of securities.

Boards of directors do not decide to borrow money or issue securities to proide retained earnings; they do so to raise ash that is needed to supplement the flow rom operations. A working flow projection may indicate a probable deficiency in working capital that should be met by intermediate or long-term financing. (Short-term borrowing does not increase net working capital.) A cash flow projection may show the need for a short-term loan. Earnings projections, on the other hand, cannot shed much light on the need for financing, although they may give a good indication of the reception the firm's securities will get in the money market—specially the long-term market.

We now turn to internal decisions about the uses of corporate funds. Since the various possible uses of funds compete with each other, decisions in this area have some tendency to merge into one grand determination of the distribution of the available funds among the several uses. Nevertheless, we must recognize that each use has its own peculiar factors that are relevant to the decision. For example, the declaration of cash dividends is usually based on consideration of both liquidity and profitability. Boards of directors usually give weight to both earnings and the availability of cash. If they foresee a cash stringency in the near future, it may affect their decision. For this purpose, a cash flow, quick flow, or working flow analysis is likely to be useful in addition to an earnings statement.

Capital expenditures is another common use of liquid funds. One major type of information that is relevant to capital expenditure decisions is differential cash flows—projected increases and decreases in cash operating costs or increases in both revenues and cash costs that are expected to result from the initial outlay. In addition, some consideration must be given to the availability of the funds needed for the initial outlay and the effect of the proposed outlay on the firm's ability to meet all of

its obligations as they come due. This requires an analysis of future liquid flows; past and/or projected statements of cash flows, quick flows, or working flows are likely to be more valuable than earnings statements.

The retirement of debt or stock is another possible use of funds. A decision on this question, aside from the incremental analysis needed to establish its desirability, requires consideration of liquidity. The management must decide whether it can spare the cash required, and in order to make this decision it needs to analyze future sources and uses of cash. Projected profits are not enough to justify retirement of securities if the profits will have to be reinvested, and lack of profits need not deter the management from contracting its capital structure if the cash needed to accomplish it will not be required for other purposes. A contracting firm may not need to provide for replacement of plant assets.

To summarize this discussion of the relevance of several asset flow concepts to selected decisions, we may say that some decisions require heavy emphasis on predictions of profitability, some require that major weight be given to predictions of liquidity, while others require predictions of both. Of the four asset flow concepts we have presented for consideration in this paper, earnings is the only one that purports to measure profitability while the other three relate more closely to liquidity. Accordingly, we conclude that all four of our asset flow measures are conceptually relevant to the decisions facing users of financial statements. Next, we shall consider the practical problems of applying the concepts.

ASSET FLOWS—MEASUREMENT,
CONSISTENCY, AND
UNIFORMITY

Conceptual relevance is an important attribute of a financial datum which is to be used in making a decision. Accuracy is an equally important attribute. A beautiful concept cannot justify the trust of the decision maker if the accountant cannot obtain accurate perceptions that will permit him to execute the concept. Theory without measurement is no better than measurement without theory.

Of the four flow concepts we have discussed in preceding pages, cash flow is the most easily measured. While one may encounter problems in the measurement of cash receipts and disbursements, surely the reader will accept the above conclusion without requiring consideration of those problems. We may, of course, find it difficult to distinguish between recurring and nonrecurring movements, but this same problem arises in the application of any of the flow concepts.

The timing of cash transactions may result in poorer comparability than would be obtained by recognition of events on an accrual basis. For example, the month of July may have five weekly payroll dates while August has only four, while next year July may have four and August five. This makes it difficult to visualize trends from month to month and year to year. Also, a cash basis of accounting for the results of routine operations provides the opportunity for control over the reported results by juggling the timing of cash payments of accounts payable.

The opportunities for manipulation of the reported results may not be quite so great when the other flow concepts are used, although we must recognize that the timing of purchases permits this type of control over reported quick flow. Working flow and earnings may be manipulated in some firms by the use of specific identification of inventory units, by the timing of end-of-year purchases on Lifo, and by the range of judgment that may be applied in writing down obsolete, slow-moving, damaged goods, etc. On the inflow side,

quick flow, working flow, and earnings may be influenced by liberal or conservative provisions for bad debts and, in many firms, by some degree of control over billing dates. However, we should recognize that cash flow is typically the most susceptible to manipulation of any of the asset flow concepts.

Quick flow reporting introduces one group of substantial measurement issues—those pertaining to the valuation of receivables. Since the amount of the inflow in a sale is the amount of the asset that came into the firm, the measurement of the amount of that asset is a prerequisite to the preparation of a quick flow statement. While we are accustomed to conditions under which we can measure accounts receivable to within one per cent of the amounts to be collected, the recent experience of Brunswick Corporation, involving a $111 million additional provision for the uncollectibility of receivables, most of which were on the books at the previous statement date, indicates that serious errors can be made in the measurement of trade receivables. Payables generally are easier to value.

Alternative generally accepted accounting principles play a modest role in reducing the intercompany comparability of net recurring quick flows. Grady lists five areas in which alternatives are available that affect quick flows.[2] Two relate to the timing of the recognition of the basic revenue flows, two relate to sales and purchase discounts, and the fifth involves accounting for property taxes. The last three are unlikely to result in a material lack of comparability, but the alternative methods of revenue recognition could make a great deal of difference in times of rapid change in the volume of business.

[2] Paul Grady, *Inventory of Generally Accepted Accounting Principles for Business Enterprises*, Accounting Research Study No. 7 (American Institute of Certified Public Accountants, 1965), pp. 373–7.

The working flow concept involves the ccountant in inventory valuation. Other measurement problems related to working ow in addition to all of those connected ith quick flow, include some relatively nmaterial ones pertaining to short-term repayments, such as prepaid advertising, nd those related to nonmonetary liabilities such as deferred credits to revenue and stimated liabilities on warranties. While hese other nonmonetary working capital omponents sometimes involve some ineresting and serious problems of measurement, the inventory area is sufficient to indicate the defects, from the point of view of he user of financial statements, that are icked up by broadening the funds concept o include nonmonetary working capital tems.

At this point in our deliberations, we hould note that as we substitute a more elevant flow concept we find accountants pplying less relevant measurement techniques. The cash flow concept requires use f only the most impeccable of measurement methods—counting the face value of noney. This method can be applied with reat accuracy and it measures a quality— resent purchasing power—that is highly elevant to the managers and investors vho may be using the data to make a decision.

The quick flow concept requires the deermination of the future cash flows that vill be involved in existing contractual obligations of, or to, the firm. These mounts must then be discounted at an appropriate discount rate to obtain their resent values. These procedures provide opportunities for error, a common one being failure to discount for the waiting period. These errors usually are not serious, although they certainly can be, but they definitely result in less accurate measurements than are made of cash and, if timing s ignored by substituting estimated future cash flows for their present values, the evi- dence being utilized can be said to be less relevant to the needs of decision makers.[3]

The working flow concept requires major concessions in the realm of measurements. The nonmonetary items are not subject to measurement by the highly relevant techniques applicable to monetary assets and liabilities. Net realizable value and replacement cost are sometimes used for inventories, but most goods are valued at some version of historical cost. Net realizable value is both current and forward looking, replacement cost is current and backward looking, and historical cost is both noncurrent and backward looking—the least relevant of all the accepted measurement methods from the point of view of decision makers. The measurements of cost of goods sold made in current accounting practice may be characterized as irrelevant measurements of a relevant flow, whereas the purchases figures that go into the quick flow computation are based on relevant measures of an irrelevant concept.

Grady lists seven cases of alternative generally accepted accounting principles that affect working flow; five of these also affect quick flow and have been previously mentioned. One of the others is a relatively minor one—the choice between carrying spare machinery parts as inventory items or depreciating them as fixed assets. The seventh—really a whole group of alternative situations—is the big one: the whole field of inventory valuation. Included in this group are (1) the choice of assumption as to the flow of costs (Fifo, Lifo, etc.); (2) the choice of standard cost or "actual" cost; (3) the choice of the portion of fixed overhead that may be included in inventory values; (4) the choice of applying the lower of cost or market rule on an item-by-item class, or total basis; and (5) the choice of carrying inventories at sale price or cost

---

[3] We believe that the valuation of receivables and payables by discounting is a part of generally accepted accounting theory.

in some industries, such as mining and meat packing.

In addition to accepted alternatives, managements choosing the Lifo cost flow assumption have an opportunity to control cost of goods sold to some extent by shifting the timing of purchases from period to period. "Dipping into" Lifo inventories also results in lack of comparability between periods and between firms. Fifo contributes its share of problems too. If the carrying costs of an aging inventory are not capitalized and/or if prices change substantially over the years it takes to develop the desired flavor, in some industries the cost of goods sold on a Fifo basis may be a poor measure of the outflow of service potential related to the shipment of goods to customers.

The measurement of earnings opens Pandora's box to accountants. In Grady's list of situations in which alternative methods of accounting are generally accepted, there are five that affect quick flow but not cash flow, two (including the group of inventory alternatives) that affect working flow but not quick flow, and twenty-one that affect earnings but not working flow. Among these were situations relating to accounting for pensions, income-tax allocation, the investment credit, depreciation and depletion methods and rates, intangibles, research, exploration and development costs, investments in unconsolidated affiliates, and business combinations. When we add to this list of alternatives the uniform practice of adhering to historical cost[4] in accounting for noncurrent assets—a uniform practice with varying undesirable effects upon the earnings of different firms and years—we can see that the concept of earnings is not measured as precisely and uniformly as the other flow concepts. Whether or not these

practical limitations offset its superior conceptual relevance to many decision situations requires a balancing that we must leave to the reader.

CONCLUSION

The value of an asset flow concept depends upon its relevance to the problems facing decision makers and on the accuracy and uniformity with which it is applied. Accounting practices include many examples of rejection of a relevant concept in favor of a less relevant one for the sake of accuracy and objectivity in the necessary measurements. The "cost principle" is the most prominent example of this priority arrangement. Accountants cannot argue that the cost of an asset is forever relevant to the problems facing readers of financial statements but they do argue that cost can be measured with greater accuracy and objectivity than a more relevant concept such as net realizable value or replacement cost.

Similarly, when choosing an asset flow concept for reporting to investors, or for reporting to management, the accountant may not choose the most relevant concept if it is too difficult to apply. We found that no one asset flow concept is most relevant to all decisions commonly made by readers of financial statements. Furthermore, the measurement difficulties and lack of comparability of earnings and, to a lesser extent, working flow calculations indicate that users of financial statements should ask accountants to give careful consideration to their choice of flow concepts to emphasize in financial statements. The proper choice is not obvious and is not always the same.

[4] We believe that it is generally accepted among accounting theorists that historical cost is often a poor basis of valuation.

ccounting and Business Research, Vol. 19, No. 74, pp. 161–169, 1989.

Cash Flow Accounting and Liquidity: Cash Flow Potential and Wealth

George J. Staubus*

Abstract—The persistence of a minority interest in 'cash flow accounting' alongside the dominant financial reporting pattern that gives cash flow statements a distinctly secondary role in the line-up of flow statements suggests that something is missing from the analyses of the interested parties. The major theme of this paper is that users rely on historical cash flow reporting for information relevant to projecting enterprise liquidity in the short run, and on financial statements based on accrual-deferral accounting for information relevant to their interest in wealth and income. An explicit distinction between the two accounting objectives (providing information for use in assessing future enterprise liquidity and providing information for use in assessing enterprise wealth and income and performance against investors' augmentation-of-wealth objective) is recommended as a basis for clarifying the issues. That distinction suggests the value of two quite different, but related, sets of data: historical cash flows and stocks and flows of cash potentials.

A number of accounting scholars have proposed that 'cash flow accounting' be emphasised more than has been common in conventional financial reporting. Lee (1972, 1981, 1984 and elsewhere) and Lawson (1971, 1978, 1985 and elsewhere) have been prominent among European advocates of cash flow accounting. The works of theorists advocating emphasis on forms of exit values (Chambers, 1966 and elsewhere; Sterling, 1979 and elsewhere) are related to the cash flow accounting proposals through their common concern with enterprise liquidity, or short-term capacity to pay. More recently, several researchers employing econometric techniques have tested securities market responses to flow variables other than conventional earnings; examples include Bowen, Burgstahler and Daley (1986, 1987); Rayburn (1986), and Wilson (1986, 1987). The cash flow issue refuses to go away.

Comparison of cash flow and exit value accounting ideas with more conventional accounting principles reveals deep-seated conflicts. It seems appropriate for one who has long argued for more emphasis on cash flows (Staubus, 1961 and elsewhere) to try once more to put the role of cash flows in financial reporting into perspective. In doing so, the contributions of Egginton (1984, 1985) and the value of his exchange with Lawson (1985) and Lee (1985) are acknowledged.

Most of these comments are intended as generally *descriptive* of pertinent financial and accounting practices observable in Western industrialised democracies, although the impracticality of pre-

cisely distinguishing between descriptive and normative statements is granted.

The conclusions, which are believed to be supported by the evidence presented, are (1) that *ex post* and *ex ante* cash flow reporting is valuable to those seeking to assess enterprise liquidity, (2) that liquidity and wealth should be distinguished more clearly, and (3) that the relationships between the key concepts and the role of cash flow potential have been neglected.

Premises

The starting point is a brief review of those features of investment activities and financial reporting that provide the base for an evaluation of the potential roles of reports on historical cash flows and on cash flow potentials.

Investment

The investment relationship is a reasonable place to commence an examination of the role of cash flow accounting in reporting to external parties. The essence of investment is the forgoing of present consumption of wealth for the purpose of enhancing future consumption (including bequests for consumption by beneficiaries). In a fundamental sense, all investors are individuals; business enterprises are only conduits. Investment success is defined as augmentation of the investor's stock of consumption purchasing power. That stock of consumption purchasing power may be under the direct control of the investor, or it may be managed by an agent—a manager of an investee enterprise.

In some cases, investments are divided into homogeneous units (shares, bonds) that are pub-

*George J. Staubus is a professor at the Graduate School of Business Administration, University of California at Berkeley.

ABR 19/74—E

licly traded, thus providing direct market price evidence of the investor's stock of consumption purchasing power—the value of the investment. In those cases, many investors seek additional evidence for assessing the value of their investments as a step towards investment decisions. In other cases, no market price for the investment is observable, so again investors seek evidence for assessing values of investments. In either case, the essence of investment value is potential consumption purchasing power, and conversion of that investment value embodied in a business enterprise to direct purchasing power in the hands of the investor depends on the enterprise's future capacity to pay. That dependency presumably explains investors' efforts to predict enterprise cash flows.

An investment analyst's predictions of cash flows may take various forms. First, the direct approach focusing on cash receipts and cash disbursements might be taken. Second, the dividend stream approach is used by many analysts (Hawkins and Campbell, 1978, p. 17). It is based on the idea that the shareholder's direct cash receipts (prior to sale of the shares) is in the form of dividends. Because dividends depend on enterprise cash flows, any well-supported projection of dividends must rest on a projection of the firm's capacity to pay—in cash, with rare exceptions. Third, the analyst may concentrate on predicting earnings (interpreted as cash flows normalised through the accrual-deferral process) and either assume that all revenues and expenses are realised in cash flows in the reporting period plus or minus an immaterial lead or lag, or adjust the predicted earnings for material discrepancies between earnings and cash flows. Any component of earnings that is not related to a recent past, current, or near future cash flow presumably is suspect. For example, if an accountant makes an upward revaluation of goodwill, the analyst is not likely to accept the offsetting entry as a component of earnings. (See Hawkins and Campbell, pp. 97–121, for other examples.) A common interpretation of certain earnings-cash flow discrepancies is as influences on the 'quality of earnings'. For example, if inflation is perceived as requiring expenditures for replacement in excess of reported cost of goods sold and depreciation, the quality of earnings is downgraded. In sum, whether the analyst thinks primarily in terms of earnings, dividends, or direct cash flows, the underlying phenomena of interest are enterprise cash flows. Prospective earnings that are not realisable in cash flows are not important to the investor. Discounting is appropriate in every case.

Many investors, of course, do not make the type of intensive analyses suggested here. They may rely on tips or qualitative judgments, or accept reported earnings without question for use in relative price-earnings assessments. But to the extent that the specific contents of financial statements are used by professional analysts in projecting the firm's capacity to meet investors' objectives, one or more versions of enterprise cash flows are the underlying phenomena of interest (Hawkins and Campbell, 1978; Hawkins et al., 1983). See Exhibit I for a summary of the relationship of earnings to share value that has underlain my own work in this area since 1961.

Financial Reporting

The decision-usefulness objective of financial reporting (Staubus, 1954, 1980) is taken for granted here, although its acceptance probably is not descriptive of practice. Perhaps those most interested in considering the uses of data on historical cash flows and on cash flow potentials are willing to accept that objective. The types of decisions that appear to be most prominent are the basic investment-disinvestment decisions, other contracting decisions, and control-oriented decisions—areas that clearly overlap and that focus on enterprise wealth and liquidity.[1] The investor's interpretation of enterprise wealth—a stock of potential consumption purchasing power—is accepted by those parties engaged in contracting and control decisions. In a money economy, enterprise wealth is interpreted as cash flow potential (Staubus, 1967, p. 660; 1977, p. 163; FASB, 1978, para. 41). The concept of cash flow potential is meant to embody the amount, timing, risk, and cost-of-capital features that determine the market value of a prospective cash flow stream. That interpretation of wealth is generally accepted, often without explicit articulation, in the world of finance (Brealey and Myers, 1984, p. 21; Copeland and Weston, 1979, p. 16). Assets are thought of as positive cash flow potentials; liabilities as negative cash flow potentials. Investors seek information regarding stocks and flows of the entity's cash flow potentials.

Investors and others making investment, contracting, and control-oriented decisions often are said to be concerned with the entity's 'performance' (Egginton, 1984). The meaning of performance is critical. Whether one visualises a corporate version of the medieval master-steward relationship, the principal/agent model, or the conventional owner/manager relationship, performance in the context of reporting to investors means achievement of investors' objectives—enhancement of future consumption—through augmentation of enterprise cash flow potential. Maintenance of liquidity is a means to that end. The cash flow potential interpretation of wealth is

---

[1]For a different but related view of the 'uses of information', see Butterworth, Gibbons and King (1982, pp. 9–17).

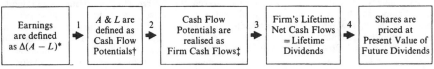

Exhibit I
Relationship Between Accounting Numbers and Share Prices

| Earnings are defined as $\Delta(A - L)^*$ | 1 → | $A \& L$ are defined as Cash Flow Potentials† | 2 → | Cash Flow Potentials are realised as Firm Cash Flows‡ | 3 → | Firm's Lifetime Net Cash Flows = Lifetime Dividends | 4 → | Shares are priced at Present Value of Future Dividends |

Link 1 is the Double Entry Tie of Income to Net Assets.
Link 2 is Realisation of Cash Flow Potentials, Subject to Measurement Errors and Omissions.
Link 3 is the Equality of a Firm's Lifetime Net Cash Inflows and Outflows.
Link 4 is the Present Value Model of Share Value.

*Earnings are defined as change in net assets other than in transactions with owners.
†Cash flow potential incorporates the amount, timing, risk, and cost-of-capital features that determine the market value of a prospective cash flow stream.
‡Accounting relies on imperfect evidence of cash flow potential for its measurements: cash at face value, estimated future cash flow, discounted estimated future cash flows, exit prices, current entry prices linked to exit prices in equilibrium, and old entry prices linked to current entry prices by the random walk pattern. Certain assets and liabilities are omitted due to unacceptable measurement weaknesses.

ccepted in the world of financial management.[2] *Corporate performance is measured by change in ash flow potential.*

Investors recognise the necessity for trading off isk and return. Information relevant to assessing isks—especially risk of loss of liquidity—is sought y investors. Therefore, information helpful in understanding and predicting the entity's liquidity s valued by investors and investor-oriented users of financial reports. The risk of illiquidity and ther risks involve uncertainties of many kinds, so t is difficult to specify standard measures of such isks or proper reporting of risk-relevant information. However, historical cash flow information is widely recognised as helpful in that regard.

Reasons for interest in cash flow accounting

Much attention has been given to the case for historical cash flow accounting in the last 15 years,

[2]In that portion of the world of finance that is oriented to securities markets, descriptive models of securities values clearly ocus on the discounting of future cash flows, as they have for several centuries. (See, for example, Isaac Newton (1686) and Eugen von Böhm-Bawerk (1891). The importance of future ash flows to portfolio managers may have increased in recent years as more of those managers have been driven by the esponsibility to provide the cash flows necessary to meet pension obligations. In the world of corporate financial management, the net present value model of investment project analysis emphasises management's overriding concern with inding projects that have net positive cash flow potential. Is here any significant evidence to challenge the acceptance of the ash flow potential interpretation of wealth and management performance in the business world?

so it is not necessary to go into great detail in this section. The works of G. H. Lawson and T. A. Lee have been especially prominent, and they extend well beyond the publications listed in the references at the end of this paper. Lee (1981) has argued for a combination of historical cash flow accounting and net realisable values assuming no continuity of enterprise activities (p. 164)—an information set that would appear to provide an excellent basis for 'liquidity management assessment' (p. 170). Staubus (1966, 1977) also deals with arguments pertaining to alternative asset flow concepts, especially flows of cash, net short-term monetary assets, net working capital, and net assets. The discussion in this section, however, is limited to historical cash flow accounting.

Departing from the descriptive mode for the present, the following observations might lead one toward historical cash flow accounting:

1. The entity's stock of cash at the reporting date is of interest because it represents the ultimate liquid asset. Interest in a stock might lead one to the related flows—how the stock arose.

2. Cash serves as the beginning and ending anchor points of sets of related activities viewed as cycles.

3. The role of historical cash flow information as a base on which to build cash flow projections is widely acknowledged. Cash flow projections are used by those who:
   (a) Are concerned about the firm's liquidity, financial flexibility and short-run survival;
   (b) Think of the firm's capacity to pay at any future time as dependent on its cash flows to that time.

4. Unreliability and lack of relevance of many measurements of net asset items—e.g., allocations of historical costs—and omission of many valuable resources and obligations from balance sheets, are recognised as weaknesses in the accrual/deferral measurements of wealth and income that make information on alternative stock/flow concepts helpful in assessing the entity's future capacity to pay. The superior reliability (observability, verifiability, representational faithfulness, neutrality) of historical cash flow data surely is a great—perhaps its greatest—strength.

The above considerations, no doubt augmented by others, justify the periodic reporting of a substantial amount of cash-oriented financial information. External reporting practices, for example those required by the Financial Accounting Standards Board's Statement No. 95 (1987), have responded to the indicated need.

The role of cash flow in financial reporting in the 1980s

Returning to the descriptive mode, this section includes observations regarding the roles for which historical cash flow information is widely accepted and a role for which it is not generally accepted, and why.

Acceptance of Historical Cash Flow Data: For Reporting on Liquidity

One can say with some assurance that cash flow reports, or flow reports on some other pool of relatively liquid assets, are widely accepted as helpful to those concerned with an enterprise's past and future liquidity. Information on historical flows is treated as a starting point for projecting cash flows, including dividends, interest payments, and principal payments to creditors. This includes judging the prospect for occurrence of a liquidity crisis. In addition, the information typically provided in cash flow statements regarding investing and financing transactions, operating cash flows, and changes in current asset and current liability items help the reader to understand the firm's activities and management's policies. If the conventional wisdom—that the two major operating objectives of business managers are to maintain liquidity and profitability—is true, cash flow reporting clearly provides information relevant to evaluations and projections of management's performance as measured by the liquidity objective, as noted by Lee (1985, pp. 93, 95).

A curious feature of the widely accepted notion that reporting flows of cash or a similar pool of liquid funds is worthwhile is that those advocating or requiring such reporting give little attention to the concept of liquidity. See, for example, FASB, 1987. An exception is Lee (1981, 1985) who does give considerable attention to the role of cash flow accounting in reporting on liquidity. Liquidity does not, however, tend to be viewed as something that exists, like wealth. Rather, it is seen as an intangible quality of a firm's financial position. The tangible version of liquidity is net liquid assets, which may be defined in relatively narrow or broader terms. Thus, the FASB, which does not define liquidity or liquid assets, calls for cash flow reporting for a pool consisting of 'cash and cash equivalents,' the latter consisting of 'short-term, highly liquid investments that are both: (a) readily convertible to known amounts of cash, and (b) so near their maturity that they present insignificant risk of changes in value because of changes in interest rates. Generally, only investments with original maturities of three months or less qualify under that definition' (1987, para. 7). An earlier view was:

We believe the essence of the liquidity concept is *short-term capacity to pay* . . . The primary attribute of a liquid asset is *quickness of convertibility to cash* . . . A secondary attribute, which we believe most businessmen expect of a liquid asset, is lack of adverse consequences to the entity from the conversion of the asset to cash. The most likely adverse consequences are (a) impairment of operating capacity and (b) the sacrifice of existing wealth, that is, a loss (Staubus, 1977, pp. 366-7).

If cash flow accounting, or any other financial reporting approach, is to be developed further in the interest of reporting on, and contributing to an understanding of liquidity, a more serious investigation of the liquidity concept seems appropriate. Lippman and McCall (1986, p. 48) suggested that 'an asset is liquid if it *can be sold quickly* at a *predictable price*.' But their approach included a 'sales policy that maximizes the expected discounted value of the net proceeds associated with the sale, and defining the asset's liquidity to be the expected time until the asset is sold when following the optimal policy' (p. 44). This position is consistent with Keynes: one asset is more liquid than another if it is 'more certainly realisable at short notice without loss' (1930, p. 67). Liquidity, in this view, is not associated with forced sales.

Three factors appear to determine an asset's liquidity: (1) standardisation of the asset, (2) thickness of the market, and (3) operational efficiency of the market. With regard to standardisation, monetary assets are more objectively classifiable than nonmonetary assets. Accountants have identified three important characteristics of future cash flows: time, amount, and uncertainty. With certainty, the liquidity of money claims is clear. Uncertainty adds a subjective factor, but financial markets are accustomed to dealing with it. The liquidity of many, but not all, money claims is readily assessed.

Turning to nonmonetary assets, those that are traded by well-established standards, as are many agricultural and mineral products, can also 'be sold quickly at a predictable price,' although the degree of predictability varies, especially with the prediction period. Other nonmonetary assets must be recognised as nonstandard and not subject to ready classification. The extreme cases are genuinely unique assets such as real property, specialized assets in process of construction to customers' specifications, and intangibles. It is possible, of course, that a nonmonetary asset could be more liquid than certain monetary assets.

Thin markets are an enemy of liquidity. 'When there are many transactions per day of a homogeneous assets such as wheat or long-term Treasury bonds, the market for the asset is thick' (Lippman and McCall, p. 47). To a prospective seller, the number of buyers in an asset market is most relevant to the asset's liquidity. 'Accordingly, the thickness of the market for an asset is said to increase with the frequency of offers' to buy (Lippman and McCall, p. 47).

Finally, the operational efficiency of the market for an asset affects its liquidity. 'If capital markets are efficient, then purchase or sale of any security at the prevailing market price is a zero-NPV (net present value) transaction' (Brealey and Myers, p. 265). That definition could be extended to other asset markets. Examples of transaction costs that are widely recognised as reducing liquidity are: brokerage commissions, transfer taxes, income taxes triggered by realisation of gains from sale, sales and value-added taxes, and search costs such as advertising, other communication costs, and agents' time. Tax advantages enjoyed when losses are realised are negative transaction costs.

'In view of this discussion, it is clear that financial assets traded in a thick, efficient market will be exceedingly liquid' (Lippman and McCall, p. 50). But that is not enough to define liquidity. With more attention to liquidity, perhaps accountants could develop the concept more fully. For now, the above-quoted 1977 definition may be acceptable.

Note that two related concepts of liquidity are relevant: the liquidity of an individual asset and the liquidity of an enterprise. The latter might involve a time dimension cut-off for both assets and liabilities. Net liquid assets might, for example, include both assets readily convertible to cash in the normal course of business within a week and liabilities due for payment within a week. (In the United States, transactions on major securities markets must be settled in cash within five business days). Dichotomous classification of assets (as either liquid or illiquid) would seem to be a crude application of the liquidity concept to individual assets, but any operational concept for comparing the liquidity of enterprises probably requires a uniform dividing line between liquid items and others, thus defining a pool of 'liquidity'. In practice, that pool of liquidity does not include such nonmonetary cash flow potentials as stocks of merchandise and materials, or real property, at net realisable values. They typically cannot be sold quickly without adverse consequences. It is not unreasonable to propose a concept of liquidity that includes such items, but that does not seem to be a popular view currently. Liquidity of an asset is a matter of degree; empirical evidence of an asset's convertibility to cash quickly and without loss would seem to be the only basis for arguing with current practice.

Rejection of Historical Cash Flow Data: For Reporting on Wealth

Now consider a role for which historical cash flow accounting is not generally accepted as suitable: reporting on wealth and income—and management's performance on the profitability criterion. A review of the status quo may not be satisfying to those committed to change, but the general reasons for preferring accrual-deferral accounting for measuring wealth and income should be acknowledged by all who are interested in the present issue. First, the opportunities for 'operating manipulation' of a cash flow measure of income are substantial. Operating manipulation consists of controlling or influencing the timing of cash transactions so as to affect the operating results of the period. Such opportunities are, of course, permitted by the rules of conventional accrual-deferral accounting, e.g., in the areas of maintenance costs, research and development, training, and other expenditures that are treated as immediate expenses even though they are investments for the benefit of future periods. But the opportunities to control cash transactions with suppliers and customers are generally recognised to be much greater. Those impressed with management's ability to manipulate conventional income by both operating tactics, as mentioned above, and by accounting choices must be even more impressed with the manipulation potential under cash flow accounting.[3] For example, imagine the potential for manipulation by a manager whose bonus is based on the change in cash balance, or on operating cash flow, in a reporting period.

---

[3]An observation based on experience with respondents to FASB proposals is that when the Board suggested requiring more up-to-date measurements of the values of wealth items, enterprise managers saw more merit in cash flow accounting. Whether that view reflected a preference for the manipulability of cash flows over 'putting themselves at the mercy of the markets' was never stated.

Related to the manipulation weakness of cash flow income are the potential 'economic consequences' of recognising cash transactions as revenues and expenses. In general, the problem is that whenever events are accounted for as having wealth effects that differ from those effects that are important to the 'principals,' agents can be expected to behave so as to maximise what is emphasised in the reports instead of what is sought by the principals. That is the weakness of present conventional accounting for 'intangible investments,' such as research and development, which are, from the point of view of owners, investments but which are treated as expenses by accountants. As between any two 'bases of accounting', the one that is further from that elusive 'economic accounting' that guides principals can be expected to have the less desirable economic consequences in the form of agents' opportunistic behaviour (Williamson, 1985, p. 47). Thus, expensing cash purchases of merchandise or plant assets (or expensing the excess of full acquisition cost over 'as-is' net realisable value) can be expected to discourage otherwise desirable purchases near the end of an accounting period. Conflicts between the measure of operating results that is emphasised in financial reporting and the measure that is of interest to principals is a weakness in any measurement system.

The preceding discussion of economic consequences leads to the third reason for preferring accrual-deferral accounting for the measurement of wealth and income: those noncash items that are recorded by conventional accrual-deferral accounting are important to principals. An owner of a merchandising business views a claim on a customer as valuable. The consumption of services purchased but not yet paid for is an economic sacrifice. The cash purchase of goods for future sale usually is not an unfavorable event. The case for such accruals and deferrals is an overwhelming one from the point of view of the owner of an enterprise who is concerned with measuring his/her own wealth and income, whether an agent is involved or not. That should not be forgotten in the context of discussions of the role of cash flow accounting.

Similarly, the purchase of long-term plant assets is not viewed by principals as sacrificing wealth. Those assets have cash flow potential. The difficulties in measuring such assets after their acquisition are acknowledged, but they are accepted as preferable to reporting acquisitions as declines in wealth—in the full amount of the acquisition cost in the case of strict cash basis accounting, or partially as in the case of a net realisable value system. Nevertheless, treatment of tangible plant assets and certain recognised intangibles contrasts with the conventional treatment of unrecognised intangible investments such as those involving training, systems development, and research and development. In the latter cases, the measurement difficulties have caused accounting to choose immediate expensing. In general, the choices represented in conventional accrual-deferral accounting result in both inclusion of certain items that are measured very crudely and exclusion from enterprise wealth of certain investments measurement of which is judged to be of negative net value. That is conventional accounting's solution to the general problem of measuring wealth and income. If a critic advocates change on the basis of measurement difficulties, should not incremental changes be tried first, rather than giving up on the measurement of wealth and income altogether?

Cash flow potential: a measure of wealth

The objects listed as assets and liabilities on conventional balance sheets have a common property: cash flow potential. Unfortunately, cash flow potential is measured poorly, partly because accounting has not set its measurement as an explicit objective. But that objective is implicit in conventional accounting measurement practices, and all widely used measurement methods, at least in the United States, deal with cash flow potential. That is most obvious in the cases of those contractual receivables and payables that are measured on the basis of future cash flows, present value of future cash flows, or current market prices. Those measurements based on the form of net realisable value that considers the asset's most likely future course—sometimes called completed-cycle NRV—clearly are focused on cash flow potential. In other circumstances, in which the continuity assumption is not justified, 'as-is NRV,' based on sale of the work-in-process, finished goods, accounts receivable, or other assets without proceeding through remaining stages of the operating cycle in the normal course of business, would be consistent with a focus on cash flow potential. 'As-is NRV' under circumstances that justify the continuity assumption clearly is a liquidity-oriented measure (see final section).

Many have not thought of entry prices of assets as being related to cash flow potential, perhaps because completed-cycle NRV is more directly related to it. Nevertheless, it should be clear that in general equilibrium in a competitive economy, the relationships between entry and exit prices make the former relevant surrogates for the latter, and often superior on the reliability and cost criteria (Staubus, 1967, p. 655–6). Lack of equilibrium and market incompleteness certainly can result in gaps between fully loaded (with fringe acquisition costs) current entry prices and completed-cycle exit prices net of remaining costs (including cost of capital), but the validity of urrent entry prices as a market assessment of cash ow potential surely cannot be denied. Similarly, •ld entry prices (historical costs) were market ssessments of that same property. In sum, conentional accounting practices do measure cash low potentials, despite not having been pur•osefully designed to find and use the most releant, reliable, and economical evidence.

Empirical research employing share prices as a riterion has tested the impact of the manifest defects' in conventional accrual-deferral accountng. The general conclusion based on more than a quarter of a century of such research (from Stau•us (1967) to Bowen (1986, 1987), Rayburn (1986), nd Wilson (1986, 1987)) is that the further the neasure tested is from conventional earnings and he closer it is to strict cash flow, the poorer the ·esults, although the value of conventional mea·urements of depreciation and depletion are still in loubt. Uncertainty regarding the value of deprecition measurements surely does not surprise proponents of serious, value-oriented measurements of plant assets, such as Baxter (1971). It is one thing to question conventional depreciation accounting; it is quite another to extrapolate such concerns to the entire accrual-deferral model.

Conclusions

Three general conclusions follow from the above analysis. First, cash flow information is valuable to users who are concerned with an enterprise's liquidity. That need should not be neglected.

A second conclusion is that liquidity and wealth should be distinguished more clearly. Conventional accounting, and some of the literature, shows confusion on this point. Reporting on liquidity and reporting on wealth/income should be set out as separate objectives of financial reporting.

A third conclusion is that the close relationship between (1) historical cash flows, (2) cash flow projections, (3) cash flow potential, and (4) wealth and income make it easy to confuse liquidityoriented aspects of past and future cash flows and wealth/income aspects. In particular, more attention should be paid to cash flow potential.

Further comments: liquidity and cash flow potential

An example of failure to make a clear distinction between liquidity and wealth is apparent in certain research focused on a decision situation in which a person needs to know the economic unit's (individual's or firm's) liquidity. For example, an accounting theorist might ask a rhetorical question regarding information needed when one is deciding to sell or hold an asset. The answer clearly includes the asset's selling price. If the asset is shares, the shareholder needs a share market quotation, but that says nothing regarding information the corporation might provide to help the shareholder assess the hold option. Another example: asking a sample of independent professional persons questions regarding 'one's assets' or what makes 'one better off' might induce images of personal and family finances (Chambers, Hopwood and McKeown, 1984). Individuals frequently need to know their liquidity. Can the bills be paid? Can I buy that new automobile or property? They rarely need to know their own net worth in order to make decisions. Their curiosity about their net worth might lead them to think about—to speculate about—such important but not always objectively measurable assets as their retirement plan, their art objects, their potential inheritance, and their personal earning power, but they rarely need to quantify and sum those and other assets for direct decision making. Therefore, if you ask them what information about their assets they use, liquidation values are likely to come to mind. In such circumstances, reports based on historical cash flows and net realisable values, as suggested by Lee (1981), might be quite satisfying. Individuals not immersed in the daily problems of business management are not likely to identify liquidity and profitability as two separate requirements for an ongoing successful business, so may not distinguish between information on liquidity and information on wealth and income.

Individuals do not buy and sell fractional interests in economic units consisting of themselves or their families, so the aggregate values of such economic units need not be known for decision purposes. *Individuals do buy and sell fractional interests in other economic units—business entities—so they do seek information relevant to assessments of the values of such entities.* The liquidity of those entities is not the primary concern of buyers and sellers of ownership interests under typical circumstances. Liquidity and value need to be more explicitly recognised and distinguished.

An observation at the core of these remarks is that cash flow potential is the implicitly accepted concept of enterprise wealth in an exchange economy. Assets have positive cash flow potential; liabilities have negative cash flow potential. Net enterprise wealth is the algebraic sum of positive and negative cash flow potentials, with no time horizon as a limit. Accounting measurements are based on evidence of cash flow potentials— evidence which varies widely in its quality. The omission of many intangible investments is an example of treating as off-balance-sheet assets those items for which the evidence of cash flow potential is unacceptable on the reliability criterion. At the other end of the spectrum, cash balances, then short-turn receivables and payables and publicly traded securities, then current nonmonetary assets, then the various categories of noncurrent, nonmonetary, physical and nonphysical assets—all of these are recognised as having cash flow potential, and are measured by reference to evidence of cash flow potential, primarily market prices. Cash flow potential is, of course, measured very poorly.

Those who have studied economics are acquainted with the perfect competition model, an abstract construct that has been found useful in thinking about the formation of prices in markets. In the theory of finance, another abstract model is widely used: complete markets. In a complete market economy, a price can be observed for anything and everything. Prices for various prospective contributions to enterprise cash flow streams (cash flow potentials), such as the contributions of various assets to the enterprise's cash flows, may be observed. Those prices provide excellent guidance for investors and other economic actors. In equilibrium, all prices in the economy are linked at levels such that no remaining opportunities for arbitrage profits exist.

In the real world, prices for the prospective cash flow streams from particular assets and liabilities, as those are understood in accounting, are not observable and market prices are not in equilibrium. Accountants and managers are not able to find quoted market prices for the 'setting-specific' assets and liabilities of the firm, even though prices for similar assets in other environments may be observed. Consequently, accountants must report imperfect substitutes for the market values of all assets except cash. The conventional accounting measurement system has been called 'market simulation accounting', defined as 'the selection and blending of pertinent observed market prices and other evidence in accordance with accepted principles of market economics to assess the price at which an asset or liability would trade in an active market' (Staubus, 1986, p. 118). Those simulated market prices are for positive or negative cash flow potentials—the generally accepted interpretation of wealth.

Reporting on liquidity—a secondary concern of investors—should not be confused with reporting on wealth. An historical report on cash flows is a useful part of the former. Reporting cash flow potentials and changes therein is the essence of the latter. Explicit recognition and responses to those two separate interests of users might be a big step towards decision-useful financial reporting.

References

Baxter, W. T., *Depreciation* (London: Sweet & Maxwell, 1971).
Böhm-Bawerk, E., *The Positive Theory of Capital*, trans. by W. Smart (New York: G. E. Stechert and Co., 1891).
Bowen, R. M., D. Burgstahler, and L. A. Daley, 'Evidence on the Relationships Between Earnings and Various Measures of Cash Flow,' *Accounting Review*, October 1986, pp. 713–725.

——, 'The Incremental Information Content of Accrual Versus Cash Flows,' *Accounting Review*, October 1987, pp. 723–747.
Brealey, R. and S. Myers, *Principles of Corporate Finance*, 2nd ed. (New York: McGraw-Hill, 1984).
Butterworth, J. E., M. Gibbins, and R. D. King, 'The Structure of Accounting Theory: Some Basic Conceptual and Methodological Issues,' in S. Basu and J. A. Milburn (eds.), *Research to Support Standard Setting in Financial Accounting: A Canadian Perspective* (Toronto: The Clarkson Gordon Foundation, 1982), pp. 1–65.
Chambers, R. J., *Accounting, Evaluation and Economic Behavior* (Englewood Cliffs, NJ: Prentice-Hall, 1966).
Chambers, R. J., W. S. Hopwood, and J. C. McKeown, 'The Relevance of Varieties of Accounting Information: A U.S.A. Survey,' *Abacus*, December 1984, pp. 99–110.
Copeland, T. E. and J. F. Weston, *Financial Theory and Corporate Policy* (Reading, MA: Addison-Wesley, 1979).
Egginton, D. A., 'In Defence of Profit Measurement: Some Limitations of Cash Flow and Value Added as Performance Measures for External Reporting,' *Accounting and Business Research*, Spring 1984, pp. 99–111.
——, 'Cash Flow, Profit and Performance Measures for External Reports: A Rejoinder,' *Accounting and Business Research*, Spring 1985, pp. 109–112.
Financial Accounting Standards Board, *Statements of Financial Accounting Concepts No. 1*, 'Objectives of Financial Reporting by Business Enterprises,' November 1978.
——, *Statement of Financial Accounting Standards No. 95*, 'Statement of Cash Flow', November 1987.
Hawkins, D. F., and W. J. Campbell, *Equity Valuation: Models, Analysis and Implications* (New York: Financial Executives Research Foundation, 1978).
Hawkins, D. F., B. A. Brown, and W. J. Campbell. *Rating Industrial Bonds* (Morristown, NJ: Financial Executives Research Foundation, 1983).
Keynes, J. M., *A Treatise on Money*, Vol. II (New York: Harcourt, Brace, 1930).
Lawson, G. H., 'Cash-Flow Accounting,' *Accountant*, October 18, 1971, pp. 386–389.
——, 'The Rationale of Cash Flow Accounting,' in Cees van Dam (ed.), *Trends in Managerial and Financial Accounting* (Leiden, The Netherlands: Martinus Nijhoff Social Sciences Division, 1978), pp. 85–104.
——, 'The Measurement of Corporate Performance on a Cash Flow Basis: A Reply to Mr. Egginton,' *Accounting and Business Research*, Spring 1985, pp. 99–108.
Lee, T. A., 'A Case for Cash Flow Reporting.' *Journal of Business Finance*, Summer 1972, pp. 27–36.
——, 'Reporting Cash Flows and Net Realisable Values,' *Accounting and Business Research*, Spring 1981, pp. 163–170.
——, *Cash Flow Accounting* (London: Van Nostrand Reinhold, 1984).
——, 'Cash Flow Accounting, Profit and Performance Measurement: A Response to a Challenge,' *Accounting and Business Research*, Spring 1985, pp. 93–97.
Lippman, S. A. and J. J. McCall, 'An Operational Measure of Liquidity.' *American Economic Review*, March 1986, pp. 43–55.
Newton, I., *Tables for Renewing and Purchasing the Leases of Cathedral-Churches and Colleges* (London: Thos. Astley, 1686).
Rayburn, J., 'The Association of Operating Cash Flow and Accruals with Security Returns,' in Studies on Alternative Measures of Accounting Income, *Journal of Accounting Research*, Supplement 1986, pp. 112–133.
Staubus, G. J., *An Accounting Concept of Revenue*, Ph.D. dissertation, University of Chicago, 1954 (New York: Arno Press, 1980).
——, *A Theory of Accounting to Investors* (Berkeley: University of California Press, 1961); republished by (Lawrence, KS: Scholars Book Co., 1971).

—, 'The Association of Financial Accounting Variables with Common Stock Values,' *Accounting Review*, January 1965, pp. 119–134.

—, 'Alternative Asset Flow Concepts,' *Accounting Review*, July 1966, pp. 397–412.

—, 'Statistical Evidence of the Value of Depreciation Accounting,' *Abacus*, August 1967, pp. 3–22.

—, 'Current Cash Equivalent for Assets: A Dissent,' *Accounting Review*, October 1967, pp. 650–661.

—, 'Testing Inventory Accounting,' *Accounting Review*, July 1968, pp. 413–424.

—, *Making Accounting Decisions* (Houston: Scholars Book Co., 1977).

—, 'The Market Simulation Theory of Accounting Measurement,' *Accounting and Business Research*, Spring 1986, pp. 117–132.

Sterling, R. R., *Toward a Science of Accounting* (Houston: Scholars Book Co., 1979).

Williamson, O. E., *The Economic Institutions of Capitalism* (New York: The Free Press, 1985).

Wilson, G. P., 'The Relative Information Content of Accruals and Cash Flows: Combined Evidence at the Earnings Announcement and Annual Report Release Date,' in Studies on Alternative Measures of Accounting Income, *Journal of Accounting Research*, Supplement 1986, pp. 165–200.

——, 'The Incremental Information Content of the Accrual and Funds Components of Earnings After Controlling for Earnings.' *Accounting Review*, April 1987, pp. 293–322.

Inflation Accounting in
Decision-Usefulness Theory

Introduction

The fundamental idea of inflation accounting — that inflation changes the size of the measuring unit so as to make the results of arithmetic operations utilizing such variable units mathematically invalid (the apples and oranges problem) — had been recognized decades before decision-usefulness theory was invented. In fact, a substantial literature on the subject was published in the 1946-1955 period, stimulated by very material inflation in the United States and other countries. But inflation accounting did not catch on. I attribute the lack of widespread interest in it at midcentury to the absence of an objective of accounting that called for it and the profession's limited understanding of it, partly due to its relative complexity. Acceptance and application of decision usefulness theory addressed both hindrances.

I gave a lot of attention to inflation accounting in the nineteen-fifties, going so far as to slip into my suggested Statement of Changes in Residual Equity (in a dissertation on revenue, 1954) the reporting of real price changes on nonmonetary assets, gain or loss on net monetary items, and the restatement of the beginning-of-period balance of the residual equity. (1954, pp. 93). My committee rejected my chapter on inflation accounting because they (quite reasonably) considered it to be outside the scope of revenue. ATOATI did include a substantial treatment of the subject as omission would have left a serious gap.

When material inflation returned to America in the 1970s, I returned to the subject of inflation accounting and found a number of gaps in the literature. In addition, I became the staff leader on the inflation accounting project at the FASB. These circumstances led to several publications on the subject in the 1970s: 1975b, 1976b, 1977c chapters IX and X, and 1979. I also drafted the FASB Exposure Draft, *Constant Dollar Accounting*, March, 1979, and then Bryan Carsberg and I became partners on the staff work on SFAS No. 33, *Financial Reporting and Changing Prices*, September, 1979, and the preceding exposure draft. Sir Bryan, an outstanding writer as well as technician, was the primary draftsman.

As I look back on the inflation accounting developments in the 1970s, I can understand the objections to adoption more clearly. Personal economic interests were a factor; managers did not want to report lower earnings, which typically would have resulted from applying constant dollar accounting. Lack of understanding was also a factor as few people cared to plow through the technicalities to learn the procedures.

In this setting, exposition, simplification, and illustrations became important. Finally, the theoretical justification was not convincing until decision usefulness theory was accepted. To me, the choice of measuring unit is a key feature of decision usefulness theory, so is included at the bottom of the diagrammatic outline, page x.

The accounting to investors side of decision-usefulness theory starts with the investor. The essence of investment is the forgoing of present consumption of wealth for the purpose of enhancing future consumption (including bequests for consumption by beneficiaries). In a fundamental sense, all investors are individuals; business enterprises, including investment companies, are only conduits. Investment success means augmentation of the investor's stock of consumption purchasing power. This reasoning leads to the conclusion that the measuring unit for assessing investment success is a unit of constant consumer purchasing power, not a nominal monetary unit of varying purchasing power. In the United States, the index of choice is the Bureau of Labor Statistics' consumer price index (CPI) for all urban consumers, although it is clear that such an index may not be perfect for measuring prices of goods purchased by investors. Thus, CPI "constant dollar accounting" is consistent with decision-usefulness theory.

Now I want to review a number of other points in inflation accounting that had not been resolved by 1975 and which I tried to resolve:

1. The best term to use to identify the procedure. Terms such as general price-level accounting, accounting in units of purchasing power, and index number accounting had been used in the literature. In my 1970s publications, I used the term "common unit accounting" to avoid identification with the monetary unit of any particular country and to emphasize the goal of using the same size of unit over time. At the FASB, the monetary units of other countries were irrelevant, so I selected "constant dollar accounting," which the Board accepted. Conventional accounting became "variable unit accounting" in my own publications and "nominal dollar accounting" at the FASB. I gave Statement No. 33 the title "Financial Reporting and Changing Prices" because it dealt with both general price level changes and specific price changes.

2. The capital maintenance issue. This is the question of how much revenue and gains in a period is required to cover the period's expenses and losses, and thereby avoid capital shrinkage, i.e., how to measure the expenses and losses. In this context, all of the period's net income is assumed to be paid our as dividends. If expenses are understated, as they might be if measured in nominal dollars, income and dividends would eat into capital. Those concerned with the issue generally focused on depreciation and cost of goods sold . Should they be measured at replacement cost so as to retain enough cash flow to replace the physical assets consumed by the period's operations and thereby permit continuance of the level of physical output? Or should those expenses be measured at constant dollar historical cost so as to maintain financial capital? Some accountants thought that the capital of the business was shrinking if it could not produce as many widgets per period as it did in the past. The decision-usefulness theory gave a different answer: the investor's capital is maintained

276

if the enterprise can maintain the consumer purchasing power of its capital, and that is more dependent on earning power in units of consumer purchasing power, not on capacity to produce the same physical product. Loss of production capability need not be a concern of the investor, or of those managers dedicated to maximization of shareholder value. For example, an oil producer with a capacity of 200,000 barrels at $6 per barrel may serve the investor as well as it did last year when it produced 400,000 barrels worth $3 per barrel. (See MAD, pp. 235-241.)

5. The monetary/nonmonetary distinction. Prior to Statement 33, writers on inflation accounting thought of monetary assets as cash or a claim to a fixed sum of money. I insisted that variability of the claim did not make it nonmonetary. It might change in amount for various reasons, such as the accumulation of interest. The important feature is that monetary items do not change in nominal amount because of a change in a specific price. A receivable that is contingent on the price of oil can be a nonmonetary item, comparable to an inventory of oil. My definitions, which the Board accepted for paragraphs 47 and 48 of Statement No. 33, emphasized that the economic significance of monetary items depends on the general price level (inflation) while the economic significance of nonmonetary items depends on values of specific goods and services, not on inflation.

7. Monetary items are the main gainers and losers from inflation; nonmonetary items have a fair chance of holding their own during inflation, but gain or lose when their specific prices change at a rate other than the inflation/deflation rate.

9. Purchasing power gain on debt. Many accountants argued that a purchasing power gain on debt was not income. I pointed out that it was, in constant dollar accounting, an increase in owners' equity other than in transactions with owners, and that it was realized as a reduction in a monetary liability without an offset.

11. The difference between earnings reported under nominal dollar (variable unit) accounting and earnings reported under constant dollar (common unit) accounting. The sources of that difference, its materiality under specified conditions, and the mathematical formulation of it were addressed in 1976b and 1977c, Chs. IX and X.

7. Tax allocation. Income tax on restatements of nonmonetary assets and liabilities should be recognized to avoid mismatching and to recognize the value of the lack of deductibility (in the case of an asset) of the restatement amount. Those restatements are timing differences. Monetary gains and losses are permanent differences between tax and book income, so require no tax allocation. (1977c, Ch. IX)

15. Reporting of real interest cost and revenue. The practice of netting a purchasing power gain or loss on an interest-bearing monetary item against the nominal interest to show the real interest revenue or cost might gain acceptance in the future if accountants in English-speaking countries ever return to the

277

subject of inflation accounting. There has been more recognition by the general public of the difference between real and nominal rates of interest since Statement 33 was issued. (1977c, pp. 428-9)

17. Constant dollar, current value accounting. In the case of comprehensive current value accounting (no historical measurements on the balance sheet), the inflation rate for the reporting period times the average residual equity gives the number for a crude one-line adjustment to convert nominal dollar net income to constant dollar net income; restatements of individual net asset items are unnecessary. More detailed restatements are necessary, however, to get the line items right. (1977c, p. 315)

19. The choice of measurement methods, which affects the timing of the reported income, and the choice of measuring unit, which affects the lifetime total income, are entirely independent choices. (1977c, pp. 256-62)

11. Application of the full set of criteria for evaluating accounting methods shows that the weights assigned to each of the criteria and the degree of the evaluator's preference for constant dollar accounting or nominal dollar accounting on each criterion affects his/her choice. Furthermore, it is clear that, in this case, those preferences depend heavily on the rate of inflation. In simple terms, the superior relevance and comparability of constant dollar accounting information are not judged worth the cost at very low rates of inflation, but clearly are when the inflation rate is very high, a possibility not ruled out in any country. The multiple criteria approach to making accounting decisions does not eliminate the need for judgment, and the decisions made by standards setters in various low-inflation and high-inflation countries appear to have been made by such an approach — 0even if the criteria have not always been assigned the weights I would have used.

Chapter IX of MAD has been selected for reprinting in this volume. That material was written in 1975 and 1976, before I got involved in the FASB project on inflation accounting. As noted above, the chapter title, Common Unit Accounting, was chosen to serve readers in all countries equally well. Constant dollar accounting sounds more familiar now. That chapter, together with Chapter X, a technical chapter on the difference between common unit accounting earnings and variable unit accounting earnings, include most of what I understand about inflation accounting, except for a few ideas for explaining it that I developed at the FASB.

CHAPTER IX

COMMON UNIT ACCOUNTING

A wide range of asset and liability measurement methods were discussed in chapters VI and VII. The emphasis was on selecting, for application to the asset or liability being measured, the measurement method that best reflected the item's cash flow potential. The approach was designed to produce a balance sheet which reported the residual equity interest in the firm's cash flow potentials. Measurement of this current stock of cash flow potentials was advocated as the key to providing information useful for cash-flow-oriented decisions. Measurement of the current stock was also considered essential to the measurement of flows, or changes in stocks of cash flow potentials over time. The group of measurement methods discussed in those chapters, including restated historical cost, appear to be useful in accounting for stocks and flows of cash flow potentials. But there is one serious flaw in that measurement system, and that flaw is the subject of this chapter.

Measurements of flows, such as the revenues, expenses, gains, and losses that constitute business income, often require comparisons of measurements of stocks at two points in time.[1] Some expense measurements, for example, involve adding a beginning balance and purchases, then subtracting an ending balance. For the result to be clearly interpretable the three measurements must be made in a common unit. And when different line items are added and subtracted on an income statement, common units are also desirable.

Accountants traditionally have considered all units of money that are denominated in the same currency to be comparable. Thus, all monetary amounts expressed in deutsche marks are

---

[1] Portions of this chapter are adapted from Staubus (1975b).

considered subject to addition and subtraction without any adjustment: "A DM is a DM is a DM." This means that our focus is
on the number of monetary units; what the money units will
buy we ignore. The alternative view is that deutsche marks, and
lire, and U.S. dollars are significant because of what one can
buy with them, and since this—their purchasing power—varies
over time, "A DM is not a DM is not a DM." The size of the
monetary unit actually varies so that adjustments must be made
to express measurements relating to different dates in a common
unit. Preparing financial statements in monetary units adjusted
for the changes in a purchasing power index, or price level index,
may be called "price level accounting," "general purchasing power
accounting," "current purchasing power accounting," "common
dollar accounting," or "common unit accounting." We will use
the latter term here to signify the currency of any country, to
avoid implying the use of a particular type of index, and to express
the basic objective of the procedure in a short phrase. Under
whichever name one may prefer, common unit accounting is, in
the mid-1970s, under serious consideration in major English-
speaking countries as an alternative to accounting in numbers
of monetary units of varying sizes.[2]

Common unit accounting is intended to make all monetary
amounts appearing on any one financial statement, and on any
articulated set of financial statements presented at one time,
comparable in terms of purchasing power. Thus, if $95 is subtracted
from $100 the remainder can be read as $5 with the purchasing
power that dollars have as of the date of the financial statement.
Application of the current value measurement methods (excluding
historical cost) discussed in chapters VI and VII does express
all measures on one balance sheet in monetary units of the same
purchasing power; such a measurement system, however, does
not achieve common purchasing power measurements on an
income statement or on comparative balance sheets. We must make
a "scale adjustment" for changes in our measuring instrument—the
monetary unit—in order to achieve purchasing power comparabi-

---

[2] Rough general purchasing power restatements have been made, and required
for income taxation, in Brazil for several years. Chile adopted a more comprehensive
system in 1974.

lity of measurements that are made at different times under
inflationary conditions.

COMMON UNIT ACCOUNTING AND THE RELEVANCE CRITERION

The mathematical basis for common unit accounting has been
explained but the relevance of the resulting data to the decisions
of users of financial statements has not. A simple example may
help us think about this aspect of the problem.

An Exercise in Current Value and Common Unit Measurement

At the beginning of period one, when a general price index
stands at 100, Jane Doe purchases a share of X Company
stock for $100. At the end of period one, Doe still holds
the stock, its market price is $108, and the price index is
at 110. Early in period two, while the price index is still at
110, Doe sells the stock for $106.

What is her income in period one? In period two? For
the venture? Make these income calculations under several
different measurement methods. Which measurement method
yields asset and income numbers that appear to be most
relevant to (a) a prospective lender's decision whether to lend
money to Doe, (b) a judgment of Doe's performance as a
portfolio manager, (c) the taxation of Doe's income, and (d)
Doe's decision as to how much she can consume and still
be as well off at the end of each period as she was at its
beginning? (The common unit principle requires that 100
purchase-date dollars be restated as 110 end-of-period-one
dollars.)

	Variable Units		Common Units	
	Historical Cost	Current Market	Historical Cost	Current Market
Period one				
Beginning	$100	$100	$110	$110
End	100	108	110	108
Income	$ 0	$ 8	$ 0	$ −2
Period two				
Beginning	$100	$108	$110	$108
End	106	106	106	106

Income	$ 6	$ -2	$ -4	$ -2
Venture Income	$ 6	$ 6	$ -4	$ -4

Now consider the following comments pertaining to this exercise:

1. The choice between historical cost and current market value affects the *timing* of the reported income.
2. The choice between traditional variable unit accounting and common unit accounting affects the *total income* over the life of the venture.
3. Common unit accounting changes reported income by changing beginning (old) balance sheet amounts, not by changing ending balance sheet amounts.
4. The difference between common unit and variable unit income over the life of the venture is $10, which is equal to the percentage change in the general price index times the beginning owner's equity stated in beginning dollars. (See chapter X for a more precise expression of the difference between variable unit and common unit income.)
5. The exercise may be considered a simple test of the relevance of data produced by different measurement methods—relevance to the types of uses suggested just before the solutions were tabulated. Assuming that no serious qualifications on grounds of cost, reliability, and so forth are warranted in this simple case, your choice of solutions indicates your view of the relevance of the alternative sets of data to the types of decisions listed. I believe that the common units, current market column includes the most relevant information. Doe's investment does not appear to have been successful in either period one or period two and she should not be required to pay any income tax on her venture.

In chapter IV we said that an attribute of an object or event is relevant to a decision if knowledge of its quantity will help the decision maker evaluate possible outcomes of available courses of action. In the next section of this chapter, we argue that the attribute of wealth that is most helpful to an individual in evaluating the outcome of a particular consumption-investment policy is the purchasing power into which that wealth can be converted over time. A change in the purchasing power potential of an individual's wealth is the measure of wealth that is most relevant to his consumption-investment decisions.

THE INDEX CHOICE AND CAPITAL MAINTENANCE

We have discussed the general objective of common unit accounting—to report in units of equal purchasing power. Now we need to examine the specifics of that objective, and to face up to such questions as "Whose purchasing power?" and "Power to purchase what?" Since we need to restate nominal units as purchasing power units in order to compute *income* rather than to prepare a balance sheet, we may find it helpful to distinguish between *capital* and *income*. The term "capital" has many meanings, but all of them relate to stocks of wealth (or interests in such stocks); "income," however, relates to changes in stocks of wealth, or flows of wealth. The term "capital maintenance" means having the same amount of capital at the end of a period as at its beginning so that the entity may "break even," or have zero income. Once we have clarified what it means to maintain capital at its previous level, the computation of income follows. Income is the excess of ending capital over the amount needed to maintain beginning capital at a constant level. To paraphrase the definition by J. R. Hicks (1946), income is the amount one can consume during a period and still be as well off at the end of the period as at the beginning. Or, income is the amount an individual can consume or a corporation can distribute and still maintain the original amount of capital intact.

What *is* required to maintain the original amount of capital intact? How much must we have at the end of the period in order to feel that we have maintained our capital? One possible answer to this is the *money capital* concept of capital maintenance: if the net assets of the firm are worth as many dollars at the end of the period as the firm's net assets were worth at the beginning, capital has been maintained. But, having as many dollars at the end of the period as we had at the beginning is not the same as being as well off—if the purchasing power of the dollars has changed. We implicitly rejected the money capital concept when we turned to the purchasing power concept at the beginning of this chapter, and we assume hereafter that it is unacceptable.

Maintenance of Physical Capital

Another possible concept of capital maintenance is *physical capital* maintenance. In this view, if we have on hand as many units of materials, finished products, and machine services as we had at the beginning of the period, or if we have enough cash to buy such equivalent physical assets, we have maintained our capital. By this approach, income realized by the sale of an asset may be computed by deducting from its selling price the number of monetary units that it would take to replace that asset. This concept of capital maintenance requires the use of the replacement cost method of measuring expenses and would require that the holding gain (or loss) be excluded from income. Thus, if two widgets were purchased at the beginning of the period for $6 each, one was sold for $9 when its replacement cost was $7, and the other is still on hand at the end of the period with a replacement cost of $7.50, the income for the period would be $9 less $7, or $2. No income would be recognized on the unsold widget. In circumstances that would make it difficult to determine and record the replacement cost of each commodity, we could use a narrow (specific) price index that reflects price changes in the categories of commodities being measured in order to approximate specific replacement cost.

Now let us consider the implications of physical capital maintenance. If the cost of goods sold is determined by replacement cost, how does a trader who buys and sells securities, or a commodities speculator, earn any income? If a trader buys and sells in the same market, replacement cost at the time of sale (the measure of cost of goods sold) must be the same as selling price, so no income is ever recognized. Or, consider the case of the two trading companies, X and Y. Suppose X invests in commodity A, which rises in price, and Y invests in commodity B, which falls. If the costs to be matched with revenues upon sale are replacement costs, A and B may appear to have performed equally well; that is, they could show equal incomes: zero. In effect, if capital maintenance means that we must be able to replace what we sold or consumed in the course of business, it makes no difference which assets we buy and hold. But surely we are better off holding assets that rise in price than we are holding assets whose prices fall! It is difficult to imagine anyone choosing a physical concept of capital maintenance in the face of this evidence.

A variation on the physical concept of capital maintenance is the *firm purchasing power* concept. It calls for the use of an index of prices of commodities that the firm purchases (including raw materials, or merchandise, and plant assets such as machinery and buildings). Such an index would measure changes in the power of the monetary unit (e.g., dollar) to purchase the things necessary for the firm to stay in business. Such a concept of purchasing power might appear appropriate for implementing the general purchasing power restatement proposal. On closer examination, however, the concept is essentially a physical capital maintanence approach and is subject to the evaluation in the preceding paragraph. If it were adopted, a firm holding a set of assets that fell in price would look just as good as a firm holding a rising "portfolio" of assets.

Some writers argue that a firm does not have income until it has provided for maintaining the same productive capacity and carrying the same inventories as it had at the beginning of the period. According to this argument, if prices pertaining to our industry rise faster than do average prices in the economy, and if income taxes and dividends are based on a computation of income that does not provide for replacing the physical assets (or their services) consumed, then 100 percent payout of reported income would require either borrowing more money or contracting the physical operations of the firm. But could not a firm be driven out of business by such policies?[3]

The argument favoring physical capital maintenance does not recognize that *maintenance of physical capacity is not necessary to maintain the real earning power and investment value of the firm.* A phenomenon associated with mobility of capital is the tendency towards a common rate of return on capital in firms with similar risk levels, if there is freedom of entry and exit. Thus, assume that Companies X and Y start out with equal capital, that X's

---

[3]An excellent statement of this position has been made by Revsine and Weygandt (1974). Another prominent advocate of the specific entity capital maintenance concept is R. S. Gynther (1974 and earlier works).

assets rise in price more than Y's, and that owners' capital is retained (or added) to permit the financing of the higher priced assets; then, further assuming fluid capital markets and competitive conditions, X's earnings must rise more than Y's if the rates of return on investment in the two firms are to be equal. Otherwise, capital would tend to flow out of one industry and into the other. In other words, maintenance of physical capital in a more inflationary industry will tend to increase the industry's real earning power. If the capital has greater earning power, it is a larger quantum of capital, so capital has been more than maintained. The firm purchasing power concept of capital maintenance is rejected.[4]

Another perspective from which to analyze the capital maintenance issue is that of project investment analysis, or capital budgeting. How can one measure the success, or income, of a project over its lifetime? If the measuring unit is stable, and assuming all equity financing and no income tax, an investment project yields a lifetime income if it produces cash inflows greater than the cash outflows associated with it. If the measuring unit is not stable, some adjustment must be made in order to net out the various cash flows. But surely that adjustment would have nothing to do with the investment required to undertake a similar project as a successor to the first. The success of the first project has nothing to do with the cost of its successor. An investor would not consider rejecting an otherwise profitable investment opportunity because he foresaw a great increase in the investment required to replace the first asset.[5]

Maintenance of Investors' Consumption Purchasing Power

We have not mentioned the decision-usefulness approach to accounting issues in our discussions of possible capital maintenance

---

[4]As an aside we may observe that if the price of a commodity rises faster than a general price index over a considerable period (presumably due to a supply constraint), its sales volume typically will decline (if there is any elasticity of demand), so the company may be able to maintain its share of the market without maintaining the same physical volume of operations. In any event, a company's "right" to maintain its physical level of operations surely is weak compared to its duty to maintain the amount of consumer purchasing power that its shareholders have entrusted to it.

[5]A conversation with Jack Hanna helped me see this point.

concepts. When we associate the Hicksian concept of income with the *objective of producing accounting data that are useful to the readers of financial statements,* it becomes apparent that it is the users' purchasing power with which accountants should be concerned. If we agree that the managers are working for the owners and that employees make only limited use of financial statements, then the major groups of users who appear to warrant substantial consideration here are investors (owners and creditors, including suppliers) and taxing authorities. It is investors' well-offness that managers are trying to maximize and that governments are trying to tax.

People invest in enterprises in order to increase their real wealth—to have greater purchasing power than they would otherwise have. The ultimate objective of all investment activities is consumption of goods by people. Investors like to know their income so they can know how much they can consume without eating into their capital. From a longer-term perspective, an individual needs to know his beginning capital and predict his lifetime income if he is to spread his consumption and bequests in a pattern that equalizes marginal utility and maximizes total utility. Knowledge of his income in the recent past and knowledge of his present capital (including income to date) are helpful in predicting future returns available for consumption expenditures. If an investor owning an interest in a business is taxed on a return of capital by a taxing authority who intends to be taxing income, or if the investor spends for personal consumption a cash return that he believes to be income but is in fact a return of capital, then accounting is not providing the information that is most relevant to those decisions, namely the change in the purchasing power potential of his wealth. For investor's multiperiod investment-consumption decisions, for income taxation decisions, and for decisions regarding managers' success in achieving owners' objectives—for all of these basic uses of income information, *capital is maintained when the investor has end-of-period wealth with the same consumption purchasing power as he had at the beginning of the period, and income is an increase in the investor's stock of consumption purchasing power.*

The argument has been advanced (Sandilands Report, 1975) that the use of a retail price index for restatement of corporate accounts is inappropriate because such a general index does not accurately measure the changing purchasing power of the monetary unit in the hands of individual shareholders who do not purchase the same "market basket" of goods as that used in constructing the index. According to that argument, the general index is imperfect for most shareholders. But if we think for a moment of the degree of perfection that is involved in other aspects of accounting, we are likely to conclude that a general index is accurate enough to be acceptable—a judgment confirmed by the millions of people (union members with cost-of-living adjustment clauses in their contracts, businessmen, and others) who rely on such indexes.

The appropriate index to use in restating accounting measurements in units of purchasing power is an index of prices of goods consumed by investors. To my knowledge, no such index has been constructed and maintained in any country. The best-known consumer price index in America is an index of prices paid by factory wage earners and clerical employees, so it is not ideal for price level restatements. Fortunately, the Labor Department plans to commence publication of a new consumer price index in February 1978. It will reflect prices paid by a broader segment of the population but will not be specifically aimed at the investor segment. Still another index appears to be needed.

In practice, the Accounting Standards Steering Committee has chosen the British retail price index and the Irish consumer price index for use in common unit accounting. The FASB, on the other hand, has, as of this date, selected an economy-wide index—the gross national product implicit price deflator—and similar indexes have been suggested for use in Australia and Canada.

Note that the extent of price change reflected by the chosen index establishes "par" for changes in specific prices. Assuming that assets are measured at their current values, if the price of a particular asset increases by the same percentage as the index, no real gain or loss occurs; only a greater-than-average or less-than-average increase would be recognized as an income item. Thus, under a *physical* concept of capital maintenance, no gain or loss would be recognized when assets were revalued to current replacement cost; the offsetting entry would be treated as a restatement of owners' equity. But if an investor purchasing power concept of capital maintenance were accepted, revaluations of specific assets other than in proportion to the change in the chosen index would result in a holding gain or loss on the asset. The chosen index is also used for measuring both the loss from holding cash and other monetary assets and the gain from being in debt during inflation.

One other point relating to capital maintenance needs to be made here. Our standard of capital maintenance must be consistent across all balance sheet items if the sums and differences reflected in the residual equity are to be clearly interpretable. For example, we must not apply different indexes in restating monetary and nonmonetary items. If a monetary asset must increase in nominal units by the percentage increase in the consumer price index in order to maintain its real value, the same is true of a nonmonetary asset. If, on the other hand, an entity purchasing power index is applied to restate nonmonetary items, it should also be applied to monetary items. A loss or gain is then reported in the amount of any difference between the restated beginning measurement and the ending measurement, whether the item is monetary or nonmonetary, an asset or a liability.

COMMON UNIT ACCOUNTING PROCEDURES

The problem that common unit accounting is intended to solve is that of adding, subtracting, and otherwise comparing measurements made in monetary units of various sizes. The first step towards the solution is the selection of the unit in which all of the measurements in question are to be stated. Since the current purchasing power of the local currency is more familiar to readers of financial statements than any other unit, the end-of-period unit is normally chosen as the base. Accordingly, all measurements pertaining to earlier dates are "rolled forward" by multiplying them by one plus the percentage change in the index between the two dates. Thus, "dating" the old measurements is a key step. The objective of roll-forward computations is to calculate the number of current units that equals—in purchasing power—the number of old units reflected in the old measurement. If, for example, the old measurement was made at a date when the purchasing power index was at 120 and it is now at 132, and if the old measurement was $60, the roll-forward computation is $60(132/120) = $66.

The increase in number of monetary units from 60 to 66 in this case is not a gain or any form of income; it is simply a "restatement" of the old amount in the current measuring unit. *A gain or loss on an asset or liability is recorded, however, if its amount as measured for reporting on the current balance sheet differs from the restated old amount.* The possibilities may be outlined as follows:

A. Measurement of an asset or liability at the *restated old amount.* In this case, no gain or loss is recognized. This procedure (described in chapter VI) is commonly applied to many "nonmonetary" items such as inventories, plant assets, and deferred credits to revenue. When applied to an asset that was previously measured at historical cost, it is called "restated historical cost." The comparable term for measurement of a liability is "restated historical receipt."

B. Measurement of an asset or liability *independently* of its restated measurement, thus recording a gain or loss.

1. Measurement at the *old numbers of dollars* (the usual treatment of "monetary" items such as cash, receivables, and payables). For example, if the firm has held $100 in currency from the old measurement date to the current date, a restatement, under inflationary conditions, would show a number greater than 100. Showing this currency on the current balance sheet at only $100 would reflect a loss, precisely what we believe has happened to its purchasing power. If a liability were restated from $200 to $220 in current units, but a current measurement puts it back at $200, then a $20 gain is recorded—a gain from being in debt during inflation. In a period of *deflation*, a gain would be recorded on holding cash and receivables, and a loss on liabilities would appear.

2. Current measurement of an asset or liability at neither the restated old amount nor the original old amount would show a gain or loss—the difference between the new measurement and the restated amount. Use of current value measurement methods, such as NRV and replacement cost, would normally produce such a gain or loss.

Now let's look at a simple illustration. The Static Company begins a year with nonmonetary assets, perhaps land, valued at $100, monetary liabilities of $40, and a residual equity of $60. The price level index used for restatements rose by 10 percent during the year and the company engaged in no transactions. The accompanying comparative balance sheets (EXHIBIT IX-1) include the old values in old units in the first column and the old values in new units in the third column; the difference represents restatements. For the ending balance sheet (column 5), the nonmonetary assets are reported at their restated beginning values while the monetary liabilities are revalued downwards to the future cash flow basis (which is the same number of nominal dollars that was recognized at the beginning of the year). Thus a gain of $4 is recorded on the debt. The residual equity shows the gain on debt as the difference between the restated beginning balance sheet amount and the ending balance sheet amount.

This EXHIBIT is a very simple example designed to illustrate the essence of common unit accounting. In this case, we measured the nonmonetary assets at the end of the period at restated historical cost, $110. While that number of dollars exceeds the beginning number by 10, it does not represent a gain or any form of increase

EXHIBIT IX-1

STATIC COMPANY
BALANCE SHEETS
19X2 AND 19X1

	12/31/1 in 12/31/1 $	Restate- ments	12/31/1 Restated in 12/31/2 $	Revalu- ation	12/31/2 in 12/31/2 $
Nonmonetary assets	100	10	110	0	110
Monetary liabilities	40	4	44	(4)	40
Residual equity	60	6	66	4	70

in the residual equity. The monetary liabilities, on the other hand, are shown at the same number of dollars at the end of the period as they were at the beginning, but a gain of $4 is recorded and it increases the residual equity from its restated amount of $66, to $70. Thus, when we compare the ending balance sheet with the beginning balance sheet in old units, we find *that the nonmonetary assets are shown at a larger number but no gain is recognized, while the monetary liabilities are shown at the same number but a gain is recognized.* If the nonmonetary assets had been measured by any method other than restated historical cost, a gain or loss would have been recognized in the amount of the difference between restated historical cost and the new measurement.

Now let's move on to a case with transactions during the year. The Two-Transaction Company, an art investor, begins the year with the balance sheet shown in the first column of EXHIBIT IX-2. The index is at 100 at the year's start, at 103 when asset A is sold for $42 on April 30, at 108 when an appraisal fee of $10 is paid on September 30, and at 110 at year-end. The year-end cash balance (monetary assets) is $52. The residual equity balance shows an income of $1.

All income statement items have been restated in $12/31/\times2$. The sale was made when the index was at 103; multiplying the original selling price by 110/103 restates it in the size of units that prevailed at year-end when the index was at 110. Those year-end dollars could be symbolized by 110$. Thus, 103$42 = 110$44.85. The asset that was sold had a year-start valuation of $30 which, when multiplied by 110/100, yields 110$33. Similarly the appraisal expense, 108$10, is equal to 110$10.19.

The loss on net monetary assets can be computed in two ways. We know intuitively that the loss occurs because of the shrinkage in the purchasing power of monetary assets held, or a gain occurs due to the shrinkage in the real burden of debt as the level of prices changes. The amount of debt owed (net of monetary assets), or the amount of monetary assets held (net of monetary liabilities), times the change in the index, determines the gain or loss on net monetary position. When the net monetary balance (or position) changes during the accounting period, the gain or loss may be computed for each portion of the period (subperiod) that the balance held steady; then that gain or loss should be rolled forward

Exhibit IX-2

Two-Transaction Company
Balance Sheets
19X2 and 19X1

	12/31/1 in 12/31/1 $	12/31/1 in 12/31/2 $	12/31/2 in 12/31/2 $
Nonmonetary asset A	30	33	
Nonmonetary asset B	50	55	55
Monetary assets	20	22	52
Monetary liabilities	40	44	40
Residual equity	60	66	67

Two-Transaction Company
Income Statement
19X2 (12/31/2 $)

Sales [42 (110/103)]		$44.86
Less, Cost of goods sold [30 (110/100)]	$33.00	
Appraisal expense [10 (110/108)]	10.19	43.19
Net operating income		$ 1.67
Loss on net monetary position[a,b]		.67
Net income		$ 1.00

[a]Loss calculated on net monetary *balances* (balance times fractional change in index, then rolled forward to year-end):

1/1–4/30: (40 − 20)(3/100)(110/103)	=	$ .64
5/1–9/30: (40 − 20 − 42)(5/103)(110/108)	=	−1.09
10/1–12/31: (40 − 20 − 42 + 10)(2/108)	=	− .22
Loss on net monetary position		110$(.67)

[b]Loss calculated by comparing monetary *transactions* in 12/31/2 units and in original units:

	Original $	Index Factor	12/31/2 $
Net liability balance 1/1	$20.00	110/100	$22.00
Receipt 4/30	(42.00)	110/103	(44.86)
Disbursement 9/30	10.00	110/108	10.19
Computed ending balance (asset)			(12.67)
Measured ending balance	$(12.00)		(12.00)
Difference: Loss on net monetary position			110$(.67)

from the end of the subperiod to the reporting date. These calculations are illustrated in note *a* of EXHIBIT IX-2; the computation procedure may be called the *balances method.*

An alternative method of calculation that achieves the same result and may be more convenient under some circumstances is to roll forward the beginning net monetary balance and every change in it (thus computing an ending balance that would have existed if the monetary items could have kept pace with inflation), and then deduct the ending monetary balance as actually measured. This method—the *transactions method*—is shown in note *b* of EXHIBIT IX-2. In practice, either method of calculation may be applied so as to recognize no more than twelve changes in balance each year in order to relate to monthly financial reports and monthly price index reports. There is no need to aim at a literal level of absolute accuracy. But we can conclude from this exercise that Static Company procedures are not adequate in active firms; it is not feasible to compute price level gains and losses by restating the beginning balance sheet and comparing it with an ending balance sheet on a mixed measurement basis.

Common unit accounting is likely to be limited to supplementary reporting for the foreseeable future. If so, ledger accounts are not likely to be adjusted to a common unit basis. Nevertheless, accountants who are accustomed to thinking in terms of a self-balancing double-entry system may want to visualize common unit accounting in terms of entries in the accounts. Such a set of illustrative entries has the advantage of showing how the procedure fits into a familiar framework. The Two-Transaction Company example will be cast into a double-entry format for this purpose. While this example includes no preferred shares, no dividends, and no nonmonetary liabilities, the entries that would be required to restate those items are also illustrated. For convenience, a "common unit restatements" account is used to assemble the offsetting (and balancing) entries associated with each restatement. (ΔI_t is the symbol for the fractional change in the price index during the period.)

(1) Dr. Loss on net monetary assets $ .67
    Cr. Common unit restatements $ .67
    (See EXHIBIT IX-2 for details
    of computation.)

(2) Dr. Common unit restatements   6.00
    Cr. Residual equity accounts   6.00
      (ΔI_t) beginning balance
(3) Dr. Nonmonetary asset accounts   5.00
    Cr. Nonmonetary liability accounts   0
    Cr. Common unit restatements   5.00
      (ΔI_t) ending balance
(4) Dr. Common unit restatements   0
    Cr. Preferred stock—inflation   0
    shrinkage(ΔI_t) ending balance
(5) Dr. Expense accounts (3.00 + .19)   3.19
    Dr. Dividends declared   0
    Cr. Common unit restatements   .33
    Cr. Revenue accounts   2.86
    Original amount times change in index
    from "date basis" to end of period.

The following additional observations may now be made regarding this procedure:

a. If all calculations are made precisely, the entries in the common unit restatements account will net out to zero, as in this example; under typical circumstances, a small balance will remain, which should be buried in the loss or gain on net monetary position.

b. When the common unit accounting procedure is applied with GAAP, the lower of cost and market test must be made after nonmonetary assets are restated; a write-down to income may be required.

c. All of the restated balances are to be used in the preparation of common unit financial statements. The usual types of closing entries should then be made, including the closing of the loss on net monetary assets in the same way as revenues and expenses. The account for "preferred stock—inflation shrinkage" is not an income account and should be closed directly to retained earnings along with dividends.

d. If the capital structure had included preferred stock (with the same total assets), either entry (1) or entry (2) would have been reduced by the amount of entry (4).

e. If dividends had been paid before the year-end, the Dr. to dividends in entry (5) would have been offset by a smaller loss on net monetary assets in entry (1) since the cash

Chapter IX

balance would have been lower for part of the year.

In contemporary practice, these entries are not likely to be journalized or posted to ledger accounts, but may well appear on a work sheet used in the preparation of common unit financial statements. EXHIBIT IX-3 illustrates how such entries may adjust traditional variable unit data to common unit data. Each debit or credit to an account other than the common unit restatements account would be supported by a schedule showing the calculation of the amount. Such calculation schedules are illustrated in several readily available reports (AICPA, 1963, 1969; FASB, 1974), but without being tied to a complete double-entry work sheet. (Consult those sources for additional assistance.)

Common unit accounting may be done as accurately and in as much detail as is appropriate in the circumstances, including a consideration of the costs of doing it. At one extreme, rough restatements may be made on the basis of published financial statements. Or, computer programs could provide for dating every entry made in variable unit accounts; then, when index data become available, the dated variable unit data could be retrieved and restated. A compromise that is likely to be popular is to restate monthly totals of transactions if the index chosen is available monthly (or quarterly summaries of transactions if the index is only available quarterly), along with common unit data from the beginning of the month.

Examples of procedures for restating published data are available (Cutler and Westwick, 1973; Davidson and Weil, 1975a). The most difficult step is ascertaining the "date basis" of the nonmonetary items. Once this has been done in some fashion, the nonmonetary assets and liabilities, the fixed portions of the residual equity, and the temporary (income and residual equity) accounts may be restated by multiplying the variable dollar amounts times the index factor (index at end of period over index at base date). The gain or loss on net monetary position can be computed for interim periods using the average balance, computed as accurately as desired, and the fractional index change during the interim period. Small errors need not be a matter for concern. The reader is encouraged to experiment.

EXHIBIT IX-3

TWO-TRANSACTION COMPANY WORKSHEET FOR COMMON UNIT FINANCIAL STATEMENTS
12/31/X2

	Data for Variable Unit Statements		Common Unit Restatements		Data for Common Unit Statements	
	Dr.	Cr.	Dr.	Cr.	Dr.	Cr.
Nonmonetary asset B	$ 50		(3) 5.00		$ 55.00	
Monetary assets	52				52.00	
Monetary liabilities		$ 40		(2) 6.00		$40.00
Residual equity (1/1/X2)		60				66.00
Sales		42		(5) 2.86		44.86
Cost of goods sold	30		(5) 3.00		33.00	
Appraisal expense	10		(5) .19		10.19	
	$142	$142				
Loss on net monetary position			(1) .67		.67	
Common unit restatements			(2) 6.00	(1) .67 (3) 5.00 (5) .33	0	0
			$14.86	$14.86	$150.86	$150.86

MONETARY AND NONMONETARY ASSETS AND LIABILITIES

A distinction must be made between "monetary" and "nonmonetary" net asset items if we are to compute the gain or loss on net monetary position, a key information output from a common unit accounting system. We should, therefore, clarify the meaning of these terms. A *monetary item* (asset or liability) is one that will entail future cash flows in nominal amounts that are not affected by inflation. The purchasing power value of monetary items to owners varies with inflation. Such cash flows typically are fixed by contract but they need not be. *Nonmonetary items* are all other assets and liabilities.

One common misconception about the monetary-nonmonetary distinction is that any item measured at historical cost or historical receipt should be restated to the current number of measuring units equivalent to the historical number and is, therefore, a nonmonetary item. But the measurement method applied to an asset, or the attribute that is measured, does not determine whether the item is monetary or nonmonetary; some nonmonetary items are measured by current value methods. There are some cases in which conventional accounting practice appears to involve measurement on a historical basis, but a little thought shows restatement of such a measurement to be obviously inappropriate. One example would be a note receivable recorded at its cost which is not equal to its face value, and on which interest is not being accrued because of doubtful collectibility. Another would be an asset or liability recorded in a tax allocation entry. This case will be discussed below.

Superimposing common unit accounting on GAAP involves measuring those items that are reported under GAAP at historical cost (most nonmonetary assets) or at historical receipt (most nonmonetary liabilities) by restating those old measurements. This means that no gain or loss is reported on those items prior to their use or liquidation; an exception is the write-down of an asset under the lower of restated cost and market rule. Monetary items, on the other hand, are normally adjusted from restated old measurements to face value, some form of future cash flow measurement, or current market value, so gains and losses on them are reported. One result is that *an error in classifying an item will affect the currently reported net gain or loss on monetary items with an offsetting error in income in the period of liquidation of the item.* For example, if a note payable were classified as nonmonetary, it would be restated upwards in a period of inflation and the gain on its real shrinkage during the period would be omitted from income. When it is paid at the nominal maturity value, a gain on settlement of the liability would be recorded. We conclude that misclassification can be a serious error.

Monetary-Nonmonetary Classification Problems

Not all assets and liabilities are easily classified as monetary or nonmonetary. In the case of convertible securities owned or issued, for example, neither classification seems generally appropriate. We would like to classify a convertible security as monetary if it is selling near its investment value as a fixed income security, and as nonmonetary if it is priced primarily on the basis of its common share equivalent. Unfortunately, that solution leaves a gray area; the call on common shares that the conversion privilege represents is always worth something, so a convertible security normally sells at a price that is at least slightly above its investment value. Drawing a line through the gray area would be extremely difficult because (1) the investment value of a convertible security is difficult to quantify, and (2) any premium of market price over investment value that would be permitted for a monetary security could only be determined arbitrarily. Consequently, it is tempting to hypothesize that both issuer and holder expect convertible securities to have, or come to have, value as a residual security, so both issuer and holder should uniformly classify them as a nonmonetary item in common unit financial statements. Is that an acceptable solution, or should we refrain from predicting conversion and treat convertibles as monetary? We could avoid the issue by measuring the attribute most relevant to cash-flow-oriented decisions—current market value—and then record a gain or loss for the difference between the restated beginning amount and the ending market value.

Cash, receivables, and payables denominated in a foreign currency are sometimes questioned. It seems clear, however, that their purchasing power is also subject to change with inflation;

since whether inflation occurs in the domestic economy or in another country will affect the amount but not the principle, monetary classification seems appropriate. However, to the extent that the monetary classification is significant because it includes all of those items on which a gain or loss can be computed by simply applying the domestic inflation factor, foreign currency items must be segregated for separate treatment similar to that accorded to bonds carried at current market value. The loss or gain on a constant balance would be the difference between the restated beginning translated amount and the newly translated balance (at the end-of-period rate). For example, $100 of lire at the beginning with a 10 percent dollar inflation rate and a 5 percent decline in the lire would yield a $15 loss and a $95 ending balance (if the lire were held through the period).

Credit or debit balances related to income tax allocation appear to be monetary because the addition to or deduction from future tax payments can be expected to vary only due to changes in the tax law, a change in the taxpayer's "bracket," or lack of taxable income, but not due to changing price levels. One way of testing whether an item should be classified as monetary or nonmonetary is to consider whether restatement of the item would result in its valuation at an amount that appears to be out of line with the expected future cash flow associated with the item so that a gain or loss would be taken on it when it is liquidated. Clearly, in a simple deferred tax case (e.g., one involving use of the installment sales method), restatement of the liability would put it at a figure larger than is needed to pay the tax due when the installment receivables are collected, so a gain would be recorded. A deferred tax liability, or asset, is a monetary item.

One final point about monetary items: ordinary preferred stock is a monetary owners' equity item. The common shareholders benefit from its decline in real value with inflation, but since that benefit does not change the total owners' equity, it is not income. It should be offset against the preferred dividend when the earnings available to the common shareholders are computed.

The Gain on Long-Term Debt

We have seen earlier in this chapter that common unit accounting treats the loss of purchasing power of monetary assets held as an income statement item; we have also seen that the reduced purchasing power significance of monetary liabilities due to decreased purchasing power of the monetary units to be paid out in the future is a positive component of income. We must recognize, however, that some accountants have disagreed with the way in which common unit accounting treats the gain on long-term debt as its purchasing power significance decreases. Individual members of two of the national standards-setting bodies have taken the position, in private correspondence, that the restatement of long-term debt is not an income item on a current basis. The best-known application of common unit accounting in the United States—that at the Indiana Telephone Company—defers the recognition of such income until the debt is retired. Another position (Saunders and Busby, 1976) is that the controversial "gain" on debt and preferred stock should be deferred as a "nonmonetary liability" (owed to whom?) and amortized at the composite rate of depreciation being applied to "property, plant and equipment" on the grounds that "treating the inflation effect of sources of property investment on the same basis as the inflation effect of the property it finances results in a realistic presentation for evaluating the overall impact of inflation" (p. 19). Since it is likely that others question the propriety of the majority view, let us consider a simple example.

The Debt and Debtless Companies

A static firm, the Debt Company, holds 1,000 units of a commodity through a period when the price index increased by 10 percent. The conventional balance sheet looks like this:

DEBT COMPANY
BALANCE SHEET
During 19x1

Commodity: 1,000 units	$100	Debt	$40
		Residual equity	$60

Upon restatement and revaluation of the debt, the balance sheet reflects income of 4 end-of-period dollars; that is, a residual equity amount $4 greater than is necessary to maintain the residual equity holders' purchasing power. The income is derived from a gain on the debt.

DEBT COMPANY
BALANCE SHEET
Restated and Revalued
12/31/x1

Commodity: 1,000 units	$110	Debt	$40
		Residual equity	$70

Is this $4 income distributable (without impairing capital)? Yes, it is if it is real at all. If the market selling price of the commodity is now $.11 per unit, the firm can sell 36 units for $3.96 and pay a cash dividend of that amount, or it can pay a dividend in kind by distributing 36 units of the commodity, leaving the following balance sheet at the start of the next period:

DEBT COMPANY
BALANCE SHEET
1/1/x2

Commodity: 964 units	$106.04	Debt	$40
		Residual equity	$66.04

If the price level again increases 10 percent, a restatement and revaluation of the debt to $40 would leave an income of $4, which could be distributed in the same manner. This practice can continue as long as the price level increases, the price of our commodity keeps pace, and the commodity is divisible enough to permit carving off a portion for sale or distribution. The earning power of the company is not reduced below its beginning-of-period level by such distributions. But note two things that common unit accounting does not do: (1) It does not, by itself, account for unrealized gains or losses due to specific price changes different than the index; current value accounting, along with common unit accounting, is needed to reflect this properly. (2) It does not report on liquidity any more than other accrual accounting systems do; a liquidity-oriented funds statement is needed for this purpose.

Now compare the Debt Company's results with those of the Debtless Company, which differs only in its capital structure.

DEBTLESS COMPANY
BALANCE SHEET
During 19x1

Commodity: 1,000 units	$100	Residual Equity	$100

Restated
12/31/x1

Commodity: 1,000 units	$110	Residual Equity	$110

Note that the residual equity in this company has only remained constant in real terms at $110 end-of-period dollars, which are equal to 100 beginning dollars. When this outcome is compared with the increase in real value of the residual equity in the Debt Company, in an amount equal to the 10 percent rate of inflation times the debt, it is clear that residual equity holders gain from debt during inflation. Under common unit accounting, the gain is recorded on an accrual basis; under variable unit accounting it is recorded upon realization of the assets. It seems impossible for any double-entry version of common unit accounting to avoid recognition of the $4 increase in the real amount of the residual equity in the Debt Company. It is, of course, possible to define income so as to exclude this particular source of "better-offness" of the owners.

To summarize in other words, a price level gain on debt represents "better-offness" of owners and is distributable to them without impairing capital. Like any other accrual basis income, it does not assure liquidity. The potential problem of a profit accompanied by a cash shortage is a risk involved in computing income on any noncash basis. But it is difficult to see how the use of cash to pay off the debt would make the gain any more distributable (as is implied by "deferring" it). Nor does paying off the debt change the exposure to inflation as the reductions in cash and debt offset each other, leaving the net monetary position unchanged. How could debt retirement (and *disbursement* of cash) be considered a realization event related to a gain? The date of realization of a gain or revenue is the date of the cash (or near-cash) receipt, which occurs, in this case, when the larger dollars are borrowed, not when the smaller dollars are repaid.

We must realize that a complete, systematic approach to common unit accounting requires recognition that the purchasing power significance of nominally constant debt and monetary assets changes with inflation; we cannot recognize restatement on unbalanced parts of the balance sheet and still have a balancing statement. The idea that debtors gain currently from inflation is as widely accepted and understood as any aspect of inflation accounting. Failure to report it as a gain would be hard to explain. Within the context of an $A = L + P$ balance sheet and income as the change in net assets other than by transactions with owners, there simply is no mathematically acceptable alternative to treating the change in purchasing power related to debt as income.[6]

COMMON UNIT, CURRENT VALUE ACCOUNTING

The two immediately preceding sections of this chapter have been devoted to common unit accounting in relation to GAAP. Now it is time to discuss common unit accounting combined with current value measurement methods.[7] To illustrate this combination, let's take the case of the Two-Transaction Company (see pp. 244–49) and add two bits of information: (1) the replacement cost of asset A at the time of its sale was $35, and (2) the replacement cost of asset B at year-end was $48. Now let's review the journal entries on pages 246–47. Entry (1) is unchanged because the monetary items are unchanged. Entry (2) is also the same as before. Entry (3), however, is revised to record the revaluation of (a) the outgoing asset A from $30 to $35 at the date of its sale, and (b) the remaining nonmonetary asset from $50 to $48 as of year-end. That makes entry (3):

---

[6] In chapter XIII we will suggest that the inflation gain on interest-bearing liabilities be deducted from nominal interest expense, that the inflation loss on interest-earning assets be deducted from interest earned, and that the inflation gain or loss on the net amount of cash, non-interest-earning receivables, and non-interest-bearing monetary liabilities be shown separately on the income statement.

[7] The common unit, current value accounting system described here is the same (in substance) as that in Staubus (1961) and is presented here through the courtesy of the copyright holder.

(3-a)	Dr. Nonmonetary asset A	$5.00	
	Cr. Revaluations and restatements		$5.00
(3-b)	Dr. Revaluations and restatements	2.00	
	Cr. Nonmonetary asset B		2.00

(The common unit restatements account has been retitled to reflect its new role.) Entry (4) is still blank because there is no preferred stock. Entry (5) is changed because the cost of goods sold is changed to $35 as of the sale date. The $35 rolled forward from 103$ to 110$ is $35(110/103) = 110$37.38, which requires an adjustment of $2.38. Added to the $.19 adjustment of the appraisal expense, the expense restatement becomes $2.57. Entry (5) is:

(5)	Dr. Expense accounts	$2.57	
	Dr. Revaluations and restatements	.29	
	Cr. Revenue accounts		$2.86

When these entries are posted to the revaluations and restatements account, along with a closing entry (6), we have:

Revaluations and Restatements

(2) Restatement of beginning residual equity	$6.00	(1) Loss on net monetary assets	$0.67
(3-b) Write-down of asset B	2.00	(3-a) Write-up of asset A	5.00
(5) Restatement of revenues and expenses	.29	(6) Loss on revaluation of nonmonetary assets	2.62
	$8.29		$8.29

You may question the accuracy of the description of entry (6). How can this "plug" figure turn out to be the *amount by which the nonmonetary assets failed to keep pace with the change in the general price level* as reflected in the index used to restate the accounts to common units? One explanation is that entries (3-a) and (3-b) have replaced entry (3), which reflected the index-based restatement, with the actual change in asset prices; the difference is, of course, the "real" loss (or gain). We should also remember that entry (5) was changed because the cost of goods sold was changed, but it still serves the same purpose.

If you still doubt the authenticity of the $2.62 loss on revaluation, consider the following proof:

	Required to keep pace with inflation	*Actual Current Valuation*	*Gain or loss*
Asset A—30(103/100)—at sale date	$30.90	$35.00	$4.10
Rolled forward to year-end (multiplied by 110/103)	33.00	37.38	4.38
Asset B, end of year—50(110/100)	55.00	48.00	(7.00)
Net loss on revaluation, in 110$			$(2.62)

So the revaluation loss on nonmonetary items is indeed $2.62 in year-end dollars. *Restating everything except the nonmonetary assets and liabilities while revaluing the nonmonetary items to current values discloses the gain or loss due to the nonmonetary items changing in real value.*

Several aspects of this procedure deserve additional discussion. One is the calculation of the revaluations of nonmonetary assets. In this case we distinguish between the revaluation of an outgoing asset and the revaluation of one on hand at year-end, but this distinction is not necessary. Consider, for example, an inventory account that has substantial activity during the year. If it is feasible to maintain up-to-date information on the current cost of acquiring an item (by purchase or production); if current acquisition price is always used to credit the inventory account when the outgoing goods are being charged to cost of goods sold or to other accounts; and if the beginning and ending inventories are stated at current values as of the beginning and end of the year, respectively; then the revaluation gain or loss can be computed as the one unknown in the "account equation." While the Two-Transaction Company does not provide an ideal example because it acquired no inventory items during the year, it can illustrate the idea of solving for the revaluation in any account. Assume that assets A and B were recorded in one inventory account:

Inventory			
Beginning inventory at current value	$80	Outflows at current value	$35

Acquisitions	0		
Revaluations		Ending inventory at	
(last entry)	3	current value	48
	83		83

With no revaluations, there are normally four types of entries in a ruled and balanced inventory account: beginning balance plus acquisitions on the debit side, and outflows plus ending balance on the credit side. Revaluations make a fifth type. If we know four of the five, we can solve for the unknown—the total revaluations. (However, physical shrinkage must not be overlooked.) That makes it very easy to calculate the *nominal* revaluation gain or loss in any account for which current value information has been constantly available. The *real* gain or loss is then computed in the revaluations and restatements account as previously illustrated.

The restatement of the revenue and expense accounts becomes very simple under current value accounting because all costs of asset consumption (cost of goods sold, depreciation, depletion, amortization), as well as any previously deferred revenues, are stated in current monetary units as of the interim date when the consumption takes place. That makes them well matched with the current revenues. Both revenues and expenses can then be rolled forward uniformly to the end of the reporting period. The net effect on income is due to the rolling forward of the difference, that is, rolling forward interim income numbers to year-end. Omission of this step may not cause a material error if the profit margin is thin. Using the revaluations and restatements account to accumulate the related entries, we see that omission of the restatement of revenues and expenses—entry (5)—would cause an offsetting error in the "plugged" entry: the loss or gain on revaluation of nonmonetary assets. That error results in a mis-classification affecting operating income and revaluation gain or loss.

Failure to obtain current ending values or current values of outgoing items will require the substitution of restated previous measurements, such as restated historical costs (or restated histori-cal receipts for nonmonetary liabilities), if we are to achieve common unit accounting. This involves the assumption that such assets (and liabilities) are still worth their original valuations in old units. That assumption could, of course, be wrong, just as the traditional historical cost valuation assumption could be wrong.

In view of the obvious difficulties that the accounting professions and businessmen in many countries have had in settling on a system of inflation accounting, it may be worthwhile to recapitulate the potential contributions of common unit accounting and current value accounting to the goal of reporting more useful information to those who rely on financial statements.

- A. The adoption of *common unit accounting* means substituting either a consumer purchasing power or general purchasing power concept of capital maintenance for the montary capital maintenance that is incorporated in GAAP. It can accomplish the following:
  1. *For the balance sheet as of a single date:* more relevant measurements of nonmonetary assets (and liabilities). As explained in chapter VII, adjusting the historical cost of an asset by the average percentage change since acquisition date in all prices included in the index typically will yield a price closer to the current price of the asset than was the historical cost without restatement. The broader the sample of assets being restated on a particular balance sheet, the closer we can expect the resulting total asset number to be to its current value equivalent. Therefore, price level restatement of nonmonetary assets tends to approximate current valuation; the more comprehensive the balance sheet, the closer the approximation. The results can be quite good for a national balance sheet, moderately good for the consolidated balance sheet of a large group, and poor for a specialized division or small company. The latter observation may be one reason why operating managers tend to be more interested in current value accounting than in common unit accounting.
  2. *For comparative balance sheets of an entity:* the roll-forward procedure that is applied to old balance sheets, as explained in the FASB and other write-ups, makes a big contribution to the comparability of balance sheets at different dates.
  3. *For the periodic income statement:* the common unit accounting system removes the inflation factor so as to

yield what economists recognize as real income over the lifetime of the entity, so the typical periodic income number is likely to be closer to real income. Putting it another way, common unit accounting "gets the income right" in the long run. Assuming that the system were adopted by all users, this feature has significant implications for an economy in which an income tax is used heavily and private sector real savings are depended upon for improvement in the standard of living.

4. *For comparative income statements:* the roll-forward feature of common unit accounting procedures makes a big contribution to the comparability of income statements and the interpretation of trends over time.

B. The adoption of *current value accounting* means measuring all assets and liabilities without use of historical cost, restated historical cost, historical receipt, restated historical receipt, or discounted values based on noncurrent discount rates; matching current costs with current revenues on the income statement; and including both unrealized and realized holding gains and losses in income. It would tend to accomplish the following:

1. *For the balance sheet:* produce the most relevant measurements of assets, liabilities, and residual equity that are possible. If added to common unit accounting, current value accounting would improve the relevance of the measurements on the single balance sheet.

2. *For the periodic income statement:* improve the timing of income by reporting it when market prices change rather than upon realization. When superimposed on common unit accounting, the result would be both proper timing and an accurate representation of long-run real economic income. Without common unit accounting, the timing would be fine, but the long-run total would be based on comparing costs and revenues in different sizes of units.

C. Looking at the whole picture, in view of the general understanding that common unit accounting procedures are much less costly and much more reliable than comprehensive current value accounting, it seems clear that the former is a much better bargain as a step towards improving financial accounting in times of inflation. In addition, it

would appear that we could have the additional advantages
of current value accounting for the particular assets and
liabilities (and associated income statement items) for which
the reliability and cost criteria can be met acceptably,
perhaps adding categories of net asset items as we gain
experience. Note that vertical comparability on a financial
statement would not be impaired (relative to GAAP) by
such partial adoption of current valuations, as there is
a lack of comparability now. Needless to say, we assume
that steps towards current valuations would be made
uniformly across firms in similar circumstances.

In summary, the combination of current value accounting and
common unit accounting can work out beautifully—if the current
value information is readily available. Common unit accounting
is much easier when combined with current value accounting
because it no longer is necessary to date and restate each nonmonetary asset or liability. Restatement of the income statement is also
easier because all amounts appearing on any interim statement
are stated in the prevailing unit of that interim period. Furthermore, the absence of current value data for a few nonmonetary
assets does not seriously affect the desirability of the combination,
provided that the restated historical measurements of the remaining items are actually entered in the accounts and kept up-to-date.
The combination provides by far the most relevant information
for users' needs and at a very modest cost over either system
alone. [8]

---

[8]Accountants would be wise to avoid the procedure, suggested by some writers,
of deducting a "capital maintenance charge," computed by applying the fractional
index change during the period to the beginning residual equity, in the computation
of net income for the period. These writers also include the gross revaluations
of nonmonetary items in income. In the Two-Transaction Company, the capital
maintenance charge would be our restatement of residual equity, $6. Together
with the gross revaluations of $5 credit and $2 debit, the net effect on income
is a $3 debit, and same as our $2.62 revaluation loss, $.67 monetary items loss,
and $.29 credit for restatement of income statement items. The information
communicated, however, is quite different. The procedure that we would avoid
says that the company gained $3 on holding nonmonetary assets (which directly
violates the idea of common unit accounting) and suffered a loss of $6, which
is described as a "capital maintenance charge." No gain or loss from being in
debt or holding money is even mentioned. I defy anyone to explain to financial

INCOME TAXATION AND COMMON UNIT ACCOUNTING

As long as common unit accounting is not accepted for computing taxable income, and assuming that the principle of comprehensive tax allocation is accepted, how should it be applied under common unit accounting? Neither the provisional standard on "Accounting for Changes in the Purchasing Power of Money" in Britain and Ireland nor the FASB exposure draft on "Financial Reporting in Units of General Purchasing Power" (1974) provides for tax allocation related to the monetary gain or loss or to the restatement of nonmonetary items. Is this appropriate? (I mentioned earlier in this chapter that the FASB treats the liability for deferred taxes as a nonmonetary item and I disagreed with that treatment.)

To test the various possible treatments of income taxes in connection with common unit accounting, let's take the example of the Land Company: at the beginning of period one, it purchased land for $200 and financed it with debt of $50 and equity capital of $150. Assume that the land was held until the beginning of period two, when it was sold for its restated book value of $220, after a 10 percent rate of inflation in period one was recognized. A tax rate of 50 percent applies to the $20 taxable gain. EXHIBIT IX-4 shows the income calculation under GAAP and under four different combinations of common unit accounting and tax accounting. The "no tax allocation" column is consistent with the FASB exposure draft. The next column reflects results under the conventional income statement approach to tax allocation by which tax is provided on any reported income unless it will never be taxed. I consider an excess of common unit accounting income over GAAP income to be taxable eventually because, as I show in chapter X, a company's lifetime income under common unit accounting is less than under GAAP (assuming inflation), so any temporary excess of common unit accounting income over GAAP income will be more than offset by future reversals. Consequently, in the long run there will be no untaxed common unit accounting

---

statement readers exactly why a "capital maintenance charge" should be deducted on an income statement. The idea that income can be affected by a loss on the residual equity is inconsistent with the generally accepted idea that income is a change in the net assets. I emphatically reject it.

EXHIBIT IX-4
LAND COMPANY
BALANCE SHEET
JANUARY 1, PERIOD ONE

Land	$200	Note payable	$50
		Residual equity	150

LAND COMPANY
INCOME CALCULATIONS

			Common Unit Accounting Tax Allocation By—		
	Per GAAP	No Tax Allocation	Conventional I/S Approach	Asset Valuation Approach	Asset Split: Mon'y/ Nonmon'y
Period One					
Gain or (loss) on monetary items	$ 0	$ 5	$ 5	$ 5	$ (5)
Income tax	0	0	(2.5)	(10)	0
Net income	$ 0	$ 5	$ 2.5	$ (5)	$ (5)
Period Two					
Gain on sale	$20	$ 0	$ 0	$ 0	$10
Income tax	(10)	(10)	(7.5)	0	(10)
Net income	$10	$(10)	$(7.5)	$ 0	$ 0
Venture					
Net income	$10	$ (5)	$(5)	$ (5)	$ (5)

gain. The fourth column is based on tax allocation by adjusting the asset value (perhaps via a contra account), as explained in chapter VI. The general principle of this fourth approach is that any difference between an asset's book valuation and its tax basis requires an adjustment of the former so that the net valuation of the asset (or liability) will be equal to the after-tax proceeds that would be enjoyed if the asset were sold for its preadjustment valuation. In other words, no instant gain or loss due to taxation should be built into an asset's valuation. The tax adjustment contra account is a monetary item.

The final column of EXHIBIT IX-4 shows the income calculations under the view that a nonmonetary asset can be divided into two parts representating two sources of cash flow potential: (1) a cash flow contribution by saving taxes, and (2) a cash flow contribution due to its basic services. The first part could be classified as a monetary item because its nominal monetary amount has been substantially fixed by the asset's purchase price and will not vary because of inflation. The latter portion, on the other hand, is a conventional nonmonetary item. If so, a purchasing power loss of $10 is suffered on the monetary portion ($100) and it more than offsets the $5 gain on the debt. The nonmonetary portion is restated from $10 to $110. This gives the asset a total restated valuation of $210 so that its sale for $220 yields a gain of $10, a taxable gain of $20, and income tax of $10.

Note that only the last two methods set up the asset valuation so that no instant net income or loss is reported when the asset is sold for its restated historical cost of $220 on the first day of period two. I prefer one of these methods. The penultimate one—tax allocation via asset valuation—may be most easily interpreted. The layman might interpret the results from period one like this: "We assume that our investment kept pace with inflation and we gained on our debt, but if we sell the land the tax collector will sock us for $10 tax, which puts us in the hole. We can postpone the tax, but sooner or later we'll have to pay it, unless our investment goes bad first, so we may as well recognize it now. It has not been a good year." Do you agree?[9]

---

[9]Cf. p. 180.

Now let's look at the tax aspect of current value accounting combined with common unit accounting. Suppose that the Land Company's assets were revalued to $250 at the end of period one and were sold for that price at the beginning of period two. Following the asset valuation approach to tax allocation, a potential selling price of $250 would involve a tax of $25 (at the assumed 50 percent rate). A potential selling price of $250 also implies a revaluation gain of $30 before tax, since it would take $220 current dollars to break even in purchasing power. The other income effect is the $5 gain on the debt. The income calculations may be summarized as follows:

Period One	
Revaluation gain, before tax	$30
Monetary gain	5
Income tax provision	(25)
Net income	$10
Period Two	
Gain on sale	$ 0
Income tax	0
Net income	$ 0
Venture	
Net income	$10

Now consider the asset valuation approach to tax allocation as applied to a going concern that reports to its shareholders on a common unit accounting basis and pays income taxes on a GAAP basis. The gain or loss on net monetary position may be ignored when the income tax adjustment on net asset values is calculated because that income item will never affect the tax paid; only restatements of old GAAP measurements of nonmonetary items need be considered. The simple generalization from chapter VI still holds. We must adjust the valuation (e.g., restated historical cost) made without consideration of taxation, by the marginal tax rate times the difference between the valuation and the asset's basis. (The possibility of grouping net asset items according to their lives, and treating each group differently, was discussed on p. 219.)

WHAT DIFFERENCE DOES IT MAKE?

In this section of the chapter we want to discuss the importance of the common unit–variable unit controversy. Assuming that a logical case has been made for common unit accounting, are the differences really material? Does anyone care? Should accountants and others be concerned? These types of questions deserve some attention before we make a decision on this issue.

First, let's consider the question of materiality. It is apparent that restatement of long-lived assets will have a material effect upon the total assets in companies with large amounts of such assets. Similarly, the restatement of the residual equity typically will be substantial. Since debt is not restated, debt-equity ratios will be reduced. But our greatest interest is likely to be in the net income number. Fortunately, we have the results of three major studies completed in the 1970s which provide us with some evidence on this point. (The substantial number of individual company data accumulated over the preceding quarter-century will not be discussed because the variations in rates of inflation and in capital structures over the decades make such data somewhat less interesting.)

One interesting study was done by the Mechanical Engineering Economic Development Committee (1973) in Britain and covers 126 companies and the years 1966–71. This study reported that aggregate profit (after interest and profits taxes) of the 126 companies, computed on a common unit accounting basis, ranged from 62 percent to 78 percent of the aggregate variable unit profit, for the six different years. Restatement of cost of goods sold was the largest factor in the differences between the two sets of profit numbers. In the early years of the period studied, when inflation rates were modest, restatement of depreciation was the second most significant factor, but as both the companies' debt and inflation increased in 1970 and 1971, the gain on net monetary liabilities more than offset the increase in depreciation. After taxes and dividends, the aggregate retained profit for the six years was £10 million on a common unit basis compared with £124 million on a variable unit basis.

The Cutler and Westwick (1973) study covered 137 companies representing approximately 75 percent of the market value of all U.K. companies quoted on the London share market. The authors have not identified the year covered, but it was probably 1971. They computed common unit income by making rough adjustments of published data. The results showed that common unit income differed from variable unit income by more than 10 percent in 107 of the 137 companies, by 50 percent or more in 34 of the companies, and by more than 100 percent in 11 companies. The three major adjustments—gain or loss on net monetary position, cost of goods sold, and depreciation—were of roughly equal significance.

Davidson and Weil (1975a) used published data to adjust the incomes of the 30 companies included in the Dow Jones Industrial Average and 30 other companies selected from the *Fortune* 500 industrials. Their data related to 1973 earnings and showed that 32 of the 60 companies had common unit income that differed from their variable unit income by at least 10 percent and 17 of the 60 showed differences of more than 25 percent. The median difference in the Dow Jones companies was 11 percent, in the other companies, 12.5 percent. The smaller discrepancies in the U.S. companies (as compared with the U.K. companies) may be due to a more sudden increase in the rate of inflation in 1973 as compared with previous years. (See chapter X for an explanation of why a sudden increase in the rate of inflation tends to increase common unit accounting earnings relative to variable unit accounting earnings.)

Variable unit accounting, according to these statistics, yields income numbers that are materially different from those that would result from common unit accounting. What difference does this make to the various parties who have an interest in the financial results of enterprise operations? Reported earnings numbers are relied upon heavily as a basis for major decisions that affect the distribution of the rewards and burdens of participating in our society. The income taxes paid by corporations and the owners of unincorporated businesses depend on a method of computing income. Reported profits are believed to have some effect upon the expectations of employees and other parties who sell goods and services to the firm. Customers and the public, sometimes through elected officials, are bound to be influenced, at least to some extent, by their perception of the profitability of specific businesses and industries, and of the business sector of the economy. All of these parties—the tax collector, employees, suppliers, customers, and the remaining public—are likely to expect more from a profitable enterprise than from an unprofitable one. We hypothesize, therefore, that the future taxes, wages, and other costs of an enterprise will be increased by increasing the *reported* profits of enterprises. If so, the overstating or understating of profits *does* make a difference. And, let's not forget, the "error" in variable unit accounting varies widely among companies.

A shift to common unit accounting as the primary evidence of enterprise success might be greeted with varying degrees of enthusiasm or antipathy by the different parties that are affected by financial statements. We should not be surprised to find managers in companies whose common unit income would be lower than their variable unit income resisting the changeover, because managers typically prefer to report successful results (of their management). Owners of closely-held businesses, on the other hand—at least those who understand the alternatives—could be expected to favor common unit accounting, especially for tax purposes. People whose rewards are tied to the stock market may resist common unit accounting on the assumption that "bottom-line fixation" would result in a reduction in share prices commensurate with the typical reduction in reported earnings. Those who believe the market is roughly efficient on this issue may not feel strongly either way.

Union officials are likely to oppose the change because they would anticipate that the reduction in profit that would be reported by most firms in the short run and by all firms in the long run (1) would strengthen managers' resistance to demands for wage increases, and (2) would eventually result in a reduction in the income taxes collected from businesses, which would have to be offset by increases in personal taxes. My own guess is that any major decrease in the collection of income taxes from business would be offset by a value-added tax, or something similar. This would be favored by those who believe that income taxes, especially on business income, encourage waste and tax evasion or avoidance. In sum, citizens and elected officials can be expected to take positions for or against a switch to common unit accounting on the basis of their appraisals of the consequences that the change would have on their own economic interests, not on the basis of the quality of the resulting accounting data as evidence of real economic results and as bases for making decisions. (Readers who recall chapter III may recognize that this paragraph implies that effects via other parties would be a key criterion in any evaluator's choice of sides on the common unit accounting issue.)

One of the simplest and most important possible applications of common unit accounting could be in the computation of taxable income from securities investments. If the tax basis of a security were increased by the amount required to keep pace with inflation or if nominal income from a security were only taxed when, on a cumulative basis since acquisition, it exceeded the cumulative restatement, the "income tax" would tax only the real income of securities investors rather than taking part of their originally invested purchasing power. Whether the tax law is changed or not, securities investors are advised to take the loss of purchasing power of money into consideration in computing the rate of return they earn on their investments. The simplest way to approximate a CUA rate of return (before tax) is to compute the return in the usual way—dividends or interest plus appreciation—convert it to a percentage of beginning-of-period market value, then subtract the inflation rate for the period. If the investor wants to know his after-tax rate of return he must deduct from his gross return the taxes he pays on the dividend and a tax provision for the capital gain, whether the gain is realized or not. If a more refined calculation is desired, one could (1) relate the return to the average investment during the period instead of to the beginning value, (2) take the inflation rate into account by restating the beginning market value in the computation of both the appreciation and the investment base, instead of simply subtracting it from the rate of return, (3) restate dividends, or interest, and taxes in end-of-period monetary units, and (4) use tax-adjusted market values in the denominator.

If this approach to the computation of an investor's real return is appropriate, then it is obvious that traditional computations based on variable units seriously overstate such returns. In fact, inasmuch as returns on securities are customarily computed on a current value basis, the percentage overstatement each period is equal to the percentage increase in the consumer price index.

Now let's see just what this means in a real case—a typical one from recent history that has been wound up. In January 1970, TRW, Inc., issued $50 million of five-year, 8 3/4 percent notes at par. These securities offered one of the highest interest rates the American market had ever seen on obligations of that quality (Standard & Poor's A). Did this represent a bonanza for investors? Suppose that the typical buyer of these securities was in the 50 percent tax bracket including state and federal income tax rates. This means that his after-tax nominal return was 4 3/8 percent. Now compare that with the rate of increase in the U.S. Consumer Price Index published by the Bureau of Labor Statistics. The percentage increases in each year were as follows:

1970	5.2%
1971	3.4%
1972	3.7%
1973	9.4%
1974	11.7%

In only two years out of the five-year life of this issue did the investor have a positive real return, and the average real annual return for the life of the issue was −2.3 percent. An after-tax annual return of 6.7 percent would have been required to break even. This translates into a before-tax nominal interest rate of 13.4 percent. This case illustrates how a tax that is intended to be an income tax can take a slice of capital in inflationary periods with variable unit tax accounting.

The above example illustrates the importance of "indexing" the input amounts that are used in the computation of investment returns to a securities holder. But does a bond holder care whether the *issuing company* adopts common unit accounting or variable unit accounting? Revsine (1973, pp. 6–7) has argued that he does not:

> . . . the creditor's potential return is fixed. Irrespective of the extraordinary profitability of the firm, the lender will receive only the agreed on interest and the principal repayment. The lender should have already adjusted for anticipated inflation in setting his required interest rate. Thus, his prime concern is whether the firm can maintain or improve its existing *nominal* dollar position. If it can, payment of both principal

and interest is likely. If it cannot, payment is jeopardized. Notice that the creditor is not harmed by a weakening in the firm's real net asset position so long as the nominal net asset position is maintained.

This position seems reasonable—at first glance. After all, the borrower has only agreed to pay back a specified number of units of money, not a fixed amount of purchasing power. But does this view really reflect the creditor's interest in financial information from the firm? One reason for a short-term creditor to be less interested in the calculation of the firm's income is that liquidity is more important than profitability to him. But a long-term creditor who uses financial statements to provide information to help him predict the firm's capacity to pay its debts as they come due must consider risk. The debt-equity ratio is an important indicator of risk. A typical firm that strives to maintain its level of physical operations during an inflationary period must increase its money capital. If its management, shareholders, and tax collectors believe that its nominal income is real, and so take it all in the forms of taxes and dividends, the increased total capital must come from debt. The result is an increase in the debt-equity ratio and a decrease in the probability of the firm repaying its creditors. I conclude that creditors may have a strong interest in the adoption of common unit accounting by borrowers and in its acceptance by taxing authorities. The following example illustrates what can happen in extreme circumstances:

> Joe X invested $4,000 of his own money in a Guzzlemobile and went into the taxi cab business. His accountant computed depreciation in accordance with GAAP and Joe set aside a cash replacement fund in the amount of his accumulated depreciation, confident that he could consume the income his accountant reported to him without fear of harming his "business." At the end of the car's life, he found that the replacement cost of a Guzzlemobile, along with the general price level, had doubled. So he went to his friendly banker and borrowed $4,000 to add to the $4,000 he had set aside, promising to pay the debt in installments. This he did, but when replacement time came around once more he again found that inflation made him unable to finance his new equipment out of his own capital so he borrowed again, except

this time he had to borrow $12,000. When he attempted to repeat the cycle the fourth time, his banker was less friendly. In fact, he refused to lend Joe the necessary $28,000 because Joe's equity would have been only 12.5 percent. Joe was out of business. Of course, he still had his $4,000, but it would buy very little. The accompanying condensed balance sheets show the essence of his financial position at the beginning and end of each asset cycle.

JOE X
BALANCE SHEETS

	First Car Beg.	First Car End	Second Car Beg.	Second Car End	Third Car Beg.	Third Car End	(Pro Forma) Fourth Car Beg.
Cash	$0	$4,000	$0	$4,000	$0	$4,000	$0
Car	4,000	0	8,000	0	16,000	0	32,000
Debt	0	0	4,000	0	12,000	0	28,000
Equity	4,000	4,000	4,000	4,000	4,000	4,000	4,000

The moral of this story is that if income is computed on a variable dollar basis, and if that income is taxed and consumed, a long period of inflation will require either new equity capital (and dilution) or an increase in the amount of debt financing required to maintain the earning power of the enterprise. Failure to maintain the earning power is likely to make it difficult for the firm to pay its debts while the alternative of increasing the debt-equity ratio increases the risk that a period of poor performance or poor business conditions will lead to bankruptcy. Long-term creditors should prefer common unit accounting.

The plight of lenders has been given substantial attention. But what about the effects of inflation on borrowers? If lenders' returns are overstated and overtaxed, are not borrowers' profits understated, and perhaps undertaxed? Indeed, they are. TRW, Inc., which borrowed at 8³/₄ percent, was able to deduct the nominal interest expense on its tax return. If its tax rates aggregated to 50 percent, its after-tax cost was only 4³/₈ percent. If it paid back dollars that had been shrunk by inflation at the average annual rate of 6.7 percent, it incurred a negative real interest cost. Under these circumstances, it seems reasonable to say that the Internal Revenue Service took part of the lenders' capital and gave it to the borrower. Can we conclude from this case that the team of inflation and the income tax collector are bound to take from the lender and give to the borrower? Not necessarily. Lenders could conceivably insist on high enough interest rates to cover both inflation and the tax and still have a real return left. For example, if lenders predict a 10 percent rate of inflation and a 50 percent tax rate and want a 4 percent real, after-tax return, a nominal interest rate of 28 percent would meet their goal. Under such circumstances, the borrower would also be paying a real, after-tax rate of 4 percent, if his tax rate is 50 percent. But it should be clear that nominal interest rates in the U.S. have not, in recent years, approximated levels required to give a lender in a typical tax bracket the 3 to 4 percent after-tax real rate of return that some people consider normal. A look at EXHIBIT IX-5 should make this point clear. Nor has this pattern been limited to the 1970s. Data accumulated by Ibbotson and Sinquefield (1976) show that investors in long-term corporate and U.S. Government bonds have earned a negative *before-tax* return for the

EXHIBIT IX-5

BOND YIELDS, PURCHASING POWER LOSSES, AND REAL RETURNS IN THE U.S.

Year	Nominal AAA Corporate Bond Yields*	Investor's Costs Loss on Purchasing Power	50% Tax	Net Real Return	Nominal Yield Required to Net 4% Real (in 50% bracket)
1970	8.0	5.2	4.0	(1.2)	18.4
1971	7.4	3.4	3.7	.3	14.8
1972	7.2	3.7	3.6	(.1)	15.4
1973	7.4	9.4	3.7	(5.7)	26.8
1974	8.6	12.2	4.3	(7.9)	32.4
1975	8.8	7.0	4.4	(2.6)	22.0

*Source: *Moody's Bond Survey*, various dates.

forty-year period ending in 1974. What has the accounting profession done to make the average citizen, or investor, aware of this pattern?

If both borrower and lender correctly predict the rate of inflation, they have the opportunity to reach agreement. The borrower, in effect, sells his tax advantage to the lender to offset his tax disadvantage. It is unexpected rates of inflation that result in transferring wealth between lending and borrowing groups. Since reaching agreement on the rates of inflation that will prevail during the life of a loan is very difficult, indexing both the contractual interest rate and the tax basis of debt owned and owed would appear to be a superior solution. Until this is done, the high and unnecessary risks involved in borrowing-lending relationships are likely to impede the functioning of the capital markets.

REASONS FOR DELAY IN ADOPTION OF COMMON UNIT ACCOUNTING

As of April 1976, common unit accounting has been used regularly by only one public company in the U.S.—Indiana Telephone Corporation. The failure of all other publicly owned, profit-seeking companies to adopt this method needs some explanation, which we can begin to provide by looking at the following areas of concern.

First, there was no demonstrable need for common unit accounting until inflation rates began to rise. Inflation was at a low enough rate through the period from 1952 to 1967 that the accounting profession and the business community did not perceive it to be a great problem. For these fifteen years, the rate of inflation did not exceed 4 percent per year and even through 1972 the inflation rate was under 6 percent in the U.S.

Secondly, common unit accounting has practical restrictions. It is costly because of the detailed work involved. It is also unacceptable for calculating taxable income. This, of course, represents the absence of a strong positive reason for adopting the method.

Third, common unit accounting is still only imperfectly understood. It has been confused with current value accounting in the minds of many people, so they have not obtained a clear perception of its effect. As a group, accountants have failed to study common unit accounting, understand its problems, learn the methodology, and prepare to apply it. Common unit accounting has not been taught generally and effectively in the accounting programs at the university level. Such imperfect and limited understanding naturally breeds mistrust: investors and analysts alike have not understood the methodology and so have not trusted it. The methodology itself is still imperfect. The ideal index is not available now; it is not even clear which index *should* be used. Nor does the methodology solve all of our price change accounting problems.

The financial community has feared, in addition, that common unit accounting would result in reporting lower earnings, which would be translated into lower share prices by an "inefficient" market. Management is reluctant to report the lower earnings that common unit accounting does yield in a majority of cases. At the same time, however, management is reluctant to report the higher earnings that common unit accounting often yields in regulated utilities. As discussed in the next chapter, a low turnover of nonmonetary assets combined with high net monetary liabilities can cause common unit income to exceed variable unit income in some periods. The managements of public utility companies may be reluctant to report to their regulatory commission on this basis because the commission may, as a result, not allow utility rates as high as they would otherwise permit. The peculiar problem of regulated industries is that the earning-power values of their assets fail to keep pace with inflation when the regulatory commissions limit their earnings to a prescribed rate of return on "invested cost," that is, historical cost of assets. This means that the current value to the company of the old assets is less than depreciated replacement cost. The proper accounting response to this limitation is to restate the cost of the nonmonetary assets on a common unit basis, then take a loss and write the assets down to historical cost—the value that the regulatory commission allows the company to recover. On this basis, Davidson, Sidky, and Weil (1976) found that only 7 of the 24 utility companies included in the Dow Jones and Standard & Poor's utilities averages had positive net income in 1974, and none had common unit accounting income in excess of 55 percent of variable unit accounting income. If, on the other hand, the commission permits the use of restated historical cost for rate making, then no such loss and write-down need be recorded.

A final clue to the failure of publicly owned, profit-seeking companies to adopt common unit accounting is to be found in the traditional unspoken doctrine of user subordination and management and accountant domination. Most external reporting decisions traditionally have been made by those who feel the costs of accounting, rather than by those who stand to benefit from it and who actually bear the costs—the investors. There is some question as to whether we have a right to expect good decisions in accounting, or in any other field, until the decision makers are able to match the relevant costs and benefits on a one-dollar, one-vote basis.

APPRAISAL OF COMMON UNIT ACCOUNTING ON THE CRITERIA OF CHAPTER III

In chapter III we discussed nine criteria by which competing accounting proposals could be appraised. It seems appropriate to apply those criteria to the proposal to prepare common unit financial statements for all major uses.

1. *Relevance* of the attribute being measured to the decision processes of users. Our discussion early in the chapter indicated that real income is more relevant to the decisions for which income data are used than is nominal money income. Common unit balance sheet data are more relevant, too.
2. *Reliability.* The present unavailability of perfectly accurate and appropriate indexes, together with possible disagreements on the monetary-nonmonetary classification of a few items, can be tallied as potential deficiencies in the reliability of common unit financial statements as compared with variable unit statements.
3. *Comparability.* A vast improvement in comparability results from eliminating the variability in the measuring unit.
4. *Intelligibility.* A modest additional effort is required to understand common unit statements.
5. *Timeliness.* Financial statement preparation could be delayed until the desired index is published. If the delay is serious, the accountant may choose to base the statements on a reading of the index for a date prior to the end of the period.

325

6. *Optimal quantity* of information. It is not clear whether the addition of supplementary, common unit statements results in a total quantity of information that is closer to, or further from, the optimum.
7. *Effects via other parties.* From the point of view of *investors,* the effect via the Internal Revenue Service (if it also uses common unit statements) would be most welcome. Managers, too, could be expected to act more in the interests of investors. From the point of view of *professional managers,* use by the Internal Revenue Service would also be desirable. Use by investors, however, assuming lower common unit income and an "inefficient market," would be undesirable.
8. *Cost of utilizing accounting data.* An analyst would do more work, costing more money, if he wanted to make calculations on both variable unit and common unit bases. But if he now tries to allow for inflation, his work would be eased by the availability of common unit statements.
9. *Cost of producing accounting data.* The cost would be increased moderately.

As pointed out in chapter III, the final decision on this issue (or any other) depends upon the weighting of the various criteria and the degree of superiority possessed by a method on a given criterion. We leave this decision to the reader.

SUMMARY

1. The computation of income requires the comparison, addition, and subtraction of measurements made at different times. Analytical techniques applied to comparative balance sheets require similar mathematical operations.
2. Defining and calculating income as an increase in the purchasing power of the owners of a business is consistent with the accounting objective of providing information useful to owners and those interested in the returns of owners.
3. When the general price level changes, the purchasing power of the nominal monetary unit changes. Such variation prevents the operations of addition and subtraction of nominal monetary units from accomplishing what is required to achieve the objectives of accounting. Common unit accounting is an adjustment technique designed

to permit more useful computations with monetary units in periods of inflation by utilizing units of equal purchasing power instead of nominal monetary units.

4. Common unit accounting requires choosing a purchasing power unit existing as of a certain date (typically the financial statement date) as the measuring unit. All measurements used in the financial statements which are not stated in that unit are adjusted to it.

5. Balance sheet items may be measured by any method desired. When they are not measured at their restated beginning amounts, a gain or loss is recorded under common unit accounting. This is normal with monetary items and with nonmonetary items measured by any current value method.

6. A monetary item is one that will entail future cash flows in nominal amounts that are independent of inflation. All other balance sheet items are nonmonetary. An entity gains or loses on its net monetary position from inflation alone, regardless of other economic events.

7. A gain on net monetary position is as "distributable" as any gain on revaluation of assets or liabilities; i.e., it is subject to the acceptability or convertibility of existing net asset items at their book values.

8. Common unit accounting is much simpler when combined with comprehensive current value accounting (as compared with the common unit–GAAP combination).

9. Income tax should be recognized on restatements of nonmonetary assets and liabilities in order to avoid valuations that cause major income effects in future periods.

10. The difference between variable unit income and common unit income typically is material.

11. The attitudes of various groups towards common unit accounting can be expected to reflect their economic interests.

12. Unexpected inflation transfers wealth from the lender to the borrower. Overestimates of inflation tend to reverse this transfer. Indexing contractual interest rates and the tax bases of securities owned and of debt outstanding can solve this problem.

13. Common unit accounting appears to be distinctly superior to variable unit accounting on the criteria of relevance, comparability, and effects via other parties but is, or may be, inferior on other criteria.

We close this chapter with two paragraphs from "The Credibility of Corporations" by Irving Kristol (1974, p. 12):

> . . . what is one to make of a corporation which proudly announces that it has just completed the most profitable year in its history—and then simultaneously declares that its return on capital is pitifully inadequate, that it is suffering from a terrible cost-squeeze, etc., etc.? In 1973, most corporations were engaged in precisely this kind of double-talk. Is it any wonder they created so enormous a credibility gap?
>
> Now, the truth is that 1973 was not so profitable a year for our large corporations. One would see this instantly if corporations reported their profits in *constant dollars*—i.e., corrected for inflation. Trade unions do this when they report their members' earnings to the world at large—*they* don't want to look like "profiteers" when they sit down at the bargaining table. Corporations, in contrast, do seem to be under a compulsion to look like "profiteers"—even when they are not, in fact, operating at a particularly profitable level.

References

American Institute of Certified Public Accountants, Accounting Research Division, "Reporting the Financial Effects of Price-Level Changes," *Accounting Research Study No. 6* (AICPA, 1963).

_____, "Financial Statements Restated for General Price-Level Changes," *Statement of the Accounting Principles Board, No. 3* (AICPA, 1969).

Cutler, R. S. and G. A. Westwick, "The Impact of Inflation Accounting on the Stock Market," *Accountancy* (March 1973), pp. 15-24.

Davidson, Sidney, Samy Sidky, and Roman L. Weil, "Dow Jones and Standard & Poor's Utilities Income for 1974 on Conventional and (Estimated) GPLA Bases," unpublished, University of Chicago, 1976.

Davidson, Sidney and Roman L. Weil, "Inflation Accounting," *Financial Analysts Journal* (January-February 1975), pp. 27-31, 70-84.

Financial Accounting Standards Board, "Financial Reporting in Units of General Purchasing Power," Exposure Draft of Proposed Statement of Financial Accounting Standards (31 December 1974).

Gynther, Reg S., "Why Use General Purchasing Power?" *Accounting and Business Research* (Spring 1974), pp. 141-57.

Hicks, J. R., *Value and Capital,* 2d. ed. (Clarendon Press, 1946).

Ibbotson, Roger G. and Rex A. Sinquefield, "Stocks, Bonds, Bills, and Inflation: Year-by-Year Historical Returns (1926-1974)," *Journal of Business* (January 1976), pp. 11-47.

Kristol, Irving, "The Credibility of Corporations," *Wall Street Journal* (17 January 1974), p. 12.

Mechanical Engineering Economic Development Committee, *Inflation and Company Accounts in Mechanical Engineering* (National Economic Development Office, 1973).

Revsine, Lawrence, *Replacement Cost Accounting* (Prentice-Hall, 1973).

_____ and Jerry J. Weygandt, "Accounting for Inflation: The Controversy," *Journal of Accountancy* (October 1974), pp. 72-78.

Sandilands, F. E. P., Chairman, Inflation Accounting Committee, *Inflation Accounting: Report of the Inflation Accounting Committee,* Cmnd. 6225 (Her Majesty's Stationery Office, 1975).

Saunders, Donald H. and Paul G. Busby, "Accounting for Inflation: To Be, or Not to Be?" *Public Utilities Fortnightly* (29 January 1976), pp. 15-21.

Staubus, George J., *A Theory of Accounting to Investors* (University of California Press, 1961; rpt. Scholars Book Co., 1971).

_____, "Price-level Accounting: Some Unfinished Business," *Accounting and Business Research* (Winter 1975), pp. 42-47.

329

Summary of the Theory

Summary of
The Decision-Usefulness Theory
of Accounting to Investors

The objective of accounting to investors is to provide financial information regarding an enterprise for use in making investment decisions. Investors commit resources to an enterprise with the expectation of receiving a return, usually in cash. Investment decisions are cash flow-oriented decisions. They are facilitated by information useful in predicting the times and amounts of returns from the enterprise to the investor. Returns to investors are dependent on enterprise cash flows. Accounting can provide evidence of the times, amounts and uncertainty of future enterprise cash flows, i.e. of cash flow potentials. Accounting to investors focuses on providing evidence of enterprise cash flow potentials.

Evidence of cash flow potentials may be available in either of two forms: stocks of future cash flow potentials or historical flows of cash or cash flow potentials. Stocks of positive cash flow potentials are called assets. Stocks of negative cash flow potentials are called liabilities. The sum of enterprise assets less the sum of enterprise liabilities is the residual equity in the enterprise. An enterprise's net assets represent the accounting measurement of the value of the residual equity in that enterprise. It is an indicator of the enterprise's future cash flows, so is used by investors for predicting their own returns from the enterprise.

Flows of net assets, i.e., historical changes in net assets, may be viewed as evidence of future changes in enterprise net assets, or cash flow potentials. Positive flows of net asset items that change the residual equity are called either revenues or gains, depending on their tendency to recur. Negative flows are expenses or losses. The difference between the sum of an enterprise's revenues, gains, expenses, and losses in a financial reporting period is called net income. A report of those four classes of net asset flows is viewed as valuable evidence of future enterprise cash flows because some of them have a tendency to recur. Such a report is also valued because it helps the investor understand the enterprise's activities and thus predict its future activities. Another class of flows that is viewed as evidence in estimating future enterprise cash flows is historical flows into and out of a pool of cash and near-cash items. That information is reported to investors in a cash flow statement.

Much of the accounting process is focused on gathering imperfect evidence of stocks of cash flow potentials and historical flows of cash flow potentials. In many cases, alternative bits of evidence and alternative ways of reporting are available. In choosing from among such alternatives, those evaluators with power to choose employ a number of criteria of good accounting:

1. Relevance of the evidence to cash flow-oriented decisions, according to economic reasoning.
2. The reliability of the evidence as a representation of the specific phenomenon it purports to represent.
3. Comparability of the evidence in relation to that of other enterprises, other reporting periods, and other evidence in the same financial report.
4. Timeliness of the reporting of the evidence, consisting of the frequency of reporting and the lag between the end of the reporting period and the presentation of the report.
5. Understandability and readability of the report.
6. Cost of accounting and of using the information reported.
13. Effects via other parties (unintended economic consequences), i.e., the anticipated favorable or unfavorable effects the reporting of the information may have on the evaluator through its effects on others.

The property of an asset or liability that investment decisions makers would like to know is its cash flow potential. When alternative bits of evidence of a net asset item's cash flow potential are available, the accountant uses the above set of criteria in choosing the evidence of net asset amount to include in the computation of the residual equity. Relevance to cash flow-oriented decisions is the primary criterion, and the commonly available forms of evidence may be ranked per their relevance as follows:

1. Cash count.
2. Discounted future cash flows or current observable market price of financial assets.
3. Future cash flows of short-term items.
4. Best-use net realizable value.
5. Current replacement cost or proceeds.
6. Equity method for equity interests.
7. Restated historical cost or proceeds.
8. Historical acquisition cost or proceeds

Application of a set of criteria of good accounting in a wide variety of circumstances results in use of the complete array of forms of evidence, or measurement methods, in practice.

The objective of investing is the enhancement of consumer purchasing power, so a consumer price index is used to restate measurements of financial statement items made at various dates at various price levels to a common date and a common size of measuring unit in a period of changing price levels.

Impact

Impact

The preceding pages include the most worthwhile of my contributions to the decision-usefulness theory of accounting. With one exception, those works were written between 1952 and 1976. As of 1999, what impact of decision-usefulness theory is discernible? I would be interested in hearing the assessments of more objective observers. The variations among them no doubt would be striking, as both the changes in the accounting scene and the extent to which those changes might be attributed to the theory clearly would be perceived differently by different observers. I offer my own brief remarks in four areas: standards setting, practice, teaching, and research.

Decision-usefulness theory has influenced standards setting in the United States primarily through the FASB's "conceptual framework," surely a decision-useful theory. The Board reaffirmed its commitment to the theory in a 1999 document, *International Accounting Standard Setting; A Vision for the Future — Report of the FASB*. Participants in the standards-setting process know they are opening themselves to criticism if they ignore the decision-usefulness objective and the qualities of valuable financial information. Thoughtful participants cannot avoid concluding that users find reporting-date measurements of assets and liabilities more relevant to future cash flow-oriented decisions than older measurements. They see that smoothing of earnings under the guise of matching costs with revenues — e.g., capitalizing and amortizing research and development costs, using self-insurance reserves, deferring losses on early extinguishment of debts, and full costing for oil and gas exploration costs — cannot be defended by the multiple-criteria approach to making accounting decisions. They understand that at least a few important market-influencing investment analysts find expanded disclosures useful. They recognize that markets are lubricated by transparency, hindered by obscurity. The theory also has made the pressures of special interest groups more apparent, even if not completely resistible. Nevertheless, until the FASB musters the courage to tackle the major issues of long standing — inventories and long-term assets — one cannot say that decision-usefulness theory has achieved complete acceptance.

The impact of decision-usefulness theory on practice is harder to detect. Some would say that preparers and their generally supportive auditors have been dragged, kicking and screaming all the way, into the conceptual framework era. That view is a bit exaggerated, in my opinion, but it is hard to disagree with the general observation that whenever a standards-setting body tries to change practice it is asking preparers to change from a method they (preparers) have chosen. It should not surprise us if they see an alternative as inferior. That is especially true when application of the alternative method would reflect unfavorably on the management's performance based on its currently preferred operating practices. One example, is a proposal to "mark to market" financial assets, thus reflecting more clearly in the financial statements the risks being taken by management and reducing the smoothing of reported earnings, as well as reporting more up-to-date balance sheet values. Another class of proposals that preparers understandably oppose would require not just different timing of reported expenses but a long-run increase. A high-profile example was a proposal to report the value of stock options granted as compensation expense. That proposal had the additional handicap of threatening to reveal greater management compensation. Decision-usefulness theory and the conceptual framework have not done much to increase the power of users of financial reports in conflicts with preparers when the latter see a threat to an important prerogative. This is not an accounting theory issue; it is a corporate governance issue. The conclusion that preparers have had considerable success in limiting the influence of decision-usefulness theory on practice is inescapable.

What can be said about the influence of decision-usefulness theory on the teaching of accounting? One might expect the typical teacher to be more theory oriented than the typical practitioner or auditor. Also, teachers might be more attuned to a public interest point of view rather than the view of a special interest group. It turns out, however, that teachers have not shown much interest in the FASB's work or in the application of decision-usefulness theory. Perhaps the best evidence is the extent to which the best-selling accounting textbooks have incorporated the theory. The common practice now is to devote one section to a summary of the conceptual framework — a portion of a chapter in an elementary text or a full chapter in an intermediate text — and then forget about it in all of the other chapters. GAAP is the bible that textbook writers choose to interpret and teach. Their acceptance of decision-usefulness theory is comparable to the adherent to a religion that shows up in a house of worship twice a year. One might say there is a gap between professed beliefs and practices, with perhaps the same types of explanations (excuses) in accounting as in religion. The theory's modest influence on teaching is comparable to, and due to, its modest influence on practice.

Despite academics' low level of interest in decision-usefulness in teaching, they have used it more widely in their research. It seems that at some date around 1967, most researchers adopted the unstated premise that decision usefulness was the test of good accounting. That development was like a neutral (neither hostile nor friendly) takeover in the dead of night. Decision-usefulness literature was seldom quoted, but all of a sudden the decision-usefulness objective was taken for granted. This change in accounting research can not be documented by reference to an explicit statement in a committee report or by a leading authority, but a careful review of the research reported in the major academic journals shows that it happened. An interesting example was the use of the market response test of newly-revealed data. The presumption generally has been that if a securities market responds to specified data, those data are useful.

Few of those studies questioned the difference between used and useful data, and the way the used data fitted into decision-useful theory was seldom addressed. Nevertheless, use in making investment decisions has been accepted as a criterion of good accounting. So decision-usefulness theory has affected research, but that effect has been more implicit than explicit.

In general, I believe that decision-usefulness theory has had a moderate impact on a field that is not easily changed — perhaps more impact than any other development in this century except the movement towards regulation and recognition by the plaintiff's bar that auditors have deep pockets. Some days I see a half full glass; some days it's half empty.

Speculating on the future of the decision-usefulness theory of financial accounting probably is not a very productive activity. To me, an interesting issue is how to explain the low level of interest, in all segments of the accounting community, in accounting theory. If the general explanation for that low level of interest is a lack of perceived payoffs to investments in theory, I am not sure what can be done about it. I can say, however, that my own investment in theory has yielded quite a satisfactory payoff. Twenty-four years between the appearance of the first crudely-written features of the decision-usefulness theory and its adoption by the American standards-setting body must be some kind of record for accounting. Now if it could only be whole-heartedly accepted by practitioners!

Publications by the Author

George J. Staubus
Publications

"Payments for the Use of Capital and the Matching Process," *The Accounting Review,* January 1952.

An Accounting Concept of Revenue, Ph.D. Dissertation, University of Chicago, 1954; Arno Press, 1980, 116 pp.

"Revenue and Revenue Accounts," *Accounting Research,* July 1956a.

"Quantitative Analysis for Investment Decisions," *The Controller,* October 1956b.

"Comments on 'Accounting and Reporting Standards for Corporate Financial Statements — 1957 Revision,'" *The Accounting Review,* January 1958.

"The Residual Equity Point of View in Accounting," *The Accounting Review,* January 1959.

A Theory of Accounting to Investors, Berkeley: University of California Press, 1961a, 149 pp. Republished in Accounting Classics Series, Scholars Book Co., 1970. Japanese translation: Hakuto Shobo, 1986.

"Nonaccounting for Noninsurance," *The Accounting Review,* July 1961b.

"Stock Valuation Reconsidered," *The Accountant,* March 10, 1962a.

"Decreasing Charge Depreciation — Still Searching for Logic," *The Accounting Review,* July 1962b.

"Direct, Relevant or Absorption Costing," *The Accounting Review,* January 1963a.

"Stock, or Share," *Encyclopaedia Britannica,* 1963b.

"Caveat Emptor Tabulas," *NAA Bulletin,* February 1964.

"The Association of Financial Accounting Variables with Common Stock Values," *The Accounting Review,* January 1965a.

"Comments on 'Future Service Potential Value,'" *The Journal of Accountancy,* July 1965b.

Book Review, Study Group at the University of Illinois, A Statement of Basic Accounting Postulates and Principles, *The Accounting Review,* October 1965c.

"Alternative Asset Flow Concepts," *The Accounting Review,* July 1966.

"Cash Flow Analyses and Projections," *Management Accounting* (London), February 1967a.

"Statistical Evidence of the Value of Depreciation Accounting," *Abacus,* August 1967b.

"Current Cash Equivalent for Assets: A Dissent," *The Accounting Review,* October 1967c.

"Asset Lives: Three Comments," *Accountancy,* October 1967d.

"The Divisional Profits Conundrum," *The Financial Times,* March 6, 1968a.

"The Cost of Capital," *The Financial Times,* March 13, 1968b.

"Plant Financing, Accounting and Divisional Targetry," *California Management Review,* Summer 1968c.

"Testing Inventory Accounting," *The Accounting Review,* July 1968d.

"Earnings Periods for Common Share Analysis," *Journal of Business,* October 1968e.

Book Review, Shinkichi Minemura, Depreciation Accounting and Economic Analysis, *The Accounting Review,* July 1969.

"Determinants of the Value of Accounting Procedures," *Abacus,* December 1970.

Activity Costing and Input-Output Accounting, Richard D. Irwin, Inc., 1971a, 144 pp.

"Return on Investment: The Continuing Confusion Among Disparate Measures — Critique," in Sterling, R.R., and Bentz, W.F. (eds.), *Accounting in Perspective,* South-Western Publishing Co., 1971b.

"The Relevance of Evidence of Cash Flows," *Asset Valuation and Income Determination,* Robert Sterling, ed. (Scholars' Book Company, 1971c).

"An Analysis of APB Statement No. 4," *The Journal of Accountancy,* February 1972a.

"Using Accounting Information to Measure Management Performance," (1972 Endowed Lecture, University of Queensland), *The Queensland Accounting Bulletin,* September 1972b.

"Empirical Research in Accounting," *Proceedings of Third International Conference on Accounting Education,* Sydney, October 1972c.

Objectives and Concepts of Financial Statements, (with W.J. Kenley), Accountancy Research Foundation, Melbourne, 1972d, 106 pp.

"The Measurement of Management Performance," *The Singapore Accountant,* July 1973a.

"Measurement of Assets and Liabilities," *Accounting and Business Research,* Autumn 1973b.

"Current Value Accounting in Financial Industries," Professional Accounting Program, Graduate School of Business Administration, University of California, Berkeley, 1974.

"The Responsibility of Accounting Teachers," *The Accounting Review,* January 1975a.

"Price-Level Accounting: Some Unfinished Business," *Accounting and Business Research,* Winter 1975b, pp. 42–47.

"The Multiple-Criteria Approach to Making Accounting Decisions," *Proceedings of the Southwest Regional Conference,* American Accounting Association, 1976a; also in *Accounting and Business Research,* Autumn 1976.

"The Effects of Price-Level Restatements on Earnings," *The Accounting Review,* July 1976b, pp. 574–89.

Statement on Accounting Theory and Theory Acceptance (with eight other members of Committee on Concepts and Standards), American Accounting Association, 1977a, pp. 1–61.

"The Use of Accounting Information in the Management of Socialist Enterprises," (with Sarah Staubus), *ICRA Occasional Paper No. 16,* International Center for Research in Accounting, University of Lancaster, 1977b, pp. 1–89.

Making Accounting Decisions, Scholars Book Co., 1977c, 676 pp.

Economic Consequences of Financial Accounting Standards (Ed. and Introduction), Financial Accounting Standards Board, 1978, 278 pp.

"Inflation Accounting," *Proceedings: InterAmerican Accounting Conference*, Panama City, Panama, September 1979.

Book Review, Robert N. Anthony, Tell It Like It Was, *The Accounting Review*, July 1984.

"An Induced Theory of Accounting Measurement," *The Accounting Review*, January 1985a, pp. 53–75.

"Differential Measurement," *Journal of Accountancy*, March 1985b, pp. 45–48.

"The Market Simulation Theory of Accounting Measurement," *Accounting and Business Research*, Spring 1986, pp. 117–132.

"Accounting Measurements in Practice, Part I," *Today's CPA*, September-October 1987a, pp. 24–27.

"Accounting Measurements in Practice, Part II," *Today's CPA*, November-December 1987b, pp. 18–20.

"The Dark Ages of Cost Accounting: The Role of Miscues in the Literature," *The Accounting Historians Journal*, Fall 1987c, pp. 1–18.

Activity Costing for Decisions. Garland Publishing, Inc., 1988, 229 pp.

"Cash Flow Accounting and Liquidity: Cash Flow Potential and Wealth," *Accounting and Business Research*, Spring 1989a, pp. 161–9.

"Accounting Measurements of Profitability and Liquidity for Financial Planning," *Proceedings: Inter-American Accounting Conference*, Asuncion, Paraguay, September 1989b.

"Decision-Usefulness Theory, Activity Costing and Market Simulation Accounting," in J. St. G. Kerr and R. C. Clift (eds.), *Essays in Honour of Louis Goldberg*. Melbourne: Department of Accounting and Business Law, University of Melbourne, 1989c.

"Activity Costing: Twenty Years On," *Management Accounting Research*, 1990, 1, pp. 249–264.

"Cherry Pickers' Friend," *Barron's*, December 7, 1992, pp. 21–2.

"The Case of the Almost Identical Twins," *Issues in Accounting Education*, Spring 1993, pp. 187–190.

"Issues in the Accounting Standards-Setting Process," in S. Jones et al. (eds.), *Accounting Theory: A Contemporary Review*. Harcourt Brace, 1995a, pp. 191–215.

"The Historical Development of Accounting in Firms: The Role of Conflicts of Interests," Special World Conference to Celebrate Fra' Luca Pacioli, Joint International Committee, 1995b, pp. 433–444.

Economic Influences on the Development of Accounting in Firms, Garland Publishing Inc., 1996a, 166 pp.

"Maurice Moonitz," *Encyclopedia of the History of Accounting and Accounting Thought*. Michael Chatfield and Richard Vargermeersch, eds. Garland Publishing, Inc.,

References

American Accounting Association, Committee to Prepare A Statement of Basic
Accounting Theory, *A Statement of Basic Accounting Theory* (AAA, 1966).
_____, Committee on Concepts and Standards Underlying Corporate Financial
Statements, "Standards of Disclosure for Published Financial Reports,"
Supplementary Statement No. 8, *The Accounting Review* (July, 1955).
American Institute of Certified Public Accountants, Accounting Principles Board,
"Basic Concepts and Accounting Principles Underlying Financial Statements
of Business Enterprises," *Statements of the Accounting Principles Board, No. 4*
(AICPA, 1970).
American Institute of Certified Public Accountants, Study Group on the Objectives
of Financial Statements, *Objectives of Financial Statements* (AICPA, 1973).
Ball, Ray and Philip Brown, "An Empirical Evaluation of Accounting Income
Numbers," *Journal of Accounting Research* (Autumn 1968), pp.159-178.
Beaver, William H., "The Information Content of Annual Earnings
Announcements," *Empirical Research in Accounting: Selected Studies, 1966*
(Supplement to *Journal of Accounting Research),* vol.4, pp. 71-111.
Chambers, Raymond J. "Measurement and Misrepresentation," *Management Science*
(January 1960), pp. 141-8.
_____, *Accounting, Evaluation and Economic Behavior* (Prentice-Hall, 1966).
Financial Accounting Standards Board, *Statements of* Financial Accounting Concepts,
Nos. 1, 2, 5, and
6 (FASB, 1978-1985).
_____, "Financial Reporting and Changing Prices," *Statement of Financial Accounting
Standards No. 33* (FASB, September 1979).
_____, *International Accounting Standards Setting: A Vision fo the Future — Report of the
FASB,* (FASB, 1999).
Ijiri, Yuji and Robert K. Jaedicke, "Reliability and Objectivity of Accounting
Measurements," *The Accounting Review* (July 1966), pp. 474-83.
Kenley, W. J. and George J. Staubus, *Objectives and Concepts of Financial Statements*
(Accountancy Research Foundation, Melbourne, 1972).
McDonald, Daniel L., "Feasibility Criteria for Accounting Measures, *The Accounting
Review* (October 1967), ap. 662-79.
Paton, W. A. and A.C. Littleton, *An Introduction to Corporate Accounting Standards,*
Monograph No. 3 (American Accounting Association, 1940).
Snavely, Howard J. "Accounting Information Criteria," *The Accounting Review* (April
1967), pp. 223-32.
Sterling, Robert R., *Theory of the Measurement of Enterprise Income* (University Press of
Kansas, 1971).
_____, ed. *Asset Valuation and Income Determination* (Scholars Book Co., 1971).